WOODWORKING
WITH SCRAPS

Other TAB books by the author:

No. 1008
$10.95

WOODWORKING WITH SCRAPS

BY PERCY W. BLANDFORD

TAB BOOKS

BLUE RIDGE SUMMIT, PA. 17214

FIRST EDITION

FIRST PRINTING—AUGUST 1978

Copyright © 1978 by TAB BOOKS

Printed in the United States
of America

Library of Congress Cataloging in Publication Data

Blandford, Percy W.
    Woodworking with scraps.

    Includes index.
    1. Woodwork. I. Title.
TT180.B63   684'.08   77-18916
ISBN 0-8306-9979-1
ISBN 0-8306-1008-1 pbk.

Contents

SECTION 3: THINGS TO MAKE

Introduction

Through most of the 20th century, the industrialized countries have been careless and wasteful. The policy of use, discard, and replace has been the guideline for almost all manufactured products. Advertisers would have us believe that we *must* have this year's product, even if it differs from last year's only in appearance. Faults in this policy are now becoming increasingly evident and, as in times past, things that last are becoming more valued.

With raw materials becoming increasingly costly and scarce, it makes sense to recover and recycle them. This particularly applies to wood; and that's what this book is all about.

New wood is becoming expensive. Some varieties are becoming rare, for certain species of trees simply do not grow fast enough to replace what we use. World stocks may still be comparatively plentiful, but certain woods are almost impossible to obtain. For some of the woods we have been accustomed to using, we now must accept substitutes or very inferior grades, despite higher prices.

All of this means that used wood may be just as good as (and often is better than) new wood. What is just as important, the old wood costs little or nothing. Crates are an excellent source, but there are many other sources of free or nearly-free wood. Pallets are made of many different woods and are often discarded. Building sites can produce valuable offcuts. At the end of a building's life, demolition can provide wood worth using again. Many manufacturing plants throw away perfectly good wood, its only fault being that it's uneconomical for them to process. Even a garage sale may provide wood that is still useful, built into some piece of useless furniture. Once the idea of salvaging wood gets you, every piece of discarded wood is seen as what it might become if you had it!

There are other factors to consider besides the conservation and economic aspects. There is always a great satisfaction in making things, but the satisfaction is even greater when you have produced something from virtually nothing. Also, few of us get an opportunity in our daily work to see a job through from start to finish: we are concerned with only part of a process. Even if our work combined with that of others produces a very satisfactory whole, it seldom produces the satisfaction and pride of the old-time craftsman who made every stage of a product himself.

Of course, not all of us have the craftsman's skill. However, what an amateur has is *time*. Much of what he lacks in skill he can compensate for with the time he can spend doing the work carefully, so the result may rival the work of a professional. Modern power tools are another boon: not every amateur craftsman has a fully equipped shop, but even if he has only an electric drill with a few attachments, he has an advantage over the oldtimers, who had to use skill and experience to match the precision of modern power tools.

The same is true with modern hand tools. For example, today's steel planes are far more accurate than the old wooden planes with their primitive adjustments. And modern glues that are much stronger and simpler to use than traditional glues will produce joints of considerable strength, even without the interlocking construction of earlier days.

Using salvaged wood is no excuse for poor craftsmanship; something made from a crate needn't look like a crate. Occasionally salvaged items can be made into something else without dismantling them completely, but in general it is better to regard crates, pallets and other salvaged wood as a source of lumber and not as something to convert. Items made from new lumber bear little resemblance to unfinished boards—the same rule should apply to using salvaged wood.

Approach your scavenged wood with this attitude. As far as possible, ignore its form and look at it as so much wood of certain sizes that you will extract and use. The way the parts were originally assembled should have little bearing on what you do with the wood.

That is the approach of craftsmanship and the approach of this book. Occasionally a piece of scavenged wood cannot be perfectly smoothed, but usually—by the time you have finished with it—it can be made at least as smooth as anything you make from new wood. As will be seen from the instructions in this book, you do not need great skill or elaborate equipment to bring wood to a fine finish. Of course, many of the things described in this book can be made from new material and some readers may do this.

The instructions in tool handling and the making of joints herein have stood the test of time and are appropriate to any type of woodwork. Where modifications are needed to suit salvaged wood, instructions are given, but anyone learning woodworking methods from this book will be acquiring traditional skills, not some makeshift techniques providing allegedly easy shortcuts that will produce inferior results.

I cannot remember the day when I didn't have a saw and a few other tools in the car, ready to salvage wood. Many of my home furnishings, the equipment in my garden and even parts of my boat are made from salvaged wood that someone else had no use for. I hope many readers of this book will get the same joy and satisfaction I did from making things out of wood that cost nothing. They will also get the satisfaction of knowing that they are doing something to recycle instead of destroy the products of nature.

Percy W. Blandford

Section 1
Salvaging Material

Chapter 1
Collecting Materials

Wood is a versatile material. There are very few other things, natural or synthetic, with such universal applications. During World War II a noted airplane designer was asked what synthetic material the scientists might produce for use on airplanes; he said that by the time all the qualities had been listed, it would be a good description of wood.

Man has used wood since long before recorded history. The needs of earlier generations were small, and although they used wood freely there was always more.

Modern man uses wood in much larger quantities. One day's issue of a newspaper, for example, requires many trees to provide wood pulp to make the paper, which is then mostly discarded the next day.

Although trees regenerate, they do not do so at anywhere near the rate they are used. Enlightened people plant trees to take the place of those felled, but in most cases they have no hope of seeing those trees grow to worthwhile size in their lifetime; with some species it may be many generations later before they will be of use as wood.

With man using wood at such a rate, some species have become rare, and therefore hard to get and expensive. We are already seeing furniture that looks like wood, but is in fact merely a veneer, or sometimes just printed wood-grain paper on a plastic or manufactured board backing. This may have to become acceptable for many purposes and could be regarded as the twentieth-century style, but it cannot stand comparison with Chippendale or Colonial. Most people prefer their furniture, and many other things, to be made of wood as in time past.

Since wood is becoming rarer and more expensive, it makes sense to recycle at least some of it. Many discarded items can yield useful material—both wood and fasteners—for anyone discerning enough to see the possibilities.

Collecting and thinking up ways of using what other people discard is something that grows on you. Apart from economy, there are the ecological concerns: you are converting to further use material that would otherwise have been destroyed, thus preserving new materials for more critical purposes and the future.

WHERE TO LOOK

Possible wood sources are all around us, for modern man is very wasteful. What someone else does not want may be useful stock to you, even if you can see no immediate use for it.

If the idea of recycling wood has only just occurred to you, you may need to look no further than your own home. A piece of broken furniture may have sound parts to use in some other project. A broken-down fence may have wood in reasonable condition that will form part of a piece of outdoor furniture. Floor boards, wall material, roof beams and similar material removed during an alteration can all be "reduced to produce," a descriptive service term meaning taking things apart so their components can be used again. If it is wood, see what can be salvaged before throwing it away or burning it.

If old wood is in such a state that it can have no further use, burning it may be a final use rather than just a means of disposal. It may be burnt for warmth, but if that is unnecessary or impracticable, it can be burned on the soil and dug in to enrich the ground, having come full circle from life to death, from use to a rebirth.

CRATES

At one time, food and many other items were delivered in wooden boxes, but cardboard boxes and cartons have pretty much replaced them. Wooden boxes may be returnable, but they only stand up to a certain number of journeys before becoming unfit for their purpose, although still sound in parts. Even many cardboard boxes have wooden parts to stiffen them or serve as a base. Ask your local store managers; they're usually quite willing to let you look over what they put out as trash.

While salvaging, be careful not to create extra work for people. They may want you to take an entire item when you only want part of it. It would be unfair to dismantle it on the spot and leave the debris for someone else to clean up. It's more polite to take the whole thing and deal with it elsewhere. Of course, you may have to partially dismantle a large item to get it in the trunk of your car, but unless you cooperate with your sources, they may dry up in a hurry.

Imported fruit and other foods frequently come in wooden containers. Sometimes the thickness of the wood is minimal and strength is provided by wire or metal strapping. In this case you will have to assess the value and take-down condition, but thin wood is good for laminating. Although thick wood has more uses, good thin pieces are worth putting into stock if they can be removed without too much damage. Some of this foreign wood is interesting because it is uncommon and may have an unusual grain. This is not always so, of course: some foreign woods are ragged, produce splinters, and have no use in any of your constructions.

One thing that has to be checked is any residual smell or fruit juice impregnation. There are ways of cleaning wood, but some smells and stains are very persistent. Some smells may be transferred to other wood, so be careful how you store and transport your findings.

Grocery stores aren't the only source of wooden containers. Many heavy or fragile items—chemicals, cleaning fluids, glass, machinery—are packed this way. This particularly applies to items that are imported. Shipping can be rough on packages, so anything that has to travel by sea may be in containers made of stout wood. Such containers are not returnable, as their origin may be the other side of the world. Much of this wood is heavy and the plywood used is thicker than most scrap, so a friendly importer of machinery may be a good source of supply.

There are delicate things that need the protection of wood. Scientific instruments may be packed in well-made crates. This also applies to musical instruments: if a piano has to be taken far, its container is likely to be wood, with construction that permits easy dismantling. Besides stores, places like colleges receive a great many items packed in wood, and often regard disposing of the packing as a nuisance. Useful wood may be broken up and burned or put out with the trash. If you let it be known that you will take such things away, they may regard it as a service, while you regard it as a way of building up your stock of useful material.

Users of engineering and other machinery will probably have to return the majority of crates, but even then there are often pieces of useful wood that fit inside to brace particular machines that do not have to go back. A machine crate is usually made of wood of quite large section, with bolts that are easy to salvage. If a large crate is non-returnable, you may be able to use it in its entirety, or complete panels may be used without dismantling it completely.

Some trucking companies use crates that they adapt to suit loads. The crates wear out, but that does not mean every piece of wood is worn out. There may still be parts worth removing to use for something else. The owners may be glad to let you take away old (or non-returnable) crates as an alternative to burning them or paying to have them taken away.

Keep an eye out for unusual packing arrangements. One type of freezer is supplied on a wooden frame that protects its base, but is no longer needed when the freezer is installed. This yields strips of easily-separated wood 3 inches by 3/4 inch in good condition. Most installation engineers would be glad to have you take these away.

PALLETS

With the invention of the fork lift came the need for pallets. Pallets are the wooden platforms into which the fork ends enter to lift a load (Fig. 1-1A). There are several sizes and methods of construction, but usually there are strips nailed to three stout cross members (Fig. 1-1B).

In use, a pallet remains under its load so it can be moved around or stacked. Until the items comprising the load are disposed of, the pallet remains with it. This means that it is often engaged by the forks, lifted and moved, then set down again. If the operator does not get the fork ends at exactly the right level, they may stab the wood instead of entering the space (Fig. 1-1C). As the power behind the forks is considerable, the outer piece of wood is the first to become damaged. Pallets may be repaired, but quite often this is not considered worth the time and effort, so the pallet is thrown away. Much of its wood may still be useful to you.

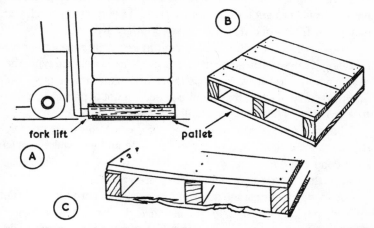

Fig. 1-1. Pallets are used with fork lifts to move loads. Damaged pallets yield much useful wood for recycling.

A user of pallets may be willing to let you have the damaged ones. He might also be willing to consider a proposal that you cannibalize damaged pallets to make sound ones in return for keeping the remaining wood. As construction is usually straightforward nailing, dismantling without damaging the wood is fairly easy.

Like packing cases and crates, pallets are often a byproduct of some other woodworking process. A lumber yard may make pallets or boxes. A furniture maker may use offcuts to make packing cases. It is worthwhile to search out sources of similar materials in different places. You may find that all the pallets in one place are made from narrow strips, while another source may yield much wider boards, due to a difference in the main product of which pallet-making is a subsidiary use. It does not matter to the pallet user how many pieces are used to make up the required surface area, but it may be of interest to you.

USED WOOD

Old and broken furniture has already been mentioned as one way to get useful wood. Besides your own and your friends' castoffs, dealers in old furniture often have pieces at the back of their stores which they don't expect to sell because they are outdated, broken or unattractive. A table with a leg missing may be beyond repair, but if the top is solid wood in reasonable condition, you may be able to visualize it cut up and made into something entirely different. It may not be possible to get it for nothing, but with the right approach you may get it for a price that still makes it attractive.

Restorers of antique furniture often get their repair material this way. If the wood in some damaged furniture is a choice type, the dealer may realize its value, but there are many newer pieces of furniture made of wood that is quite good, but not of particular value to a restorer. These pieces should be cheap.

Furniture sales may include pieces for which there are no bids. If you examine the furniture before the sale and see which pieces have good wood in them, you may be able to buy them dirt-cheap because they're not appealing as they are.

Also check out garage and rummage sales. There may be little interest in a shaky bookcase, for instance. Perhaps it is no longer effective for its original purpose, but there are boards in it that could be used again. If you are lucky, you may come away with it at a bargain price.

Anything made of wood is worth your attention: pick it up, turn it over, look inside it, and thoroughly check it as a wood source and not as the piece of furniture it is at the moment. Something may have been spilled inside. It may have been attacked by borers, or part may be rotted. The seller has no responsibility for the quality of the wood—what you buy is your responsibility. If you find it is useless when you get it back to your shop, you will have to charge off the cost to experience.

Watch for houses that are being dismantled. Wreckers tend to move swiftly. Wood may be mixed with stone, bricks, plaster and other debris. What could be useful wood may become mangled and broken as it is pushed into piles, so if you are to salvage such things as floor boards, studding and roof beams, you may have to be on the spot at the right stage in dismantling. As with other salvaging operations, get permission. Find out who is supervising the work on the site; if he is cooperative, he may suggest the best time to come and forage amongst the debris. Permission from the man at the top is always advisable—know his name and quote it if someone asks what you are doing.

Some items in a dismantled building may be used again by those doing the work or by a builder associated with them. Doors for instance, may be taken off carefully for use elsewhere or, if it is a very old house, there may be something like a fireplace that has antique value. These things are not for you. They may form part of the return that the wreckers hope to get from their work by selling such items to those engaged in restoration elsewhere. Make sure you know what you are allowed to take and be careful not to exceed your allowance, nor to do anything that increases the work of the wreckers. If you scatter debris in your search for wood and leave it for others to clean up, you will become unpopular and that source of supply will be lost.

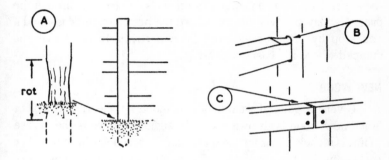

Fig. 1-2. Outdoor woodwork tends to rot at ground level or where water can be trapped, but when these parts are cut out, some useful wood can be recovered.

Another source of supply, at least to the rural searcher, is discarded fencing. A fence post rots first near ground level (Fig. 1-2A). The part buried in the ground may still be in good condition and the section more than six inches above the ground may be unaffected. What is in the ground is not worth bothering with, but the upper part is probably too good to burn, although no longer big enough for fence construction. In horizontal rails, any rot will be in places where water can be trapped, such as where ends go into sockets (Fig. 1-2B) or are nailed (Fig. 1-2C). If there is rot any-where, the spores of decay may be present in apparently sound wood some distance from the obvious rot, so cut well back and burn the scrapped parts so spores cannot move to previously sound wood.

19

Wood that has been used in a fence or other outdoor construction will have weathered. There are a few indoor applications where a weathered finish is required, but usually such wood is best used for something else outside. Weathered wood is not usually impaired in strength, and it's certainly well-seasoned. It may be reused for a similar purpose, but the beauty of the weathering will really distinguish such items as a carved name board.

Dumps can be a valuable source of old wood, hardware, and other usable material. Smaller dumps are best, for the larger operations sometimes bury waste almost as soon as it's dumped. They're also unsympathetic to requests for permission to sort through their trash.

But the smaller operations can be a goldmine. If you get to know the supervisor, you can usually get permission to sort through the piles. He may give you tips on where the better material is—and if you stop by often—may even have particularly good material dumped where it's easily accessible.

NEW WOOD

Given the general wastefulness of modern society, quite a bit of brand-new wood is thrown away. In addition, there is the phrase "Time is money." This means that a stage is reached where the labor costs outweigh the economies of using certain wood. Two pieces of wood may be too narrow for whatever is being manufactured. Glued together, they could be used, but the time cost of making the joint would not be economical, so the narrow pieces are thrown away. Someone producing a series of standard wood parts may come to a piece with a knot or split. He has to discard it, although most of the piece could be used for something else—by you, if you have made arrangements to collect these things.

The same thing may happen in a lumber yard. If wood is being cut to suit the needs of a customer, there may be many offcuts that are too short or too narrow to sell at standard prices. In fact, the original customer may have paid for them. You may not get them for nothing, but they should be quite cheap. It is probably best to buy a trunkload of "firewood" rather than pick over the offcuts too carefully. If it is seen that you want particular pieces of wood, the salesman may charge you higher prices than if you take them as part of a miscellaneous collection of oddments, allegedly for firewood.

Plywood manufacture is another process that depends on uniformity. If anything going through does not conform, it is discarded. If a particular run is making sheets 8 feet by 4 feet and at the end of the line comes a piece 2 feet long, it is thrown away; yet it may be a pack of perfectly good veneers or, if glued, a perfectly sound piece of plywood. For better-quality plywood, veneers containing knots, splits, or other flaws are cut out as the long line of veneer from the revolving log is fed towards the manufacturing line. There may be a piece 4 feet wide and several feet long with just a small flaw that would make several square feet of good veneer for another purpose, but it does not suit quantity production of plywood, so it has to go.

If you are within reach of a plywood factory, it is worthwhile enquiring what happens to the scrap material. Usually it's a problem to the factory—you may find they burn it periodically or continually. If you can get permission to pick over the scrap before it is burned, this can be a valuable source of free plywood and veneer.

A building site is another place where new wood may be obtained. When a carpenter has to cut a piece of wood to size, the remainder may be a useful length. If there is a place where it can be used soon, it may be picked up again, but otherwise it is likely to join the pile of other spare and wasted materials.

Obviously, you cannot just walk onto a building site and help yourself. On some sites there is a security problem concerning new material: you should obtain permission to forage among the waste piles or you may find yourself suspected of intent to thieve. If you get permission to take away waste wood, it is advisable to arrange to stop by at intervals; otherwise, wood discarded early may become soiled with other building materials. If you can arrange to pick up scraps at frequent intervals, rather than wait until the bulk has accumulated, the quality of what you get will be better.

TRANSPORT

The occasional small piece of salvaged wood is no problem to transport. A surprising amount of wood is discarded along the roadside, so it's worthwhile to carry a coarse-toothed saw in your car. If you see a piece of abandoned wood that is too big for your trunk, you can cut it to length on the spot.

Smaller crates can be carried intact in the same way. If they will not fit in the trunk, they may travel on a seat, but be careful of torn wood and projecting nails. Pieces of carpet or blanket material may be used to protect car upholstery. Many people receiving something in a crate are fairly ruthless in breaking it open, so look all around it and break off splinters or knock in projecting nails. A claw hammer should join the saw as part of the salvaging kit in your car.

If you are salvaging long wood, it is a pity to cut it to fit the car trunk, for much of its value to you is in its length. If you have no other means of transport, a roof rack on a car will take a considerable amount of long wood. The type of rack used for a boat is best. If you carry the wood directly on the car roof, pad the roof with blankets or similar material. Tie the wood together as well as to door handles or other secure points. Also tie down the ends to control bounce. If the load is longer than the car, make sure you conform to local laws about overhang.

In some cases, such as dealing with offcuts from a factory or the wood from a dismantled building, it may be a question of all or nothing. If you approach one of these places for permission to collect surplus wood, the answer may be that you can clear out all their waste wood, but you are not invited to pick it over and be selective.

You will have to decide if you are to take up the proposition. You may find yourself with a storage and disposal problem. Will you be able to keep all that might be useful at some future date? Can you dispose of all that will be no use to you and may be no use to anyone? If it is a once-only offer, the problem is not so great, but if the only way you can get what you want now is to offer to remove future scrap wood, you will have to weigh the advantages and disadvantages in relation to your circumstances.

Some of the best crates tend to be big. Some of the best sources of supply of old pallets or offcuts prefer you to take everything, even if only on one occasion. These loads are too great for a car, and it may be worthwhile borrowing a truck for the occasion. The value of what you are getting—to you, although probably not to anyone else—may justify renting a truck.

Much depends on what you want to do. If you only want scrap wood to use on occasional projects, the transportation problem is small. However, salvaging wood to reuse tends to get more engrossing, until you reach the point of looking at almost anything wooden with a view to reusing it. The actual collection of wood becomes almost as much a hobby as making things from it.

What starts as a hobby may develop into a business. You may make and sell things from salvaged material, sometimes combined with wood bought for the purpose. Your material costs are then low, so you can allow yourself a reasonable payment for labor, while still offering goods at reasonable prices.

If you are able to maintain a supply of offcuts by arrangement with a lumber yard or plywood factory, such pieces can be squared up and made generally presentable to sell to craft workers. If you reach this stage, you will certainly need your own truck. Your source of supply may regard you as someone who comes regularly and clears out his scrap wood. You may regard him as the place where your business is founded.

Chapter 2
Types of Materials

The collector of scrap and salvaged wood from various sources is liable to accumulate a very large range of wood and wood products. Some of these cannot be recognized in the form in which they are found and some not even when they have been planed and sanded, for the number of types of trees used for lumber is more than any one person can expect to recognize. There are scientific ways of classifying woods, but these are beyond the scope of the wood salvager and unnecessary—it is sufficient that a piece of wood has an attractive appearance, although you may not know what it is.

Trees that yield wood for our purposes are broadly divided into hardwoods and softwoods. In most cases these are descriptive terms, but there are a few softwoods that are harder than some hardwoods. The names do not really indicate comparative hardness. Hardwood lumber comes from broad-leafed trees, most of which lose their leaves during the winter. Softwood comes from narrow-leaved trees, such as the cone-bearing firs and pines, that keep their leaves during the winter. A scientist may have a more exact definition, but these broad classifications will serve our purpose.

Which wood is used depends on many factors, primarily availability. In most areas, softwood is cheaper and more available. However, in some locales, the dominant wood may be a hardwood: in the tropics for instance, there are few softwoods. If crate production is subsidiary to some other woodworking, the type of wood will depend on the other activity.

This applies worldwide, and also within the United States. The yellow pine—a softwood—may be most readily available in the south, but in some eastern states a hardwood may be more readily available for crates. If the packing case has come from a foreign country, a knowledge of the trees grown there may guide you.

Most wood obtained via salvage will be softwood. It is not easy to see what type of wood is used when it is rough-sawn and dirty, but scraping or planing to expose a smooth surface will allow the grain to be examined. Most softwoods are lighter than hardwoods. The surface is softer and more easily dented with a metal tool edge. Grain is mostly a light creamy brown. Where there are prominent grain lines, they are in two shades of the same color, but in many softwoods the grain lines are not very prominent. If the lines are easy to see, this is usually due to the presence of resin; this may be obvious from feel or smell.

Hardwoods vary more in appearance than softwoods. They can be almost any color, but browns and reddish browns predominate. The annual rings do not usually cause grain lines of much contrast, and in most cases the wood surface is more closely knit, so it is hard and more resistant to denting.

The difference between softwoods and hardwoods is more obvious if you examine a few known examples, for descriptions and pictures cannot fully describe the qualities that define soft and hard woods. The differences are important. If you want to make a piece of furniture that will polish well, you must use a hardwood. Softwood can be painted and has many construction uses, but for a polished furniture finish you would be disappointed with softwood.

Some hardwoods from the tropical countries are red, may not be very hard (although they are hardwoods), and are often called mahogany, although many of them are really other species. Some have a rather open grain and tend to split and splinter, so it is difficult to do good work with them; others will take a good finish and may be made into very attractive polished wood articles. With an unknown reddish wood you will have to do some experimental work to check its qualities.

The U.S. and other countries use systems of grading wood, primarily for structural applications. Straight-grained wood is graded better than wood with twisted grain, knots and other flaws. This is important in building carpentry, but if the wood is to be used decoratively, a twisted grain may look better than a straight grain. About the only wood that's useless to a salvager is that which has warped and twisted excessively. Even then it should be looked at to see if it might be made into something after cutting into shorter lengths or narrow strips to minimize the distorted shape.

Wood *sections* describe wood that's been sawn but not planed. A two-by-four measures two inches by four inches after sawing. After planing it can be as much as 3/8 inch less in each dimension, i.e., 3 5/8 inch by 1 5/8 inch, but it's still called a two-by-four. Standard sections are more applicable to softwood than hardwood, as these are the usual building woods. Sawn size is also referred to as the nominal size.

Some crate material is planed, some is only sawn, and sometimes it is a mixture of the two. Quite often the machine planing is quick, so there are prominent ridges; it may have been planed with one pass, so parts are left rough from the saw. An advantage of planing is that it allows a much better examination of the quality of the wood. You can see the grain, and knots and flaws are obvious even if the planed surface is dirty. Sawn wood has a rough overall appearance that hides what is underneath. It is easy to assess the worth of planed wood, but if it has a sawn finish, you may have to dismantle and plane it to find out if the wood is worth bothering with.

If the thing you are considering is sawn wood; or in such a condition that you are doubtful about its value for salvage, it may be possible to plane an edge so you can see the grain. With a little experience you can tell if it is hard or soft and identify the probable species from a small planed area. The way the wood planes will also indicate if it is seasoned. A smooth easy shaving from a sharp plane indicates seasoned wood that will be easy to make into something else. If the wood drags on the plane with an apparent wetness and the surface is rough, the wood may still be of value, but it will have to be seasoned before it is used.

SEASONING

In a living tree, sap forms the new wood around the outside of old wood. Sap is not as plentiful in the winter as in the summer, so trees are usually felled in the winter. Even then there is quite a bit of moisture in the wood which must be dried out by a process called *seasoning*.

Logs are cut into large boards and stacked so air can circulate around them (Fig. 2-1A). In the past, the only method of seasoning was the natural one: the stacked boards might have been sheltered under a roof, but otherwise they were open to the air and dried out naturally. The usual period for most woods was one year for each inch of board thickness, so the process was a long one. Today wood is dried artifically in a kiln in a much shorter time.

Much wood used for packing cases is seasoned, because it comes from the same source as wood for other purposes. But it may not be, for *green* wood may be quite satisfactory for a one-use-only crate.

The term "green" has nothing to do with the color of the wood, but means the wood was not seasoned before being made into something. Seasoned wood is not absolutely dry; it still contains a small amount of moisture. This means it is compatible with the atmosphere and is unlikely to take up or give out much moisture, so it will remain stable. Excessively wet or dry wood may warp or expand and contract as it adjusts to a satisfactory moisture content (Fig. 8-1).

Wood that is being seasoned tends to dry more on the outside and at the ends first. Sometimes the ends of boards are painted to prevent too rapid drying, or battens may be nailed across (Fig. 2-1B).

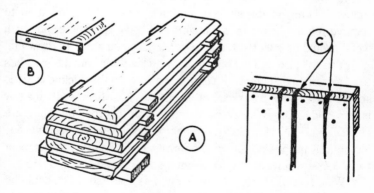

Fig. 2-1. Wood has to be stacked (A) so air can circulate for it to season naturally. Ends may be nailed to prevent splitting (B). If unseasoned wood is used in a crate, joints will open and boards will crack (C).

If green wood has been used to make a crate or other form of packing, its seasoning will have started during the time between cutting to size and dismantling by the finder. If this is a sufficient length of time, seasoning may have been completed, but it is probable that ends will have split and edges that were close will now have open joints (Fig. 2-1C). Providing the wood is still reasonably flat, it still has possibilities.

If the wood is still green, boards should be stacked in the same way as for natural seasoning. It is unwise to try to hasten seasoning by putting the stack in a hot place: the result is likely to be warping and twisting.

WOOD SIZES

The framing members from crates and other sources are usually not very different in their sectional dimensions. Although they may not always be square, they are fairly thick in relation to their width. In a crate they are used for corner members, with the sides fastened to them in both directions. In house construction they support floorboards or are used for stud to support wall paneling.

Such wood serves a key purpose in the original construction and will usually be valuable for a similar purpose in anything you make. Such pieces may also be the source of wood to carve or turn on a lathe, particularly if you are lucky enough to have found an attractive hardwood. When you make anything of *carcass* form (with paneled sides) fixed to a frame of solid wood) these pieces will form the frame. When you dismantle something there is a temptation to remove the flat boards and paneling and leave the frame, but such wood should be collected to give you a balanced stock to draw on.

You will also find flat boards varying in width from a few inches to a foot or more. Their width depends mainly on the thickness of the source tree; some trees cannot be cut into boards more than a few inches wide. Others may make very wide boards, but they are normally cut down into narrower boards, except when needed wide for special purposes. An exceptionally wide board may warp or twist, even when carefully seasoned and handled.

Wide boards are useful for many purposes, so they should be carefully removed to avoid splitting or other damage. The best wide boards for reuse are upwards of 5/8-inch actual thickness. Thicker boards in sound condition are valuable stock. Thinner and narrower pieces have more limited uses due to their size, although laminating allows building them up to bigger sections. For instance, many narrow offcuts can be glued together to make up a wide board. A drawer side 5 inches deep may be made up by gluing pieces of different (narrow) widths.

Wide boards less than 5/8-inch thick may still be worth keeping; much depends on their condition. Some imported fruit crates are made of wood so thin as to barely survive one trip. This is not much use when salvaged unless it is reasonably flat and without flaws. If it is rough-sawn, there would not be much wood left if the surfaces were planed. However, some of it may be laminated and may have possibilities for outdoor construction where its rough surface would not matter. If you are able to get crates or other things made from thin wood, save the best of it, but thicker wood will be of more use to you.

The place of wide boards is often taken by plywood. As plywood sheets can be much wider than any board and have good strength with less thickness and weight, plywood is attractive to crate makers when its price is reasonable. There are many grades of plywood. It might be expected that only the cheapest and roughest grades would be found in crates but, as with other materials, if the crate has been made as a subsidiary to something else, the plywood may be quite good. Even if the main structure of a crate is poor quality plywood, it is possible that better plywood will be found supporting a machine or propping a part inside.

Much plywood is made of fir, which has a coarse grain, particularly after it has been cut as a veneer from a rotating log. In the cheaper grades there are knots in the surface veneers. In a slightly better grade one side is free of knots. Farther up the scale comes plywood with no visible knots.

Plywood can be made from many types of wood, depending on need and availability. Plywood for furniture or cabinet work frequently has an outer veneer that matches the solid surrounding wood. Plywood from many foreign countries is made from a reddish mahogany-like wood that is smoother than fir.

At one time much plywood was made with a glue that was not waterproof, but most modern synthetic glues are water-resistant, if not fully waterproof. If the plywood in a crate has delaminated—started to come apart—it has been made with a glue that does not stand up to damp conditions. This is not worth keeping, although you may have to remove it to get at other material you want.

Thinner plywood is mostly three-ply and worth having for panels and similar applications. Thicker plywood has five or more plies. In a given thickness, a large number of thin plies results in a stiffer panel than a lesser number of thicker plies. Sound plywood 1/2-inch thick or more is valuable salvage. Not only is new plywood of this thickness expensive, it is a good base material for many things and can be used for veneering and marquetry.

Plywood from a building site may be anything from the roughest grades to some with special surface treatments. It may have an attractive decorative veneer or the surface may have a plastic coating—a thick coat for a table or a thin decorative treament for a wall panel. All of these things are valuable stock, even if the pieces are not very big. It is always possible to work them into a small item and feature their special finish.

Hardboard is a manufactured board with a wood base but no apparent grain. Usually one surface is smooth and the other has a checkered effect where it has taken the impression of the mesh on which it has dried. Usual thicknesses are 1/8 inch and 1/4 inch. Sheet sizes are similar to those of plywood.

Hardboard can be used for some of the same purposes as plywood, but it is not as strong and most of it has little resistance to dampness. Its most likely reuse is as bottoms of drawers, backs of cabinets and similar items. The smooth side, if it is undamaged, will take paint and other finishes well. It can also be used for marquetry or as a backing in a picture frame. Some artists paint very effectively directly on hardboard. The manufactured surface of hardboard is very smooth and should not be sanded. Scratched hardboard surfaces cannot be restored by sanding, but they may still have uses in less important places. Some interior paneling that is apparently wood is actually hardboard with a plastic or veneer film that simulates wood. Offcuts of this material have many possibilities in making small items; in most cases the surface is hard and waterproof, so it can be used on tables or for tray bottoms.

Hardboard may have a painted or enamel surface that's much harder and smoother than could be obtained by brushing. Pieces of this material are worth saving. Even if the color is not what is finally required, the manufactured finish is a good base for smooth brush painting. Hardboard may also be supplied with a metal (usually aluminum) surface. This needs careful cutting and working, but it can be used where a metal protective surface is needed.

There are sheet plastics that have possibilities. Formica and similar sheet materials may be found already attached to plywood, but if they have to be removed from an old bar top or other working surface, they can usually be pried away so the old glue on the back may be sanded to make the material suitable for use again.

DEFECTS

Besides splits, knots, shakes, and other obvious natural faults, old wood may be suffering from rot or it may have been attacked by borers, often called "wood worms." Rot has been mentioned in connection with fence posts, where its presence is usually obvious, but an old crate that has had a part wet for a long time may have rot that's not so obvious.

If wood feels spongy and soft or gives a dead response when knocked, suspect rot. It may now be dry, but at some time it has been damp and spores of decay have taken hold. Rot cannot be reversed. There is no satisfactory treatment. The damaged wood and some of the surrounding sound wood has to be burned. Unless it has plenty of sound wood elsewhere that can be cut away, it is usually best to ignore a rotten crate.

If you have accepted a crate and discover rot, burn the rotten part. Do not keep it with the idea of using it for something less important: the spores may move to other wood and infect that. If you use wood that has been near rotten wood, treat it with one of the preservative solutions available.

The presence of borers is indicated by a number of small holes. The worms are actually grubs deposited by a flying insect; they burrow into and eat the wood, and do not emerge to the surface again until ready to fly away. They may honeycomb the wood below the surface, sometimes to the extent that it collapses. Usually, the effect is not as serious as that—most wood that has been attacked can be used again. The grubs are only active for a few months around July. At that time, if there are live worms in the wood there will be wood powder around the holes. In any case, the wood should be treated with one of the fluids intended to kill the pests. If the infestation seems bad, discard the wood. The borers appear to favor certain woods and sometimes only parts of those woods. Sapwood is more likely to be attacked than heartwood.

CLEANING

Preparation of rough wood for further use is dealt with in Chapter 4, but quite often the wood as dismantled is dirty and contaminated with oil or other fluids. They should be removed before attempting to bring the surface to a good finish or your tools may be blunted or clogged.

The best way to deal with dirt on wood is the same as with dirt anywhere: wash it. But do not soak it in water too long for wood is absorbent, particularly along the grain, and water will seep into end grain a long way and take a long time to dry out. It is better to place the wood on a surface where water can run away and use hot water and detergent to scrub the surfaces. Wash away all detergent and dirt with clean water, but keep the water flowing so it cannot settle anywhere, especially not on end grain. Set the wood to dry where water can run off all surfaces. Allow plenty of time for the wood to dry naturally: forced drying with heat may cause warping.

Detergent will remove fruit juices and many other stains, but it may not be very effective with grease. Kerosene or gasoline will dissolve grease, but may spread their own stain in doing so. A liquid intended for cleaning paint brushes may be more effective.

Hard paint can be removed by scraping after softening with a blowtorch. This may mark the wood, which won't matter if you paint it, but if the wood is to get a clear finish, use a chemical paint stripper. However, read the instructions, particularly about how to neutralize the stripped surface; otherwise there may be a chemical left that might harm the wood or affect a later surface treatment.

Some stains may be quite deep in the wood. It is unlikely that these can be removed completely, but the surface can be made to look better by wiping it with a solvent. It may be possible to reduce the color with domestic bleach, but this may affect the wood color as well. Then the only way to get an even effect would be to bleach the whole surface, and this may not match the surrounding wood.

Any hard deposit on the wood may be better treated mechanically. The crate's contents may have dripped a resin that has hardened or you may find lumps of hard mastic. The bond to the wood is not usually very tight, so it is often possible to lever under the material and get it off in one piece with little damage to the wood surface. This is better than softening the material to a paste that may cause more trouble.

Beware of broken glass, metal particles and similar things. If the contents of a crate have broken it may be impossible to get rid of embedded glass and metal. If the wood can be used without treatment it may be worth keeping, but the surface would damage your tools. Be certain to remove all nails and other fastenings, or you may find yourself spending a lot of time sharpening and repairing tools.

Chapters 3
Dismantling
and Salvaging

Care in taking apart a crate or other wooden article will result in more usable wood than will a hasty or rough approach. It is worthwhile spending time planning the work before starting on what may seem to be the obvious part. Careless work can result in splits or marked wood that will be no use for anything important. Sometimes the parts are joined in a way that defies dismantling and the only way to get anything useful from the assembly may be to cut off the joined parts. However, it is often possible to withdraw fastenings that were intended never to be dismantled.

Any crate or packing case was put together in a sequence which is usually fairly obvious. Dismantling should be in the reverse order. In a box type, the bottom was probably put on last and the longer sides are fixed to the ends.

In nailed construction there is a choice of removing the nails or driving the wood pieces apart so the nails come with them to be removed later. In a simple construction, with sides nailed to an end (Fig. 3-1A), the sides may be driven outwards, but do not be tempted to merely hit them directly with a hammer. This will produce too local a shock that may split the wood and will certainly mark it. Instead, put a piece of scrap wood across the inside and hammer fairly lightly along it to loosen the nails (Fig. 3-1B). If there is an opposite end to be dealt with in the same way, do a little at each end rather than completely separating one end first. If you must

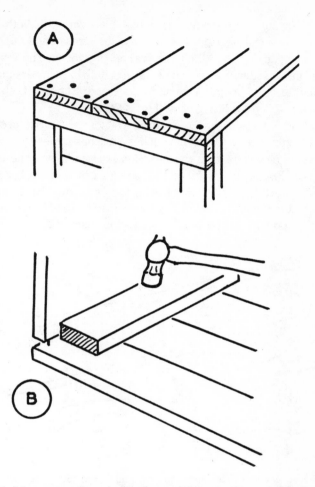

Fig. 3-1. A hammer and wooden block are sufficient to dismantle most crates.

make direct hits anywhere, a mallet is less liable to damage the wood than a hammer.

DISMANTLING TOOLS

Several tools used in woodwork construction can be used for dismantling, but there are a few special tools intended for the purpose. The word "wrecking" is sometimes associated with them. This is unfortunate, as their correct use separates parts with a minimum of damage and does not wreck the material in the process.

A ripping bar (crowbar) is a tool-steel rod with both ends flattened to a chisel shape. One end may be straight and the other slightly angled (Fig. 3-2A) so there is a heel to pivot on. The leverage can be increased by curving one end (Fig. 3-2B). Such bars may be two feet or more long, to give ample leverage. Either or both ends may be notched for lifting nails (Fig. 3-2C).

Another ripping chisel has the ends offset and a variation on the nail notch provides a slot to slide under a nail head; then the bar can be levered on its end to lift the nail. Stanley also makes a one-ended nail claw (Fig. 3-2D) 11 inches long and a more compact bar made from flat stock (Fig. 3-2E) that can be carried in a tool kit. Length is important for leverage, so if a ripping bar is to be used in dismantling heavy wood with long nails, a large tool is essential.

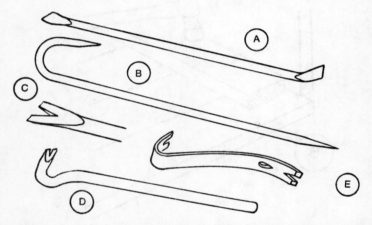

Fig. 3-2. A variety of levers are used for prying and removing fasteners.

A ripping bar can lever a joint open a considerable way in one action (Fig. 3-3A). The straight end may be needed to make an entry; then the shaped end is put in the joint. If it is a wide joint with many nails, lift only a little at each point, then progressively separate the parts to avoid cracking.

It is possible to open joints with an ordinary woodworking chisel, pushed in and levered. There is a flooring chisel (Fig. 3-3B) intended for lifting floor boards, but with its two-inch-wide blade and long steel handle, it is stronger and provides more leverage than a normal chisel. Such a wide chisel will also work with a twist (Fig.

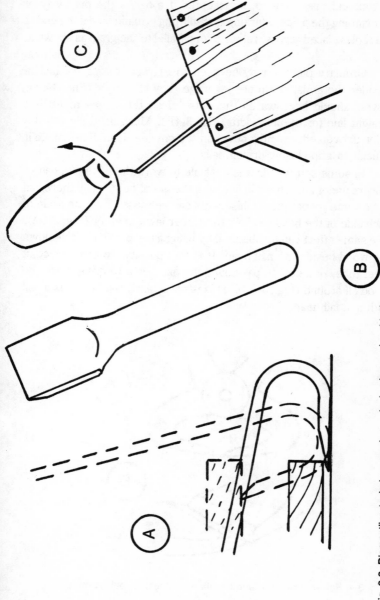

Fig. 3-3. Dismantling techniques using a ripping bar and a chisel.

3-3C). A ripping bar will also sometimes work better if it is twisted as well as levered.

Of course, a ripping bar will dig into the wood. This may not matter and may have to be accepted if a bar is the only way of dismantling the piece. Marking and splitting is minimized if the end of the tool is placed across, rather than parallel to the grain as shown in Fig. 3-3C.

Ordinary pincers may be used to extract smaller nails. The broader the ends, the more leverage they can apply (Fig. 3-4A). Bevels should be towards the outside, so the edges meet in a straight line for the full width (Fig. 3-4B). Much-used pincers develop uneven edges and a bevel on the outside. Both flaws make it difficult to grip closely-driven nails.

In some soft woods it is possible to work the edge of a pair of pincers under a nail head in line with the grain, but usually there has to be some preparation. Chisel cuts can be made along the grain of each side of the head to allow the pincer jaws to enter (Fig. 3-5A). The same effect can be obtained by using a nail punch to drive down the wood beside the nail head. It is also possible to use a piece of steel tube, of a size to pass over the nail head, to drive down the wood all around (Fig. 3-5B). This is particularly useful if it is a nail with a small head.

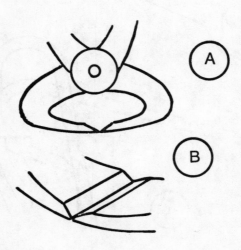

Fig. 3-4. Pincers with an inside bevel are the best for pulling nails.

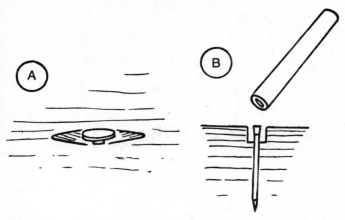

Fig. 3-5. Chiseling or punching the wood surrounding a nail may ease its removal.

Pincers are limited to nails that can be pulled easily. Ordinary nails about two inches long are about the limit, but the type of wood also affects tightness. For larger nails there are special nail pullers. Their patterns vary, but they usually have a pair of pincerlike jaws with a levering piece projecting to one side. The long handle has a sliding weight (Fig. 3-6) which, when dropped, produces enough force to drive the jaws into the wood beside the nail head. The action of levering tightens the jaws and the nail comes out.

Using pincers or a nail puller may damage the wood surface, but if the existing surface is good and damage is to be avoided, a scrap of plywood can be used to lever over (Fig. 3-7A). If the nail is long, a block of wood can be used after the first levering, to give a second purchase (Fig. 3-7B).

In some plywood construction, power-driven staples are used instead of nails. Although the tops are narrow, the legs may be quite long. They are difficult to grip with pincers, although the narrow jaws of a nail puller will go under the top. The alternative is to start loosening with a screwdriver. Insert a corner and twist or drive it (Fig. 3-8). When the center has been lifted, or one leg has started coming out, there should be enough metal to grip with pincers or pliers.

If parts of a crate are held together with nuts and bolts that have rusted, it may be possible to free them with penetrating oil or

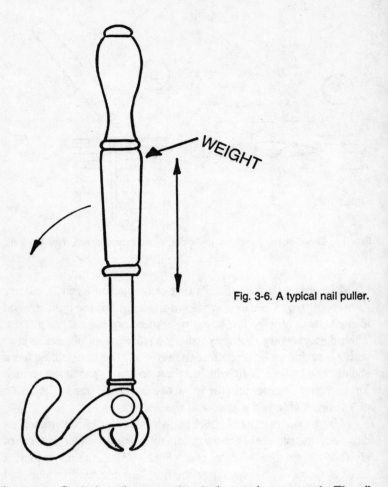

WEIGHT

Fig. 3-6. A typical nail puller.

kerosene. Soak them for some time before trying a wrench. The oil may enter the wood; if this risk is to be avoided, the bolt or nut may be cut. If the situation allows, a hacksaw can be used or, if the saw won't fit, a hacksaw blade alone to cut through the bolt between the nut and the wood (Fig. 3-9A). Bolt cutters (Fig. 3-9B) rely on great leverage to make the cutting edges go through the bolt or other iron or steel rod. Cutters with two-foot handles will cut through 3/16-inch bolts; larger sizes can cut bolts up to half-inch diameter.

The alternative to cutting the bolt is to split the nut; this is probably a better way for rusted crate fasteners since cutting the bolt would usually damage the wood. Splitting the nut to free it from

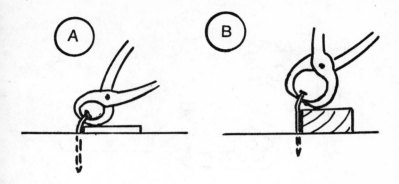

Fig. 3-7. Leverage is improved and the suface protected by use of blocks.

the bolt can usually be accomplished without affecting the wood. The tool engages the nut and two cutters are forced into it by tightening a screw (Fig. 3-9C). The capacity of one common splitter is a nut 3/4-inch across the flats.

Before attempting removal, clean slots by driving the edge of a screwdriver across them (Fig. 3-10A). This is important. Trying to turn a screw with rust or dirt in the slot may result in the screwdriver lifting and damaging the edge of the slot, hindering further attempts at removal. If a screw has rusted into the wood and defies turning, a tap with a hammer on the screwdriver may loosen it (Fig. 3-10B). If this fails, put the red hot end of a metal rod on the screw head. Hold it there long enough for the heat to penetrate.

A square screwdriver or one with flats on it can be levered with pliers (Fig. 3-10C). Press hard to hold the screwdriver in the slot and lever with a jerking action. Make sure the screwdriver end matches

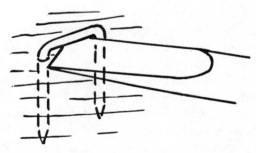

Fig. 3-8. A screwdriver will raise staples so they can be grasped with pliers.

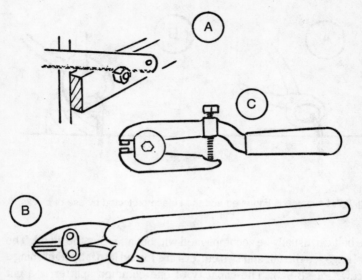

Fig. 3-9. Other means of convincing balky fasteners: (A) hacksaw blade; (B) bolt cutters; (C) nut splitter.

the slot. If it is loose, rounded (Fig. 3-10D) or too narrow (Fig. 3-10E), the leverage applied to the screw is diminished considerably.

Another way of getting maximum leverage on a screw is to use a screwdriver bit in a bit brace (Fig. 3-10F). As with any screw turning, lean heavily on the end of the brace to keep the bit in the slot. If you are not used to turning screws, remember: when looking at the screw head turn counterclockwise to loosen it. With a stubborn screw it sometimes helps to give it a slight turn in the driving direction before unscrewing.

Some light packing cases are joined with bifurcated (split) rivets (Fig. 3-11A). The two ends can be lifted with a screwdriver and squeezed parallel, or nearly so, with pliers, and the rivet pushed or punched out (Fig. 3-11B). If ordinary rivets are used, they will be used over washers. The burred end can be center-punched and drilled into enough to loosen the washer (Fig. 3-11C). Then punch the remains of the rivet out.

If a nut refuses to turn on a bolt, look for accidental or intentional burrs on the bolt end. The only way to free this is to grind or file the burred end away. If the nut will then unscrew you have a nut and bolt to use again.

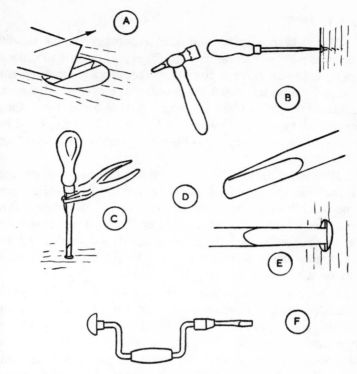

Fig. 3-10. Stubborn and rusted screws need special treatment.

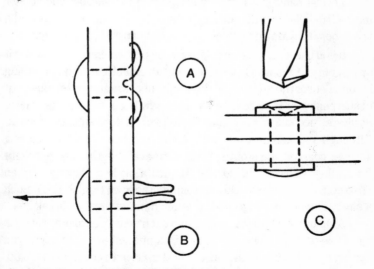

Fig. 3-11. Rivets should be drilled, then punched out.

43

CUTTING APART

The makers of crates and other containers are not usually concerned with ease of dismantling. Their objective is to make a packing case that will not come apart accidentally—they do not expect it to be any use after it has delivered its contents undamaged. Because of this, the construction may be such as to defy dismantling without causing damage to the wood. In such a case it may be wiser to cut away the fastened parts so the wood is removed in a state fit to use.

If the wood is in clean sound condition, it may be possible to use the same saws you use for finish work. But many crates have grit embedded in the grain or have old nails or other metal fasteners that are not immediately apparent. In that case it is wiser not to use saws that are also used on finish work, as damaged teeth would affect the quality of the finish work. It is better to keep saws for dismantling work or to use saws with disposable blades.

A useful saw for hand work is the bow saw (Fig. 3-12A), which is intended for cutting small logs or for pruning trees. If the crate is wet, this will cut without binding. The teeth are fairly coarse and often have gullets (Fig. 3-12B) to carry away sawdust. This is valuable when cutting green or wet wood, but not so important with dry wood. Teeth can be in several sizes, but are generally coarser than normal hand saws. The finest sawteeth available should suit most dismantling work. Although these blades can be sharpened a few times, they do not last long and are cheap and easy to replace.

If you use a portable circular saw, be certain there is no hard grit or nails in the wood. Otherwise an inadvertent cut into something hard may take the edge off all the teeth, necessitating a tedious bout of sharpening or replacement. A saber saw (jig or bayonet saw) uses easily-replaceable blades, and is well-suited to dismantling work. Although frequently used with a fine-toothed blade for cutting shapes, coarser and stouter blades are available that are excellent for cutting across crate boards. If such a blade is damaged by an obstruction, it can be quickly and simply replaced (Fig. 3-12C). Such a saw will leave an edge with the minimum of surface breakage.

Although you may be tempted to cut freehand across a crate it is advisable to draw a line. If the line is continued over the edge, you can joint points or sight across the bottom face to check for obstructions that would interfere with sawing or damage the saw. Some crates have blocks and attachments inside that were used to secure the contents. They can usually be removed before taking the main structure apart, but if sawing is hurried, the presence of a fitting may not be realized until the saw teeth hit it (Fig. 3-12D).

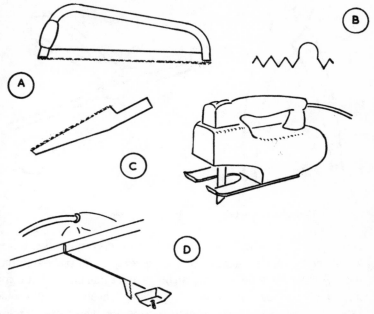

Fig. 3-12. Both hand and power saws are useful for dismantling.

METAL BANDS

Many wooden crates are bound with wire or flat metal strips. This is worth salvaging, if it's stout enough to be made into parts for outdoor woodwork, etc.

A convenient tool for cutting wire is a pair of end cutters (Fig. 3-13A). The meeting edges are sharpened and they extend wider than the handles, so they can be fitted across wire even when it is half embedded in the wood (Fig. 3-13B). These are more convenient than side or diagonal cutters, which cannot exert much power in the situation pictured. A pair of end cutters 7 inches long will deal with wire up to about 1/16 inch in diameter. Larger cutters will handle thicker wire.

Flat steel crate binding is usually quite thin, and can be cut with snips. Some have straight handles, while others have handles like

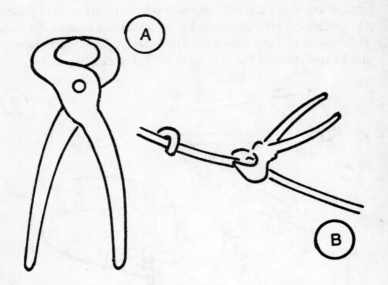

Fig. 3-13. End cutters are best for cutting binding wire.

scissors (Fig. 3-14A). It is the length of handles in relation to the length of the blades which provides leverage and makes cutting easy. Almost any type of snips can be used for thin bands, but if you buy a tool especially for this use, a total length of about a foot should be satisfactory. Some cutters have broad points, which give stiffness when cutting across sheet metal, but for breaking through bands, a fine point is easier to get under the tight metal.

Wire binding is often held on with stout staples which can be eased out with a pointed tool. Lighter staples may respond to a tool like an ice pick, but for tougher jobs use a pointed punch with a hammer (Fig. 3-14B). Once the staple has been eased away from the wire it can be lifted out with pincers. Bands are usually nailed on. It may be necessary to pry out the first few nails with an extractor or the end of a screwdriver, but then you can usually pull the binding (using gloves) free—the nails will either come off with the band (Fig. 3-14C) or their heads will be left accessible.

SALVAGING

Use care when dismantling even a small crate so that uneven strains do not cause cracking or splitting. As one part is cut through,

46

another joint may suddenly be loaded, twist, and drop. Support the part being cut, or have an assistant ready to hold it as it is cut through. A side may be removed completely if help is available, and then the crate turned over for removal of the other side. If you are working alone on a side whose width is made of several boards, leave one board in place while removing the others.

Use caution with very large crates: Some have sides heavy enough to hurt you badly if they fall.

Many crates are made with unseasoned wood, which shrinks as it dries out. If there are nails restricting shrinkage, cracks will develop (Fig. 3-15A). Whether to cut off the cracked end or keep the wood intact depends on what is to be made from it. If there is no immediate planned use, it may be advisable to store the wood as it is. If the planned use is for narrow strips, they may be cut beside the crack (Fig. 3-15B). If the wood is needed in its full width, the cracked end may be cut off (Fig. 3-15C). If the wood is stored carefully it is unlikely that the crack will spread further.

Nails and screws may not seem worth saving, but any amateur craftsman knows that a varied stock of fasteners is valuable. Apart from the economy of reusing fasteners, salvaging provides such an assortment that you'll have just the right size for almost anything.

In a packing case it is usually the head of a screw or nail that suffers the most. As this is the visible part, it is often the state of the head that decides if a fastener is worth keeping. Much can be done to revive appearance. Nails can be straightened on an iron block (Fig.

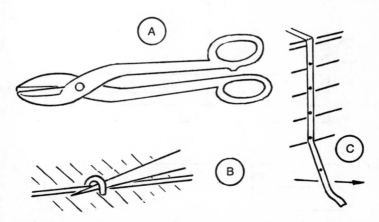

Fig. 3-14. Nailed strips and staples may require shears and a pointed punch.

3-16A). Always strike the bend, not the end. It may help to squeeze the nail in a vise. Screw heads can be brightened by holding them in holes in a wood block so they project slightly, then rubbing them on a piece of abrasive paper supported on a flat surface (Fig. 3-16B).

If the slot in a screw head has been damaged by the screwdriver twisting out, a hacksaw blade can be used to make the slot fractionally deeper (Fig. 3-16C) and the head can be cleaned up with a small file. Dirt or rust can be scraped out with a screwdriver blade. To avoid damage to screw threads, hold the screw between blocks of wood or make vise clamps from aluminum or copper (Fig. 3-16D).

The kinks can be hammered out of salvaged wire. It can be stored straight if it's not too long. If long, roll it, but not tightly or it may be difficult to get curves out later. Loops not less than 18 inches across are advisable. Thin metal strip will probably have been punched for nails; the ragged holes can be hammered flat before rolling the strip for storage.

If the steel wire or strip is rusty, it's a good idea not to clean it off unless the metal is to be used immediately. The first attack of rust

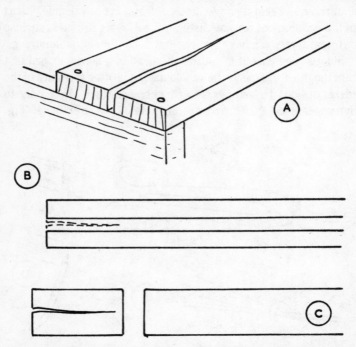

Fig. 3-15. Much salvaged wood will require treatment of cracks.

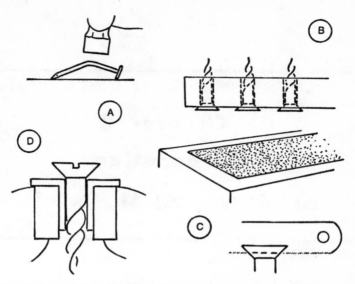

Fig. 3-16. Many salvaged fasteners can be reused with a little cleaning up.

on steel actually provides a protective coating that resists further rust. If the rust is cleaned off, the bright surface will rust again unless it is well protected, and the resulting pits will be deeper than if you hadn't cleaned it. If steel is still bright, the risk of rust can be avoided by coating with a rust-inhibiting fluid. Wiping with an oily cloth is not very effective, but will serve if a suitable fluid is unavailable.

Chapter 4
Preparation
of Salvaged Material

Salvaged wood and other materials may be unready for immediate use. Even when it has been washed and dried, it may be rough, with a surface that does not give much of a clue to what's underneath. Before you can determine what wood it is and what use it may have, the rough outer surface has to be removed.

If there is no doubt about the surface being free from grit and other hard substances, you may plane it. Unfortunately, used wood may have hidden pieces of hard substances that would harm a plane cutter. A chip out of the edge of a hand plane is a nuisance and necessitates much time spent in grinding and sharpening. Resharpening a power plane is even more work, so you need to be certain that the wood is clear of debris before using edge tools.

Paper labels will usually come off if thoroughly dampened. This should be tried first. If the paper does not float off it can probably be scraped away while saturated. A knife blade used sideways will work, or a chisel can be drawn across on edge (Fig. 4-1A). Wallpaper scrapers with wide blades and long handles, such as the Red Devil Zipaway Stripper (Fig. 4-1B), will take paper and adhesive off crate wood.

Some hook scrapers (Fig. 4-1C) have a blade with a slightly curved serrated edge that will remove paper labels. They're also useful for removing lettering or other marks that have been painted or stenciled on the wood. With any type of scraper, use a firm action.

Try to get right through the paint or other material in one stroke, if possible, so a thin sliver of wood comes away as well. This is better than many light scrapes, which can work the paint into the grain.

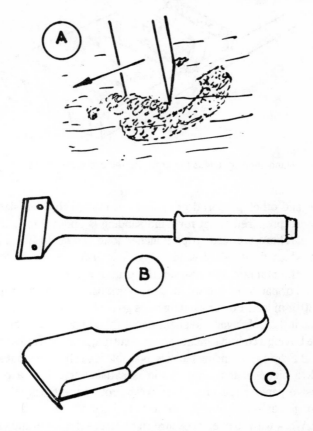

Fig. 4-1. Scrapers and chisels are useful for removing labels and crate markings.

If the wood has a rough surface and the marks have not penetrated very deeply, a surprisingly quick result can be obtained by hand-sanding across the grain with a coarse abrasive. Sanding with the grain tends to push any ink or paint into the grain, but cross-grain rubbing usually removes all the offending material with the fibers of wood that are rubbed off.

"Sand" paper is made in a variety of grits. Garnet is the natural grit, but most papers (quite often cloth) are coated with aluminum

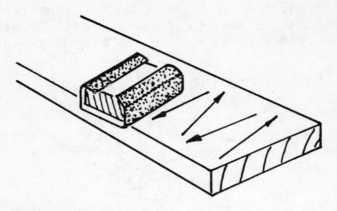

Fig. 4-2. Hand sanding across the grain will remove some marks.

oxide and other prepared grits that are graded to even size. The standard prepared sheet for hand sanding is about 9 inches by 11 inches. There are also strips 9 inches long and about 3 1/2 inches wide which fit standard sanding blocks. Grits are numbered; the lower the number, the coarser the grit. For preparation of rough printed or painted crate wood, use 36 grit paper. (The finer grits go to 220 or more.) Power sanding belts go to even coarser grades than 36, so if the only available sheet paper is too fine, it may be worthwhile buying a coarse sanding belt and cutting it up for hand sanding.

If a clip-type sanding block is available it can be used, but for this work a piece of flat scrap wood is satisfactory. Use a piece of abrasive paper large enough to wrap around the block (Fig. 4-2). Wear gloves—coarse grit can be very hard on the hand.

Work with an even pressure right across the wood and vary the area covered with each stroke to obtain a reasonably even surface. If one part does not clear at first, work over it and the surrounding area as much as needed, but be careful not to work in a hollow that will need considerable corrective action later.

A disc sander on an electric drill is a simple and cheap way of preparing a rough soiled surface. The backing pads are hard rubber, 7 or 9 inches in diameter. Either will do, but the smaller is better for small electric drills, as the drag on the periphery of the disc can put a heavy load on the drill. In addition to possible damage to the drill, slowing the disc makes it less effective.

Sander discs are available in the same grits as hand sanding sheets. A disc usually attaches to its backing pad with a cup-shaped washer and screw sunk into the center of the pad. Make sure this screw is as tight as possible: if a disc pulls away, it usually tears so it cannot be used again.

When using a disc sander, hold it so the shaft is slightly off perpendicular to the work so only part of the disc actually cuts (Fig. 4-3A). If the disc is held flat against the wood, it may be impossible to control. Keep the sander moving and do not use excessive pressure on the surface unless there is a particularly bad place to sand off. At first the movement of the cutting face can be across the grain (Fig. 4-3B). This will leave a pattern of scratches that will be fairly obvious as they cross the grain lines. When the surface is fairly clear, change to movements along the grain (Fig. 4-3C). You will still get curved scratches, but as they are nearly in line with the grain they are less obvious.

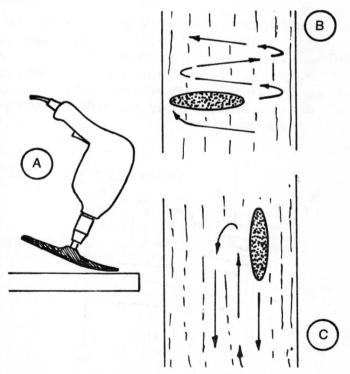

Fig. 4-3. With a disc sander, sand first across, then with the grain.

A belt sander is a more costly tool, and would not be justified for this purpose alone, but it is useful for many other woodworking operations as well. The belt on most belt sanders is between 3 and 4 1/2 inches wide. It is made in a continuous loop as much as two feet long, but the actual sanding area is about 4 inches long (Fig. 4-4). This will remove a lot of wood quickly, so keep the tool moving or you may make grooves from the edge of the belt or hollows under the working surface of the belt. As with other sanding, a belt sander gets rid of roughness best when used across the grain, but the surface will finish better when it is used along the grain. Belts are changed easily: use coarse grit for quick removal of a rough or marked surface, then a finer belt with the grain to give a smooth surface.

Wood salvaged from a building site is often spattered with concrete. Concrete may contain grits that are harder than those of abrasive paper, so trying to sand off concrete may merely ruin your abrasive sheet.

The blobs of concrete are usually not tightly bonded to the wood surface. A screwdriver may lift a blob clear and leave little marking of the surface. If more force is needed, a cold chisel and a hammer (Fig. 4-5) should be effective. If the wood is covered with concrete or the concrete is difficult to remove without tearing the wood, it may be wiser to discard the wood: any grit remaining in the grain will blunt saws, planes and other cutting tools.

WORKING AREA

Fig. 4-4. The working area of a belt sander is only a small portion of the belt.

Fig. 4-5. A cold chisel and hammer will remove lumps of concrete.

One new type of sander uses a large number of rotating abrasive flaps that brush over the surface. These can be used for rough and finish sanding, and work well on shaped as well as flat surfaces. Some of these tools are large and heavy so they are only suitable for use on a bench-mounted spindle; the lighter versions fit in the chuck of a portable electric drill and are of more use for salvaging wood.

Sand-o-Flex wheels (Fig. 4-6A) have abrasive strips rather like brush bristles. The ends of these strips hit against the wood at high speed, causing overall abrading. As the ends of the strips get worn, they can be fed outward by an adjustment at the hub. Diameter across the bristles is 6 inches and the standard tool fits a 5/8-inch shaft, but can be adapted to fit 1/2-inch or 1/4-inch shafts and chucks. The width of the abrasive is 1 inch. If the tool is on a fixed shaft the wood should be moved around for even sanding. If the tool is driven by a portable drill, it should be moved over the surface.

A less complicated tool is the Grind-o-Flex, which does not have a provision for feeding out more abrasive strip when the ends are worn. Instead, the flaps of abrasive cloth are permanently bonded between steel flanges. Various grades of grit are obtainable, including 40 grit, which will be suitable for preparing rough salvaged wood. The usual grinder is about 6 inches in overall diameter and 1 inch wide with a 1/2-inch hole which can be adapted to fit a 1/4-inch-drill chuck (fig. 4-6B). Both of these tools can be used on other materials besides wood, e.g., for cleaning steel or smoothing plastic after shaping.

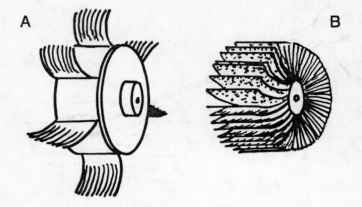

Fig. 4-6. Flap-action sanders will quickly smooth an irregular surface.

Another tool with a similar whipping action that should not be confused with the sander is the Roto Stripper (Fig. 4-7A). It uses steel arms for such tasks as stripping paint and removing rust. The device fits an electric drill and can be used to clean painted wood without using chemicals or burning. If wood is only partly painted, this is a good way of dealing with the painted portion and marks without affecting the clear parts.

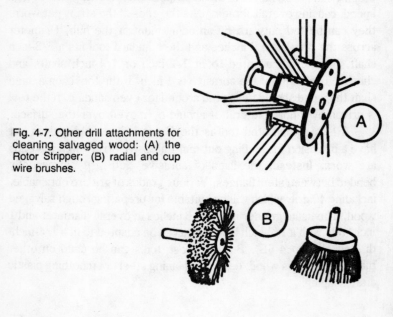

Fig. 4-7. Other drill attachments for cleaning salvaged wood: (A) the Rotor Stripper; (B) radial and cup wire brushes.

Radial and cup wire brushes (Fig. 4-7B) are not really wood-working tools, but mounted in the chuck of an electric drill, are suitable for removing local marks. Steel wire brushes will remove rust from steel and can be used to brighten heads of old screws.

If the surface is known to be free of anything that would damage a plane cutter and you decide to hand plane without any earlier preparation, the best tool is a jack plane. An old-fashioned wooden one may be kept for this purpose, as it is capable of a coarser cut than a modern steel plane—which is superior in other ways.

For cleaning off surface roughness and getting a reasonably smooth surface with a minimum of cuts, set the mouth of the plane as wide as it will go, (Fig. 4-8A). Sharpen the edge so it curves to take a deep cut at the center, tapering off to nothing at the sides (Fig. 4-8B). Set the cap iron farther back than normal, about 1/8 inch back from the apex of the cutting edge (Fig. 4-8C).

Make a few trial cuts to determine how coarse you can set the plane: it will vary from wood to wood. You may be able to plane along the grain, but if the grain is coarse and tends to tear up it may be better to make the roughing cuts at an angle to the grain (Fig. 4-8D) or even at a right angle to it. The aim at this stage is not to make a finished surface, but to remove the old surface.

Surfaces are the main problem, but edges may be in need of preparation if they are rough and damaged. Damage to an edge may be more serious than to a surface. The best treatment may be to draw a straight line and saw the original edge away (Fig. 4-8E) if the sacrifice of a little width is acceptable. If the edge is dirty and contains grit but you wish to retain most of its width, use a sander. You may have to plane later to get the edge straight, but this removes the old surface, providing a clean base to work from.

Another useful cutter is the Surform tool which cuts like a rasp, but is self-cleaning. Its replaceable blade is sheet steel perforated with teeth. The plane version (Fig. 4-8F) works well on edges. Rasps and files are valuable, but use only the type intended for working wood. A file intended for metal will clog almost immediately if used on wood. A coarse rasp has a cutting action very similar to a Surform tool, but needs cleaning with a wire brush occasionally.

BUILDING UP A STOCK

The avid collector of surplus wood will accept all that comes his way and will build up a stock that grows haphazardly. This is satisfac-

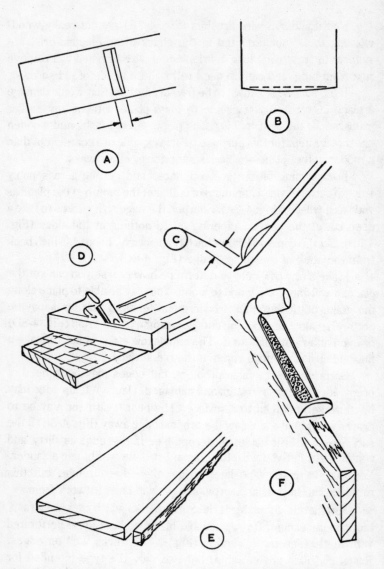

Fig. 4-8. Set the plane for a coarse cut when working on rough wood. A Surform tool can be used on rough edges.

tory, for a varied stock allows tackling a great number of different projects and may, in fact, suggest things to make.

Another advantage of a large and varied stock of wood is that they will be stored for some time. This allows them to settle into a stable condition. Even if they have been seasoned, the dismantling and hauling process may open cracks or cause slight distortion. It's far better to have these flaws develop while the wood's in your stockpile than after you've made something from it.

If you have certain projects in mind, you will know what surplus material you are looking for. However, be as flexible as possible in your designs: something attractive may turn up that is different from what you were planning. It would be a pity if you were tied so rigidly to a particular design that you could not adapt to take advantage of a new find.

There are some general principles to serve as a guide to foraging and salvaging. Wide pieces and long pieces are better stock than narrow and short pieces. Large pieces can always be converted to small pieces, but it is usually impossible to go the other way around.

This means that you should cut, transport, and store pieces as big as convenient. If any assembly is difficult to dismantle and you are unsure of what you will do with it eventually, it may be better to keep it in a partially dismantled state than reduce it to boards. For instance, you may go to a lot of trouble to remove balky fasteners but end up making something that would not have required their removal.

There are certain basic sections that are always good stock as they find a place in many types of construction. Strips of substantial section, such as 2 inches by 3 or 4 inches is always worth having. Large sections are particularly useful in outdoor construction: sheds, decks, benches, etc.

Small section strips are always good stock. Whatever you make will contain strips as frames, drawer runners, doorstops, and many other things. If you have plenty of strips, you will be saved the trouble of cutting down larger sections. Anything from 1 inch by 2 inches downwards, in as long a length as you can get, is worth keeping.

Wider pieces of solid wood at least 5/8 inch thick should form the backbone of the collection. For most furniture, wood of this thickness is generally needed for strength and stability. Wood nearer 1 inch thick is better for cutting joints. If you can find 1-inch boards 6 inches or so wide, you have the foundation for all sorts of construction.

Plywood is becoming increasingly available to the recycler as it progressively replaces solid wood in new items. In fact, the proportion of plywood to solid wood is so unbalanced that it's sometimes difficult to use it all for lack of solid wood to frame it. There is a limit to what can be made with plywood alone. So you may be selective in salvaging plywood. Discard the roughest and do not bother with any that is delaminating. That indicates a poor glue was used, and anything made from an apparently sound part of it might be spoiled by delamination later.

Large plywood sheets should be kept intact, even if they give you storage problems. You will value the size when you make things from it later. Parts can be cut around each other on a large piece with less waste than when cut from small pieces. Of course, large sheets are worthwhile for their size when making large items such as table tops.

Plywood of any thickness has uses. Much thin plywood is used in smaller packing cases and anything where there is not much load on the panel. This and hardboard can be used for hidden parts, such as drawer bottoms. Keep all the thin plywood you can get, but particularly treasure thicker plywood.

Although large pieces of plywood are good stock, keep narrow strips and small pieces too. Thin narrow strips will bend to such shapes as the edge of a guitar. Thick narrow strips of plywood may be substituted for solid wood in some construction. You won't want to make just large things, and there are many small objects that can incorporate very small pieces of plywood.

Most of the stock that you accumulate will be solid wood and plywood of the more utilitarian type. It can be made into many useful things, but they will not be of cabinet quality, and will not stand comparison with polished furniture made from new selected hardwoods. However, there are some exceptions.

Crates that are subsidiary products from woodworking places devoted mainly to other things may contain surprises in the form of pieces of good quality hardwood or plywood faced with select veneer. You may hoard these pieces until you have enough for a special project, or buy new wood to supplement your finds. Hardwoods should be kept separately from softwoods as a good hardwood gives you scope for more ambitious woodwork.

STORAGE

The object of storing salvaged wood—as with any wood—is to keep it in as good condition as when it was put into store so it is suitable for use when needed. Some items may be kept only a short time before a use is found for them, but others may be kept a long time. Care is needed to keep them in good condition.

Stored wood should be under cover, protected from rain and excessive sun. Even if the wood is to be used for outdoor woodwork, it should be kept dry, for wet wood cannot be worked with tools and may warp and crack.

Wood stored indoors will dry out more than wood stored outdoors, assuming the indoor wood isn't kept in a damp basement. Using wood this dry on outdoor projects may cause problems, for the wood may absorb moisture when moved outside and warp or break joints. If the wood is stored indoors, avoid overheating it: keep it away from heaters.

Short lengths of strip material—up to 3 or 4 feet—can stand on end in a rack (Fig. 4-9A). Longer wood should be stored flat. One way is a rack with arms extending from the wall at fairly close intervals (Fig. 4-9B). Be careful that strips put on it rest flat. It is easy to put a number of long strips of various sections on a rack, then take one away to use, leaving some of the others caught up on neighbors and no longer straight and flat throughout their length. This will lead to permanent distortion.

If you have a long wide board that you do not expect to use for some time, it may form the bottom of a pile on a long rack, preventing thin wood from sagging between the supports. As long wood is used, its offcuts can be transferred to the upright rack.

Anyone who salvages wood tends to be reluctant to waste any of the stock he builds up. This means you will have a number of short ends that are too small to put in the upright rack, yet you want to keep them. Really small pieces may go in a box. Pieces up to about 2 feet long may go on shelves under a bench (Fig. 4-9C). As you can see only their ends, you may not know exactly what is there if a large pile develops. If there is space above the bench, it may be better to arrange an open, clearly visible shelf made from lengthwise battens (Fig. 4-9D).

Plywood of much size is probably best stored on edge. Placing it against a flat wall will minimize distortion of thicker sheets, but thinner sheets should rest either against thick ones or a few upright straight strips (Fig. 4-9E). Smaller pieces of plywood are best kept flat; they may go on the same shelf as the short pieces of solid wood. If there are a great many pieces you could use some of your thin strip wood to make a sort of open cage in which plywood pieces stand on edge (Fig. 4-9F).

When crates are dismantled, quite a few metal fastenings will be recovered. Nails and screws that you expect to use frequently can be in open-topped boxes and discarded plastic and metal food containers. If you have a good stock of fasteners and want them within reach, a sectioned box can be made from offcuts (Fig. 4-9G).

For nuts and bolts and any unusual fasteners that may not be used quickly, it is better to use closed storage containers as a protection against rust. There are many cans and other metal containers that can be used, but screw-top glass jars offer good protection as well as allowing you to see what is inside. They can stand on a shelf or the tops may be attached under a shelf and the jars screwed into them (Fig. 4-9H). This puts your storage in a place that might not otherwise be used, but you have to make sure the jars are tightly screwed home and cannot vibrate loose.

If you store anything partly dismantled, make sure there are no projecting nail ends or other parts that could damage people, other wood, and possibly prevent the item from being stored flat. Get rid of projections; there may be broken pieces from other sides or internal parts. Clean off panels until they're flat on both sides; then they can be stored on edge like plywood. Such pieces may conveniently go behind the plywood leaning against a wall, supporting the sheets. If there are two similar partly dismantled parts, store them face to face or back to back, so they keep each other flat.

Storage is a very important step between finding wood and making it into something different. If the input of salvaged material increases, do not let its quantity overwhelm you so you throw it all into a pile and neglect it. Even if you have no immediate use for it, get it under cover, keep it flat, and if you have time, separate and sort your stock.

Stack green wood properly to season. Remember to look for signs of rot, even if you are unable to find the time to store wood properly. Rotten wood may contaminate previously sound wood, so cut it out and burn it promptly.

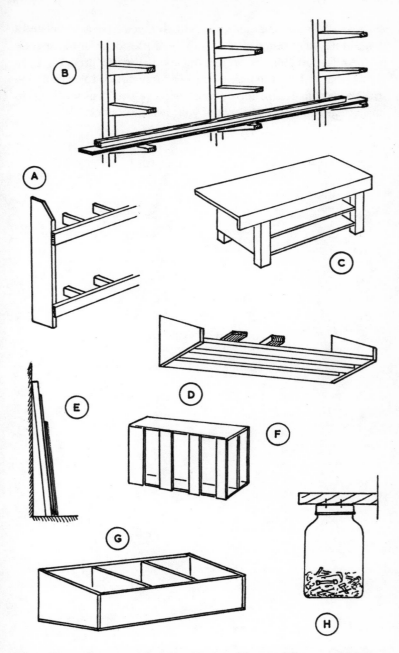

Fig. 4-9. Salvaged wood should be stored carefully to avoid warping and twisting. Small items can be stored in boxes and jars.

Get to know your stock, particularly if you have accumulated a large store; knowledge of what is there sparks ideas for making use of the material. Planning projects can be a two-way process: if you know what you want to make, you look for materials to make it; you can also accumulate materials which will give you ideas for things to make that will best make use of your available stock.

Chapter 5
Adapting Crates

Quite often the existing form of some surplus material may suggest what could be made. In that case there is no need to completely dismantle the box, pallet or other assembly. At other times the existing thing may be unlikely to have a use as it is, or it may be so damaged that it must be taken apart to recover the sound wood.

Sometimes the construction is such that any attempt to fully dismantle will result in much splitting or other damage. In that case it may be better to take away the crate and store it dismantled only as far as necessary for compact storage.

A typical assembly that might be worth keeping intact is a small wooden box in good condition. It may be regarded as a unit to use with similar boxes to make storage shelves. It might be fitted with a lid and used to store anything from children's toys to shoes or blankets. It could be converted to many things by the addition of legs or feet. It could be used outdoors as a hutch for an animal, or it might hold soil to grow things. All sorts of uses are suggested by small sound boxes. The point to remember is that it does not make sense to dismantle a box if you later use the wood to make a similar box.

Larger boxes are often constructed with two framed facing panels, possibly with nails driven through and clenched; the other two sides and the bottom are directly nailed to them and much easier to remove. In that case it may be best to remove the bottom and sides, but not attempt to take apart the clench-nailed panels.

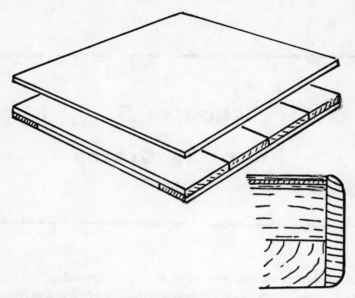

Fig. 5-1. A substantial but scarred panel may be veneered to provide a presentable surface.

These framed panels may later be built into a project where their strengthened framing will be an advantage. A framed panel makes a good base for many constructions. Two framed panels may be joined as they were in the original box to make an open framework or some form of rack. A framed panel becomes almost a shop pallet; you can use it as a base or stand on which to assemble anything you are making. If it looks good enough it may make a table top or a stool seat.

If a framed panel is not very presentable but it is strong, it may be possible to cover it with good plywood or plastic to give it a good surface. Then the edge can be framed with thin strip so the base is not visible, but is of value for its strength (Fig. 5-1).

PALLETS

A pallet is likely to be discarded only if it is damaged. If you only get one pallet, it is usually advisable to dismantle it completely and store it as pieces. But if you get several matching pallets they may suggest a construction without being taken apart. The cross members are stout: several pallets put together can make a floor for a shop or a garden shed. There is no need for boards on both surfaces, so one layer could be removed and used to repair damage on the other surface.

If your shop is in a basement or other room with a stone or concrete floor, pallets with the boards from one side removed can be used to stand on. This has at least two advantages: wood is more comfortable than stone or concrete to stand on, and if you drop tools, the wood surface will not blunt them or break them (Fig. 5-2A). Of course it may be necessary to raise the bench by the same amount, although a short person may be glad of the added height of the pallet.

Pallets with the boards removed from one side can be used in pairs, with those removed boards used to complete the box (Fig. 5-2B). With an open construction they can contain garden rubbish. With a closed construction, you have a strong box.

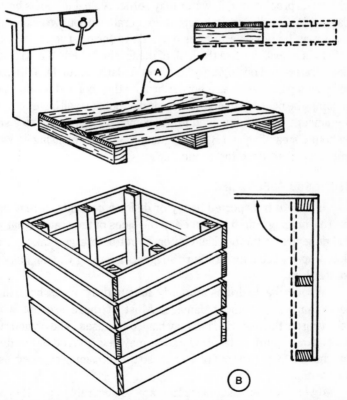

Fig. 5-2. Pallets may sometimes be used for table tops, stands, and boxes without complete dismantling.

LARGE CRATES

If you are fortunate enough to obtain a very large crate, big enough to walk into, you may consider using it as a shed. Its adaptability depends on its construction. It will have been designed to lift with the opening or lid upwards, and may not have much rigidity stood on edge.

If a large crate seems to have possibilities for a shed or similar structure, examine it for diagonal strength. If a side is made of many boards, it may be liable to push out of shape. This might be cured by a diagonal brace, without having to take anything apart. The open side may be the weak direction, but your design could include framing for a door or window that will also brace that side.

A greater problem with using a crate as a shed is the fact that whichever way you put it, it will have a flat roof. Even if you cover it with waterproof material, water may settle. A sloping roof is better. Can you make a diagonal cut across your crate without wrecking it? If so, it may be possible to alter one side to form a roof.

Finally, will you like the look of the finished shed? If it still looks like a crate stood on edge, you may not find it acceptable. With paint and added parts, such as a border around the roof and windows cut in, it may be possible to disguise its origin, but you will have to weigh the amount of work involved in: A, converting the crate to a shed without dismantling and B, dismantling the crate and using its wood to build a shed from the ground up.

OTHER SUB-ASSEMBLIES

If a crate transported heavy or delicate contents, it may have internal bracing bolted or braced to the sides of the crate. What you find depends on the original contents, but before you take it completely apart, see if its structure suggests anything you might incorporate it into.

Wooden cable drums are fairly substantially made, but usually defy dismantling without damage. Most of these are not worth salvaging for the material, but may have other uses. The obvious use is as a round outdoor table. One side may be removed or cut down and the hub fixed to a concrete base, so the remaining side serves as a table top.

If you recover assemblies that are so securely joined they will not come apart without damage, yet you cannot think of any way of using them as they are, there is still a possible use: concrete forms. Concrete has to be retained while it sets. The wood in forms usually suffers from contact with concrete, and the wood in these assemblies can substitute for wood that might serve for something more important.

WEATHERPROOFING

Before deciding that a particular piece of salvaged material will be useful outdoors, check that it will stand up to weather. If it is an old crate that has been used many times and obviously has been left outdoors without damage, it should be suitable for any outdoor use you wish to make of it.

The weak points in an assembly for outdoor use are fasteners and glue. The majority of woods used for crates should have a reasonably long life if used for something outdoors. Some may tend to warp and split more than others, but not many are likely to succumb to rot, except after many years. Hardwoods are mostly more duable than softwoods, but a resinous softwood has good weather resistance. A prominent grain in softwood or unusually heavy weight usually indicate the presence of resin.

Nails in a crate or packing intended only for a single use are often quite thin and sparse. Rust would cause some of them to break in quite a short time. If an assembly of this type is to be used without dismantling, reinforce it with nails that are stouter and longer than the existing ones. Ideally, the new nails should be zinc-coated or otherwise protected against rust.

Most modern synthetic glues are convenient to use and waterproof or highly water-resistant. However, there are other, cheaper glues with little resistance to moisture that may be found in crates or cases. Do not assume that any glued joint will withstand exposure to rain, but with modern adhesives it probably will. However, if there is any doubt, the only satisfactory test is to try soaking a part of a joint with water.

More of a problem than glued joints between solid wood parts is plywood. As with solid wood, plywood is more likely to have water-resistant glue than other sorts, but other glues are used in the cheapest crate plywood for economy. It was not so very long ago that much plywood was made with non-waterproof glues, so any obviously old crate with plywood parts should be suspect.

Examine plywood for cracks where plies have come away. Look for puckers that indicate glue giving way and allowing the outside veneer to spring up. Examine exposed edges, particularly those that might have been facing down when the crate was in use. Almost certainly it will have spent some time standing in a puddle. If the plies have separated along this edge, the plywood is of no use for outdoor construction. If the edge shows marks from wetting, yet the edge joint is still intact, the plywood should be weatherproof and the crate parts may be used for an outside purpose with reasonable confidence.

Any wood used for outside purposes should be protected in some way. If the crate part is not very large, it can be soaked in wood preservative. Otherwise the preservative may be brushed on, but do not treat it like paint. The object is to thoroughly impregnate the grain, so put preservative on liberally. Apply more than one coat and, ideally, continue applying until no more can be absorbed. Absorption is greater through end grain. If a part is too large to soak completely, but the end grain can be immersed, leave it for several hours to soak the liquid up. This is particularly important for anything that will go into the ground. Some preservatives should not be used in the vicinity of plants, so check what you use on window boxes or other plant containers.

Preservatives may be colorless or in a few basic colors. They do not obscure the grain pattern. Some can be used under paint, and some may not be followed with anything else. Check the instructions with the fluid.

Paint does not penetrate like preservative. Instead, it makes a protective opaque film which does not let moisture penetrate—at least not immediately, depending on the type of paint. Paint is useful to the salvager mainly because it hides uneven coloring, printed markings, and other disfigurements with an evenly colored coating.

If crate material is to be painted, it must be dry and free of grease or oil. Grease and oil may act as preservatives, but they will not hold a film of paint. They should be removed by scraping and the use of degreasing fluid.

The first coat of paint may have to be thinned slightly; this allows it to penetrate the pores of the grain and get a better grip. Further coats will adhere to the first coat and the whole finish should remain intact for a long time. Paints vary greatly, so check the instructions and specifications on the can. Make sure the paint you choose is intended for outdoor use. Indoor paints are made in a greater variety, but they are not as durable.

FINAL CHECKS

Before embarking on a project that will use parts of crates or other things, be certain that you will be satisfied with the results and what you are making will perform its function at least as well as if you had made the item from wood obtained by complete dismantling. Many of these sub-assemblies can be as functional in their new job as they were in the old one, but sometimes a construction that is good enough for its job in a crate may not stand up to a different use.

Final appearance is important. There is no reason why anything made from crate material should not be as good as a similar thing made from new material. If you use a part of a crate without fully dismantling it first, it may be difficult to disguise the origin of the wood. Since most of us do not want furniture that will constantly remind us of its crate origin, we attempt to cover or disguise it, or employ the part in a way that gives it a new look. If a piece of camp furniture looks like part of a crate, it doesn't matter, but for other purposes aim to make something that looks fit for its purpose and not like an adaptation of something else.

Chapter 6
Matching
Projects to Materials

With the great variety of types and sizes of wood available to the recycler, it is not always easy to assess the possibilities of what you have collected. It would be a pity to start making something and find during construction (or after completion) that you have wasted time by using unsuitable materials.

Wood is certainly a very adaptable material, but there are many varieties of wood and their characteristics differ considerably. There are certain properties common to all woods, but particular species have properties that make them suitable for particular purposes. In a few cases the properties are such that the wood is useless for construction.

Wood from a tree with many branches will be full of knots, which occur where the branches join the trunk. Such trees usually have been grown in open areas. If a similar tree has grown in a forest, there will be few or no low branches, so knots are few.

This means it is difficult to be specific about the qualities of a particular species, but softwood that has frequent knots is not much use except for the roughest carpentry. The same wood free from knots, or with only a few small ones, may be quite good for construction work, although it cannot be given a very satisfactory furniture finish. It may be used for internal parts of something that has a hardwood exterior.

Softwoods are the usual construction wood for items where the wood itself is not intended to provide decoration. The wood may be painted, or it may be faced with plywood, plastic or one of the many types of decorative sheet. For external woodwork, things that are utilitarian rather than decorative, fittings and shelves for kitchen and workshop, or any of a large number of objects that are practical rather than decorative, you can use softwood. Most wood from surplus sources is softwood.

Some hardwood may be suitable only for purposes similar to softwoods. Some are rather coarse-grained and would be difficult to bring to a good finish, so they must be kept for rough work. If you have doubts, try planing a specimen. This should show immediately the possibilities of that piece of wood. Even if you do not have much of that type of wood, it is probably better to keep what you have to make a small item of furniture, some decorative article, or possibly a carved or turned item, than to use it with other woods in a utilitarian structure.

Besides the types of wood you have, you must consider their sections and shapes. Plenty of flat wood means broad solid surfaces are possible. Plenty of wood of square or near-square section may suggest framed-and-paneled construction. Square-section wood in lengths that would make table legs or similar things may be kept in sets of four for this purpose. Square-section wood, preferably hardwood, can be turned on a lathe. Even the smallest pieces can be turned into tool handles, chessmen, small knobs, and similar things.

Batten wood will find uses with plywood, but if you recover some good strips of knot-free softwood of even size in batten sections, it is probably worth using in something more ambitious where the wood is not just backing for a panel. Shelf brackets, racks of many sorts, and light fencing can all be made from good strip wood.

PLYWOOD

Much of your salvaged material will be plywood. The poorer quality may have uses as backs and bottoms of case construction, but there are definite limits to its use. So be selective about poor-quality plywood. Better plywood is a different thing—it is all good stock.

Small pieces of good plywood can be made into pads to go under plates or vases or form the basis for decorative panels, pyrography (wood burning), pokerwork, or other tooling. Keep your small pieces—there should be a use for them all.

Bigger pieces of plywood need to be thick if they are to be rigid without framing, but even a big sheet of 1/4-inch plywood stiffened by edge framing will be strong enough for many things. If the plywood itself is to take a load, as in a base, thin plywood would need a lot of framing and even then might sag under local loads. For that purpose it is better to use 3/8-inch or 1/2-inch plywood. You should find plenty of this in large, heavy-duty crates.

If the plywood is obtained that is faced with special or unusual veneer, it is worth keeping. Although American plywood is usually made of fir, other woods are used in foreign plywood, so imported crates may give you some variation. Birch is a more close-grained wood than fir and is found in some European plywood. Reddish woods similar to mahogany are used in some tropical plywood. Both of these woods will take a clear finish better than fir plywood. It may be possible to find plywood that matches your solid hardwoods, enabling you to make furniture of even grain and color.

Faced plywood will suggest some special uses. It can probably be made into a framed panel, the bottom of a tray, or some other object with the panel as the featured motif.

Besides using plywood for flat panels and general construction, it can be curved; it is much stronger curved than flat. Plywood may be bent around solid wood top and bottom pieces to make strong curved sides to a cabinet. Pulled to a complete circle around a solid base, it will make a round box. But do not attempt a compound curve—a sheet of plywood can be curved in only one direction.

Do not expect too much of salvaged hardboard, particularly if its surface has been scratched or otherwise damaged. Its quality varies. Good hardboard is quite strong with a tough surface, but some is not very superior to cardboard. Most should be used only for backs of pictures, bottoms of drawers, and similar things. It may be used in the shop for mounting drawings, bottoms of nail boxes, and anywhere that filling a space is more important than providing strength.

Perforated hardboard may be found in crates. With its regularly-spaced holes, this peg-board is useful for tool racks, using bent wire clips that can be made or bought. A good-quality piece may have a similar use in the kitchen or office.

Some salvaged wood has holes that do not affect strength, but spoil its appearance. It is often possible to design a project so these holes can be hidden. If holes show, they can be plugged: if a painted finish is used they should not show. The wood may also be built into a bench, or used for outdoor carpentry, where a hole will not matter. If used as a structural member alongside a door or opening, it may be possible to face the flawed wood with plywood to give a smooth surface.

Examine your stock for predominant sizes and sections. If you find you have a large stock of boards of one thickness, regardless of width, you may be able to design something that takes advantage of this uniform thickness. Construction will be simplified and you'll be making the best use of your stock.

Section 2
Tools and Techniques

Chapter 7
Tools

The number of tools available is increasing every day—anyone coming new to tool selection may be bewildered. But woodworking is one of the oldest crafts; some woodworking tools have been developed over centuries, and it is fairly safe to assume that what has been designed and improved by generations of craftsmen is unlikely to be suddenly superseded by something entirely new. This principle can guide you in selecting hand or power tools. If a tool does its job in a way that derives from traditional tools, it uses proven basic principles, even if it has some new feature that takes advantage of modern technology.

Most households have at least a few basic woodworking tools. However, many household tools are used by a variety of people for a variety of purposes, and may not be in very good condition. A hammer with a loose head, a saw with teeth missing, a chisel that has hit too many nails, or a drill with rounded edges cannot do good work and will only lead to frustration. It may be possible to put such tools back into condition, but for good-quality woodworking, it may be better to get new ones. The quality of work is affected by the tools. Apart from what they contribute by their efficiency, the feel of good tools makes the craftsman more conscientious.

A tool's quality is usually reflected in its price, and good tools are a worthwhile investment. A cutting tool made of inferior steel will never take or keep a sharp edge. This means that a cheap saw may never cut properly, and soon reaches a stage where brute force rather than the cut of the teeth takes it through wood. A cheap chisel or plane blade is more easily sharpened, so periodic blunting is not as serious, but the edge dulls so quickly that the work is never as good as could be achieved with better steel.

The nearest thing to a revolution in woodworking tools in recent years has been the introduction of electric hand tools. Power can now be taken to the work instead of having to take the work to a stationary power tool, or do the job by hand. Of course, power tools cannot do every woodworking process. They lessen the labor and make accuracy easier for some processes. For processes where mechanical accuracy is important, some power tools can easily do what used to require great skill and experience with hand tools. However, anyone who hopes to get far with woodworking needs to know how to handle hand tools. It is unwise to rely too much on power tools. They are a great help, but most jobs are better finished—and some done completely—by hand.

This means that the value of a tool must be considered in relation to alternative tools and the work to be done. It may be better to buy a good variety of hand tools than to spend all your budget on one power tool. It is good policy to have a large range of simple tools. For instance, a pump-action screwdriver may seem attractive, but for its cost you could buy many plain screwdrivers in different sizes; they will deal with many more sizes of screws.

There are certain basic hand tools that every woodworker should own and know how to use and maintain. These are the tools a woodworker always uses, even when he has expanded his tool kit to embrace many hand and power tools.

The tools for dealing with crates and other sources of recoverable wood were described in Chapter 3. The tools described in this chapter and the next few chapters are those needed to make things from the wood that has been salvaged.

SAWS

Saw teeth are shaped so they cut the wood fibers and make a *kerf* (groove) that the saw will pass through without binding. The cutting is done by the leading edge of the teeth, which can be sharpened with a file or by grinding in a machine. The kerf is caused

80

by setting (bending) alternate teeth in opposite directions (Fig. 7-1A). Two types of saws are needed, depending on the direction of the cut. A saw cutting across the grain must sever wood fibers: its teeth are given definite cutting edges (Fig. 7-1B). For cutting with the grain the teeth need more of a planing action (Fig. 7-1C). Teeth intended for work across the grain will cut with the grain, but will be less efficient. This means more effort to push the saw. As sawing with the grain is usually done with a power saw, most craftsmen manage with hand saws designed for cross-grain work.

The general-purpose saw may be called a hand or panel saw (Fig. 7-1D). In times past the handle was artistically shaped, but modern plastic handles are more functional. The thrust line (at a right angle to the grip) should pass through the middle of the blade (Fig. 7-1E). There are many sizes: a blade 18 inches long will do, but length is not critical. The teeth are more important. They are graded by the number per inch; 10 per inch is a reasonable choice, if you have another saw for finer work (Fig. 7-1F).

For cutting joints, sawing wood to length on the bench, and similarly exacting work, the hand tool of choice is a backsaw (Fig. 7-1G). This has a rectangular blade stiffened by a back. Length is usually 10 or 12 inches and teeth are of the cross-grain type, 14 or 16 per inch. This may be called a tenon saw and a smaller version (8 inches) with finer teeth may be called a dovetail saw, although both saws are used for many things besides the named joints.

There are several narrow saws for cutting curves. A keyhole saw has a blade like a saber saw (Fig. 7-1H) and its name indicates one of its uses. For larger curves there are sets of saws that fit a common handle. They are bigger than keyhole saws, but like them are fairly thick to provide stiffness (Fig. 7-1J). A better saw for fine curved work is a coping saw (Fig. 7-1K). This has a thin blade held in tension by a spring frame. A finer saw of similar type is called a fret saw. It can be used for most delicate fretted work and may be used on thinner plywood from crates.

The power tool that has taken over from the hand saws for curves is the saber saw (see Chapter 3). Blades are available with teeth for coarse or fine cutting, intricate shapes or straight cuts, and work on plastics and other materials. If much work is to be done in wood, an electric saber saw is worth having.

The portable circular saw has uses in cutting crate wood to size, but it does not do much that could not be done by a careful worker

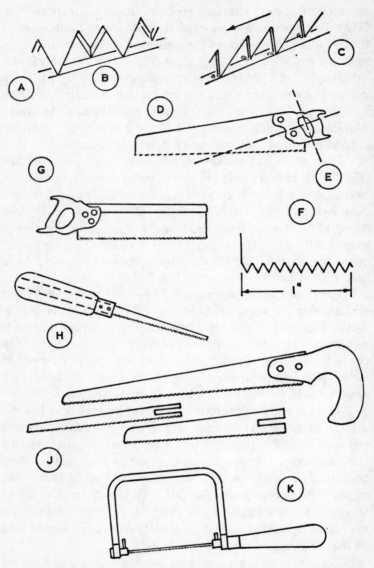

Fig. 7-1. There are many types of saws, with different types and sizes of teeth for cutting with and across the grain, and for cutting curves and straight lines.

with hand saws. It does it with less labor, and may be justified on that count. It may also produce greater accuracy if used with a fence or guide, but for careful close work, such as making joints, it is safer to use hand saws.

A fixed circular saw (table saw) is useful for cutting wood to new sections, but there are many other tools that should be acquired before it.

For rough work, as when cutting old and soiled crate wood to make signs or rustic furniture, the bow saw (see Chapter 3) is better than any of the finer hand saws.

CHISELS

The number of end cutting tools listed by some manufacturers runs into the hundreds, especially if they include carving and turning tools. An ambitious woodworker will find that he wants several chisels, but not as many as in the past: power tools have reduced the amount of chopping of wood needed. However, early work can be done with only a few chisels and others obtained as the need arises. It is seldom wise to buy so-called sets of chisels, or other tools. You will almost certainly get some you do not want. Some sets are made to meet a low price and are not as good quality as can be bought individually.

The basic chisel has a rectangular blade fitted to a wooden or plastic handle (Fig. 7-2A). A tang on the blade fits into the handle, engaging a shoulder that prevents it from driving in further if the handle is hit. Some craftsmen prefer hardwood handles of a particular shape, but the more common plastic barrel-shaped handles are satisfactory and will stand up to hammering. If the chisel is fairly stout, it may be described as a *firmer* chisel. A similar but more slender chisel is called a *paring* chisel. This is for delicate hand work and is not intended to be hit.

Firmer chisels may be bevel-edged (Fig. 7-2B). This will do just about all that can be done with a plain firmer chisel and will also go into corners, so it is worth paying a little extra for bevel-edged firmer chisels. Paring chisels may also be bevel-edged, but a firmer chisel will do most paring, so there is no need for paring chisels in the first tool kit.

A stouter chisel is a mortise chisel (Fig. 7-2C). This was used for chopping out mortise joints and needed to be stiff, but with the modern practice of drilling out the waste from a mortise, what chiseling has to be done can be done with a firmer chisel, so mortise chisels are practically extinct.

Chisels are made in widths from 1/8 inch up to 2 inches or more. A good first chisel is a 1/2-inch bevel-edged firmer chisel. A need will soon be felt for something narrower: 1/4-inch may come next. A broad firmer chisel is useful for heavier work and for paring; a 1 1/4- or 1 1/2-inch may be chosen. You can buy other chisels to suit varying joint widths as you need them.

Chisels get shorter as they are sharpened. This reduces their reach, but otherwise a short chisel is as useful as a long one, and such used chisels may sometimes be bought inexpensively. Almost any

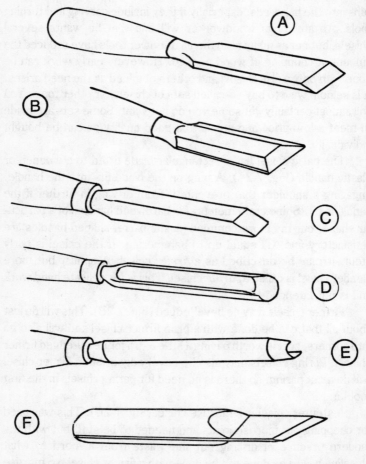

Fig. 7-2. Chisels, gouges, and knives take many forms; many types are needed if you do much woodworking.

size will find a place in a craftsman's kit. Chisels for turning wood on a lathe are long and without a shoulder against the handle. Wood-carving tools are lighter than firmer chisels and may taper in width. Details of these two types are given in later chapters.

A curved chisel is called a *gouge*. If it is sharpened on the inside it is described as *in-cannelled* (Fig. 7-2D). If it is sharpened on the outside it is *out-cannelled* (Fig. 7-2E).

Except for whittling, there is little woodworking use for an ordinary knife, but one that cuts at the end is used instead of a pencil for precision marking, particularly where an end has to be cut. The traditional knife (Fig. 7-2G) has given way to utility knives with disposable blades.

There are no power tools that take the place of the chisel, although some may do similar work. A mortising attachment on a drilling machine may cut a slot that does not need the attention of a chisel. A power router will cut grooves and hollows that would otherwise have to be cut with gouges and chisels. Despite these uses, a woodworker needs his chisels for many trimming and fitting operations.

PLANES

A plane may be thought of as a controlled special-purpose chisel. A chisel-like *plane iron* (actually a steel blade) projects through the base of a plane. Some planes use a single iron, but general-purpose planes intended to produce a broad, smooth surface also have a *cap iron* (Fig. 7-3A). This breaks off shavings as they come through the plane mouth and reduces the risk of the cutting action tearing up the wood surface.

It is still possible to buy planes made of wood or steel with wood soles. A few dedicated craftsmen may argue that these are better tools, but a steel plane is much easier to adjust and will maintain a true sole, so it is preferred.

A short general-purpose plane may be described as a *smoothing* plane. A medium-length one (14 inches) is a *jack* plane (from "jack-of-all-trades"). A longer one is a *trying* or *jointer* plane. All work on the same principle, but differ in the lengths of their soles (Fig. 7-3B). Differences in their use are described in Chapter 8. If only one plane is bought at first, a useful one is a Stanley #4 or #4 1/2 smoothing

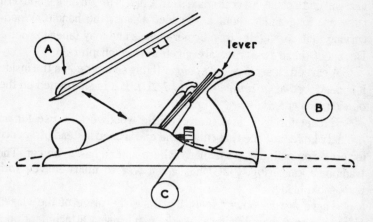

Fig. 7-3. Planes vary in their sole length, but most have a cap iron above the cutting iron.

plane. It can be used for several planing jobs, but you will soon need a longer one also.

In a steel plane, the cap iron is held to the cutting iron with a screw so it can be adjusted up and down. Another screw near the main handle moves the irons up and down (Fig. 7-3C) and a lever controls the tilt of the blade. There may also be a means of adjusting the width of the mouth.

A block plane (Fig. 7-4) can be used in one hand. It has a single cutting iron, fitted with its bevel upwards, and is particularly suitable for cutting across the grain. Its small size makes it suitable for trimming ends, beveling edges and other light cuts.

There are a great many other special planes. Some have been replaced by power tools, but others are still available, and should be bought as you need them.

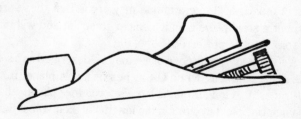

Fig. 7-4. A block plane is used for light work.

The old-time cabinetmaker used wooden planes with shaped soles to make moldings, but such work is now done by a power shaper or spindle molder. Similar to molding planes are *rabbet* or *fillister* planes for making rabbets (Fig. 7-5A) and *plow* planes for making grooves (Fig. 7-5B). Metal versions of these tools will be needed if power tools for the same purpose are not available.

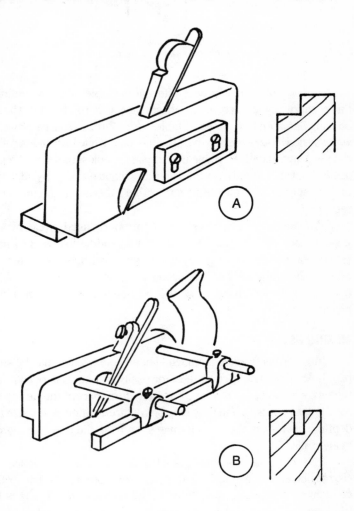

Fig. 7-5. A rabbet or fillister plane (A) cuts rabbets; (B) grooves are cut with a plow plane.

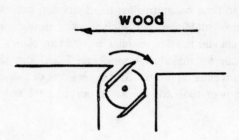

wood

Fig. 7-6. A power plane, or jointer, uses rotating cutters.

A power plane works on a different principle. Two, sometimes three sharp knives are mounted so they can rotate in a shaped opening between two plates or tables (Fig. 7-6). In a large plane, or *jointer*, the wood is pushed over the machine while the blades rotate at a very high speed. Portable power planes look something like jack planes, and are moved over the wood as in hand planing. By adjusting the flat surfaces in relation to each other, the depth of cut can be regulated.

When a power plane is sharp and properly used, it can make a good surface, but for the finest finish it should be followed by hand planing or power sanding. A power plane with blunt cutters or moving the work too fast will produce a surface with many visible hollows, and more hand work will be needed to give a furniture finish.

MAKING HOLES

Most projects made from wood need holes. They may be small pilot holes to enable screws to enter easily without risk of splitting, they may be holes for dowels, they may form part of the design (as hand holes or racks), and they may be required in almost any size and depth. This means that a craftsman soon finds the need for a great many drills.

Portable drills are most people's first power tool choice. Of course, holes can be made with hand tools, but an electric drill is convenient and usually described by its chuck capacity, the smallest being 1/4 inch, and other common sizes, 3/8 inch and 1/2 inch. The larger-capacity drills are heavier. Although they may take small bits as well as large ones, their weight and size make them less

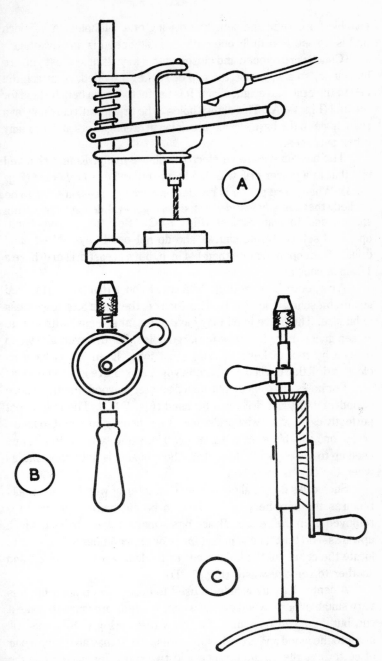

Fig. 7-7. (A) a power drill mounted in a stand; (B) a wheel brace; (C) a breast drill.

suitable for careful and sensitive drilling of small holes. A 3/8-inch drill is a good first drill; one with variable speed is an advantage.

Chucks are opened and closed with a key. If this is lost you are in trouble, so always use the clip or socket provided, or attach the key to the drill with a light chain. It is useful to have a bench stand for the drill (Fig. 7-7A). This allows holes to be drilled with certainty at a right angle to the base, giving precision in drilling joints and for many other purposes.

The alternatives to an electric drill are many. Round-shanked bits that fit a power drill will also fit a hand drill or *wheel brace* (Fig. 7-7B). When more power is needed and greater pressure has to be applied, there is a *breast drill* of similar general design, but with a shaped end to lean against (Fig. 7-7C). Both tools have hand-operated self-centering chucks and do not need keys. Most hand drills will not open to more than 1/4 inch, but a breast drill may have a 1/2-inch chuck.

A carpenter's brace (Fig. 7-8A) has a chuck that takes a tapered square bit shank (Fig. 7-8B). The shank is the same size regardless of bit size. The brace itself may have different sweeps, with a large sweep giving more leverage for large holes, but the average sweep offered by tool makers will suit most jobs. Even if you have an electric drill there will be occasions when a bit brace is also needed.

For holes up to about 1/4-inch diameter in wood, multi-purpose (wood/metal) twist drills can be used (Fig. 7-8C). The hole is not perfectly clean with twist drills, but as it is usually intended to take a screw or nail, this does not matter. The same type of drill can be used up to the capacity of the drill if hole quality is not important, as when the hole is for a bolt.

Such drills do not allow for the character of wood, which really requires the periphery of the hole to be cut before the waste is removed from the center. Brace bits—made in sizes from 1/4 inch upwards—do this. The simplest *spade* or *center bit* has a long spur to locate the center of the hole, a cutter to cleanly outline a circle and another to remove waste (Fig. 7-8D).

A center bit may wander if used to make a deep hole, but it is very suitable for plywood or thin wood. It needs pressure to make it cut, but if the central spur has a screw thread (Fig. 7-8E), this will pull into the wood and provide some pressure. It may also have a pair of cutters at the circumference and two more for slicing out the

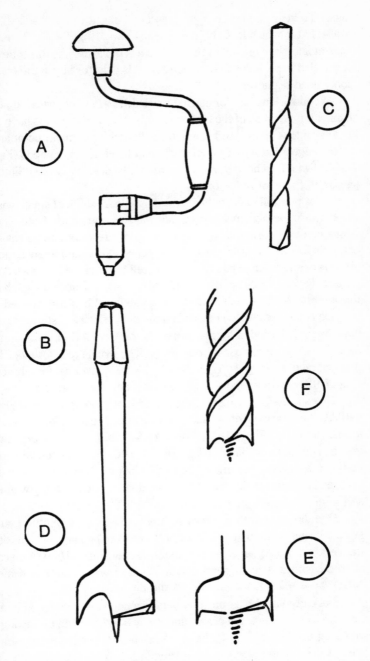

Fig. 7-8. A carpenter's brace and a variety of bits.

waste. To keep the bit straight in a deep hole, it can be backed by parallel flutes which lead the waste chips away (Fig. 7-8F). Several types of flutes are used, but the principle is the same. As this type of bit will also make holes in thin material, it is a better buy in the commonly used diameters.

Woodworking bits for use in power drills are made with parallel shanks, but because of the higher speeds, the working ends have to be different. A high-speed spade bit is flat with a straight point and cutting edges that would be ineffective at hand turning speeds (Fig. 7-9A). Twist bits have very similar ends, backed by twisted flutes similar to those of brace bits.

Most bits will make only one size of hole. A stock of small twist drills should be accumulated to suit screws and other fasteners. Brace or power drill bits will be needed in a few common sizes—certainly 3/8 inch and 1/2 inch for dowelled joints, and a few larger sizes as needed. Some bits can be adjusted to cut circles over a large range (Fig. 7-9B). One of these bits will take care of larger holes, but for anything less than about 3/4 inch, individual bits are needed.

Do not bother with *spoon* and *gimlet* bits, which are still sold but have been superseded by the more accurate twist drills. Countersink bits are used to flush screw heads. The usual type, for electric drill or brace, is a *rose bit* (Fig. 7-9C). A screwdriver bit for a brace (Fig. 7-9D) provides more leverage than any screwdriver.

Holes in metal are started and located with a center punch (Fig. 7-10A). It can be used on wood, although a pointed tool like an awl or ice pick is better (Fig. 7-10B). For holes for small screws, a bradawl may be a better tool than a drill bit (Fig. 7-10C). It is started with its cutting edge across the grain, then given half turns each way as it is pressed in. It severs the grain fibers but does not remove any wood, so the driven screw gets a better grip.

One difficulty with a power drill is controlling its depth of cut since it drives a bit so fast. Where holes have to be carefully limited to a depth, a depth gauge can be fixed to the bit (Fig. 7-10D). A piece of wood with a hole through it (Fig. 7-10E) will serve the same purpose, as will a piece of tape on the bit.

Bits can make holes up to about 3 inches in diameter. Above that size a circle has to be drawn and the waste removed by sawing with a jig or similar saw. If the work is suitable for mounting in a lathe, a hole of any size can be turned in it.

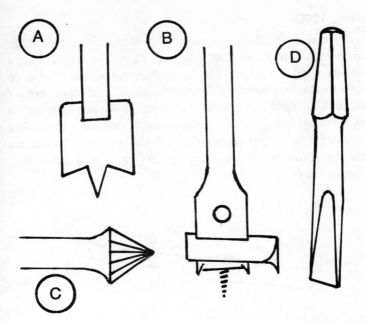

Fig. 7-9. Drills are not just for making holes. They can also countersink and drive screws.

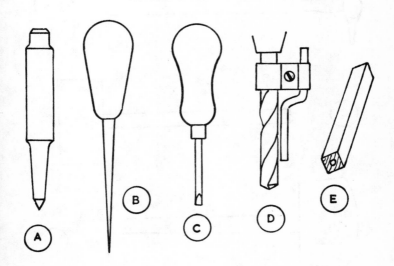

Fig. 7-10. Punches and awls are useful small tools. Drill depth gauges can be bought or improvised.

DRIVING TOOLS

A hammer is probably the most common tool in the world. Each trade has its own idea of what a hammer should be, so there are a great many types available. Almost any hammer will hit a nail or do similar things, so a hammer already owned will probably serve for work with salvaged crates and other wood. If you buy hammers, a very light one (4- or 6-ounce head) is useful for delicate work, while a 16-ounce (or more) claw hammer (Fig. 7-11A) will serve for general purposes. A hammer with a straight peen (Fig. 7-11B) will get into awkward places.

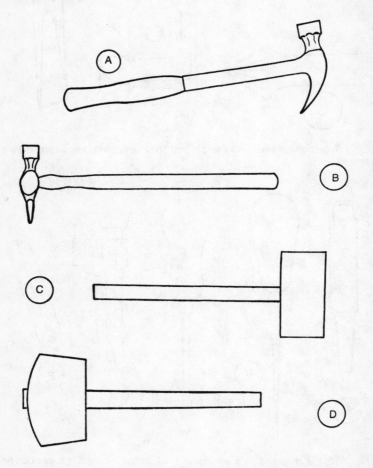

Fig. 7-11. A variety of hammers and mallets will be needed for woodworking.

A hammer delivers a hard blow that will mark wood. If a softer blow is needed, the tool is a mallet, which may have a round wooden head (Fig 7-11C) or the traditional rectangular one with a tapered rectangular handle (Fig. 7-11D). Some mallets have plastic faces, which are also effective.

Most screws have slotted heads (Fig. 7-12A), but there are screw heads with crossed hollows, the best-known being Phillips heads (Fig. 7-12B). These were originally designed to prevent power screwdrivers from slipping off during quantity production, but hand screwdrivers deal well with them. The size of slot or crossed hollow varies according to the size of the screw. Although one screwdriver end may suit several sizes, you'll need different screwdrivers for widely different sizes. It is important that the end of the screwdriver fits the screw; tips are usually soft enough to be filed if necessary.

A long screwdriver is easier to use than a short one, but some short ones are needed for use in confined spaces. The handle should give a good grip. It may be round with flutes or other devices to prevent slip, but the most comfortable and sure grip is a handle that is elliptical in section (Fig. 7-12C). These were traditionally made of close-grained hardwood, but are now more likely to be plastic.

It is possible to buy screwdriver handles that accept several bits so one screwdriver will deal with several sizes of screws. Some incorporate a ratchet for driving or withdrawing screws without removing the bit from the screw. The pump screwdriver is a little more sophisticated: pushing the handle up and down turns the screw. These special screwdrivers have attractions, but many experienced craftsmen prefer the feel of plain screwdrivers. The brace bit (Fig. 7-9D) provides additional leverage for large screws. If the brace has a ratchet action, it will work in confined spaces.

If a nail has to be driven where a hammer cannot reach, or the nail head has to go below the surface, a nail punch (Fig. 7-12D) is used. The punch may have a flat end or be slightly hollow to reduce the risk of slipping. A few punches with different-size ends are worth having.

There are power screwdrivers and screwdriver attachments for electric drills, but their main advantage is in quantity production. A craftsman making individual things usually does better work with hand screwdrivers. There are special tools for driving nails and

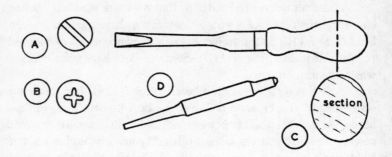

Fig. 7-12. The most popular screw-head configurations are the slot and the Phillips head.

staples used as substitutes for nails, but they are of little value for the sort of work we are considering.

MEASURING AND MARKING OUT

A satisfactory finished wooden article and the accuracy of its construction depend on careful measuring and marking out of the pieces of wood. "Measure twice before cutting once" has a lot of truth in it.

Measuring is a means of comparing. Whether we use inches and feet or millimeters and centimeters or some other measure, we are just adopting a system that allows us to note the size of one part and compare it with another. If one part can be held alongside another it has to match, there is no need for measuring. Direct comparison is always best if it is possible. If several parts have to be the same in whole or in part, mark them together.

A steel rule is a better tool for measuring than a wooden or plastic one. It is also a more reliable straightedge for checking flatness or drawing a line. For distances greater than the length of the rule, a tape measure can be used. The old-time cabinetmaker used a *rod*, which was any straight piece of wood on which he put all the key measurements (Fig. 7-13A).

The tool for checking a right angle is a *try square* (Fig. 7-13B), which should be steel with a 12-inch blade. An alternative tool is a *combination square*, which has a stock that slides on the blade (Fig. 7-13C) and will check 45 degrees as well as a right angle. These are the vital functions, but some combination squares will check other angles and may include a level. For comparing other angles, the usual tool is an adjustable *bevel*; its blade can be locked at any angle to the stock (Fig. 7-13D).

It is worthwhile making a straightedge as long as the biggest thing you are likely to make. Bevel one edge of a length of straight-grained, well-seasoned wood. Check the planed edge by drawing a line along it and turning it around to see if it matches the other way (Fig. 7-13E).

With some crate wood it will be necessary to plane a surface true. A pair of *winding strips* can be made; they're used to sight along to check for twist (Fig. 7-13F). They are just two identical straightedges thick enough to stand on the wood.

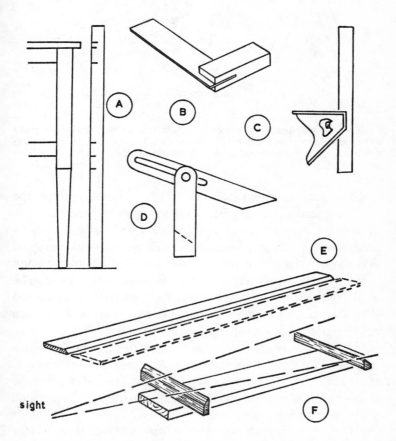

Fig. 7-13. Tools for checking accuracy and marking out are important. Some can be improvised.

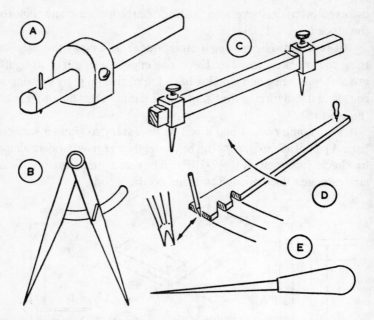

Fig. 7-14. A marking gauge scratches lines parallel to an edge. Curves are made with dividers, trammels or improvised compasses. A pencil may be sharpened to a chisel edge or a spike used to scratch an accurate line.

For marking lines parallel to an edge, the best tool is the traditional marking gauge (Fig. 7-14A). It may be metal or wood. You can pay more for attractive hardwood with brass inserts, but a plain one will handle most needs for a long time. One with two spurs that can be adjusted in relation to each other ensures uniform marking of mortises and tenons. A combination square can also be used, adjusted so the blade extends the right distance and pulled along the wood with a pencil against the end. A similar device is a notched piece of wood cut specially for the job.

A pair of pencil compasses, such as are used for drawing circles on paper, can be used on wood, but it is useful to have a larger, stouter pair of dividers (Fig. 7-14B) that will open to 10 or 12 inches. Besides scratching circles on wood, they are used for stepping off distances and comparing sizes.

Less common tools are a pair of *trammel heads* (Fig. 7-14C), which fit on a piece of wood to make a compass of much longer reach. Some will take a pencil in place of one of the points. The piece of wood can be any length: a short piece will allow the trammel heads to substitute for dividers, and there is nothing to stop you from drawing a curve with a 20-foot radius if you have a beam that long. An alternative for large curves is a length of wood—notched if there are several radiuses to be marked—with an awl at the center of the circle. This sort of marking is done with a pencil, but a round point soon blunts and a thick pencil line is not very accurate to work to. The point will last longer if it is sharpened to a chisel end (Fig. 7-14D). Special carpenter's pencils are made with flat-section lead to give a longer-wearing point.

To mark accurate cross-grain lines, particularly those that will be cut to, a knife is better than a pencil as it severs the grain fibers and makes a clean edge. A *scratch awl* (Fig. 7-14E) is sometimes used instead of a knife, but it does not make a clean line.

HOLDING DEVICES

A work top at a convenient height is needed. For simple light work it may be an ordinary table, but something more substantial is needed to stand up to heavy work without springing or moving. Its front edge, at least, should be stout wood that will not rebound under hitting and will give firm support when sawing, planing, and performing other heavy operations.

Height should be about 30 inches, but if you are making your own bench, try holding a plane as you would over a piece of wood 2 inches thick. That will show you a suitable height. Err on the low side—that is better than having to lift tools too high. Length should be at least 5 feet and width, 2 feet (Fig. 7-15A). Legs and framing may be wood, although steel is good. If the bench is to stand free from walls, it should be heavy enough not to move about. If it can be braced to a wall, that is helpful, but avoid locating it in a corner where movement of long pieces of wood will be restricted.

A vise is best slung under the bench top (Fig. 7-15B). A vise that stands above the bench may function just as well as one under, but it is a nuisance when you need the whole top of the bench clear for a large job. The vise should be fitted with wooden jaws to avoid damaging work. If possible, make the bench with a front apron level with the inner vise jaws (Fig. 7-15C). This acts as a guide to anything projecting from the vise and will accept pegs to support long wood (Fig. 7-15D).

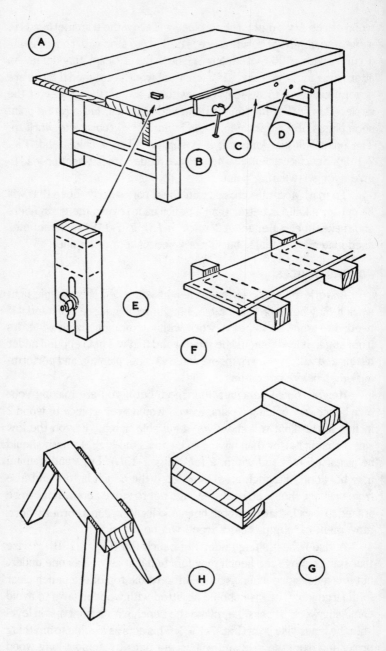

Fig. 7-15. To do good work, the wood has to be supported firmly and securely on a bench or trestle, with the aid of bench stop and hook.

Holdfasts work like a vise and hold work flat on the bench. They are useful, but not essential in a first tool kit. What is important is something to plane or push against at the end of the bench—the left end if you are right-handed. A strip of wood nailed on may do, but will have to be replaced occasionally.

Metal bench stops are also available, but it's better not to have metal where there is a risk of a plane blade hitting it. A simple adjustable stop that has only wood projecting can be made from a piece of hardwood fitted through a slot in the bench. A wing nut on a bolt through a leg provides adjustment (Fig. 7-15E).

A bench hook or, preferably, a matching pair can be made. It should be regarded as disposable since it will be cut and scarred. Two narrow hooks (Fig. 7-15F) are needed, even for short wood, but a wider bench hook (Fig. 7-15G) can be used alone. In order to do accurate work you must maintain a true surface on the bench top, so chopping with a chisel and similar work should be on scrap wood or the bench hook—not directly on the bench.

For lower work a pair of trestles is ideal (Fig. 7-15H). Their tops should be 15 to 18 inches from the floor. They are used for sawing and assembly of furniture, and provide a comfortable working height for dismantling some crates. Alternatives to trestles are old chairs with the backs cut off, boxes, or crates. Trestles are easily made from salvaged 2 × 4s, using (or not using) the prefabricated leg brackets available at most hardware stores.

Clamps serve as portable vises and are used to pull and hold parts together. The most useful type is the *C clamp* (Fig. 7-16A), available in sizes from a few inches capacity to a foot or more. They can be obtained with deep throats or with an extra screw at a right angle to the frame for exerting pressure on the side of the work. Hand screws made of wood (Fig. 7-16B) serve similar purposes; some may be adjusted to handle work with non-parallel faces.

For light work there are *spring clips* (Fig. 7-16C) that work the same way as paper clips. Sliding clamps adjust on a bar to give varying capacities (Fig. 7-16D).

Sliding bar clamps will deal with much greater distances than fixed clamps. They may be bought with their own bar or as just heads to fix to a steel pipe (Fig. 7-16E). Most clamp uses require two clamps, so buy them in pairs.

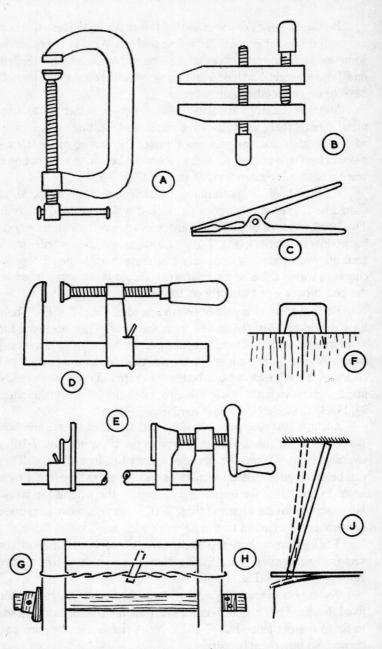

Fig. 7-16. A good selection of clamping devices is always useful. Some can be improvised.

There are other ways of pulling parts together. *Pinch dogs* are made of steel with tapered inner surfaces (Fig. 7-16F); when driven into the end grain of two meeting boards, they force the boards together. Wedges can be used against temporary blocks (Fig. 7-16G), rope can be twisted to draw joints tight (Fig. 7-16H), and parts can be levered together (Fig. 7-16J).

FINISHING TOOLS

Some of the tools suggested for cleaning wood during dismantling of crates described in Chapter 4 may also be used for finishing things made from the wood.

There is nothing as good as a plane for putting a good surface on flat wood, but there are curved surfaces and joints with the grain running in several directions that may be better finished with other tools.

Files, Rasps, and the Like

At one time woodworkers used only a few files and rasps. A file has its teeth made with crossing grooves and a rasp has individually raised teeth. Both tend to clog quickly and have to be cleaned with a wire brush. They still have their uses, but their place has largely been taken by the Surform and many similar tools. These have thin steel blades with teeth similar to those of a rasp, but each tooth has a hole that passes the wood as it is removed. A blade fits a framed handle (Fig. 7-17A). When it blunts it is removed and replaced. The tool is available in the form of a file or a plane; the blade may be curved in cross-section (Fig. 7-17B) or in length (Fig. 7-17C).

Another newer tool is the Aven Trimmatool, which has a blade with teeth across its width. An adjustment allows the blade to be curved in its length from flat to concave or convex (Fig. 7-17D) for exactly following curves. When working on crate wood that is not good enough for finished cabinetwork, but is for exterior carpentry, a Trimmatool or a Surform tool will round edges and remove the rough ends left by a saw.

The traditional tool for curves is a *spokeshave,* which may have a flat sole for outside curves (Fig. 7-18A) or a curved sole for hollows (Fig. 7-18B). It works as a two-handled plane. Most are metal, with the blade controlled by a wedge; some have angle and depth adjust-

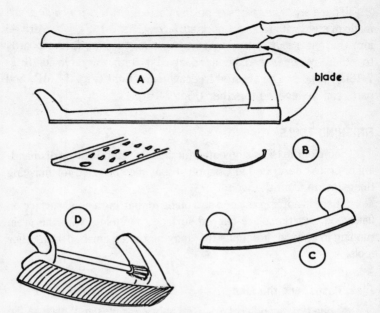

Fig. 7-17. Files and rasps for wood have largely been supplanted by more versatile and efficient tools.

ments. An older version has a wooden stock and the blade arranged to give thinner shavings (Fig. 7-18C).

Although the name seems to indicate that the spokeshave was used for shaping wheel spokes, the wheelright actually did most of

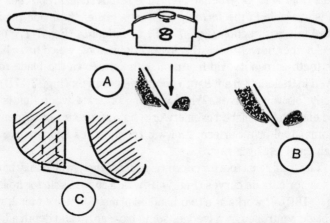

Fig. 7-18. The traditional tool for curves is a spokeshave.

that job and many others with a *draw knife* (Fig. 7-19A). It may be difficult to obtain now, but it can be used for many shaping jobs, particularly when using large rough wood for outdoor construction.

Hook-type scrapers used for the first smoothing of crate wood or the removal of painted markings can also be used for producing finished surfaces. Some makes offer different blades for rough and finishing work (Fig. 7-19B). The old-time cabinetmaker use a flat piece of steel as a scraper (Fig. 7-19C); its sharpeneing and use are described in Chapter 8. It is also possible to use the edge of a piece of broken glass in the same way.

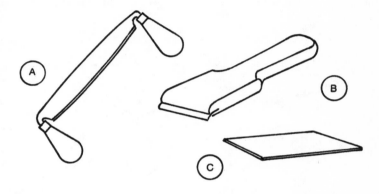

Fig. 7-19. A draw knife (A) is a traditional shaping tool; scrapers (B and C) can be used for finishing as well as removal.

Sanding and Sandpaper

"Sandpaper" is a terrible misnomer, since sand hasn't been used on abrasive sheets for a long time, and almost all sheets are backed with cloth, not paper, particularly for power sanding. Typical abrasives are powdered glass, garnet (which is longer-lasting) and a variety of manufactured grits. Today, nearly all abrasive papers are bonded with waterproof glue. Any with non-waterproof glue should be warmed to drive off moisture before use; otherwise, the grit will come away as soon as the paper is used.

Systems for grading abrasives are not uniform. Some manufacturers use a number that indicates the number of particles of grit per square inch. An earlier system rates paper from many zeros to 3, with the higher numbers coarser. Another system is in multiples of one hundred, with the lower numbers coarser. Most suppliers also rate their product as *fine, medium,* and *coarse*, which is the safest way to order until the exact favored grading is known. Abrasives for power use are coarser than for hand sanding, since the higher speed gives a smoother surface. Avoid grits intended for metal: they may leave a color on wood.

For hand sanding the paper may be used loose in the hand on shaped parts, but for flat work it is better to tear the paper into pieces and wrap one around a sanding block. There are sanding blocks that clip the paper, but one can be made of plain wood, a piece of cork, or wood faced with hard rubber, of a size that allows a quarter-sheet to wrap around and be gripped (Fig. 7-20A).

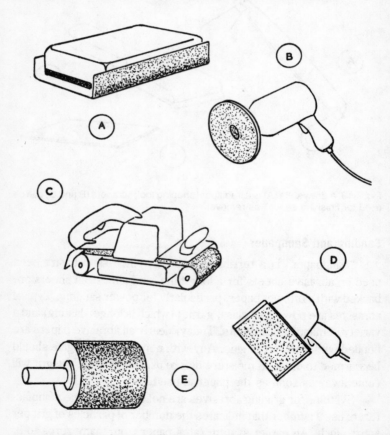

Fig. 7-20. A flat surface should be hand sanded with the abrasive paper around a block. For power sanding there are disc, belt, drum and, oscillating sanders.

A disc sander uses abrasive discs over a flexible backing on a spindle that can be used in the chuck of an electric drill, or the entire unit can be bought as a specialized tool (Fig. 7-20B). Although a disc sander works quickly and can be used to level unevenness, its rotating action leaves curved lines showing on the surface. Much subsequent work may be needed to remove these scratches, so a disc sander has limited woodworking uses.

A belt sander uses a continuous band of abrasive which goes over a pad and two rollers. It rotates at high speed and is controlled with handles like a plane (Fig. 7-20C). As the movement is a straight-line action, any scratches can be in the direction of the grain; with a fine abrasive belt they will not show.

An orbital sander moves a flat rectangular panel covered with abrasive paper with an orbiting action at a very high speed (Fig. 7-20D). This is a final finishing tool and gives a power finish that is nearest to hand sanding.

Sanding drums turn a ring of abrasive cloth with rubber or plastic backing on a spindle (Fig. 7-20E). These are useful for dealing with edges, particularly curved ones, but are not for surfaces.

There are other ways of sanding using fixed machines, with belts or discs. These are as much for shaping as for finishing, and would not normally be justified for a small shop dealing with salvaged wood. The Grind-o-Flex and Sand-o-Flex sanding wheels that use flaps of abrasive cloth, suggested for cleaning off rough crate wood (see Chapter 4), can be used with finer grits for finishing wooden things.

OTHER POWER TOOLS

Anyone setting up a shop to deal with salvaged wood will probably find he can do almost all he wants with hand tools, with an electric drill as his first power tool, followed by a jig saw.

Another tool you may eventually want is a router. It has a high-speed rotating cutter mounted in a frame that acts as a guide or gauge (Fig. 7-21A). When the cutter comes against wood it cuts cleanly in whatever direction it is moved. A plain cutter can make a groove across or with the grain or in a winding direction. If the cutter is shaped to make a groove with a rounded bottom, it will simulate carved name boards (Fig. 7-21B). Other cutters can round or mold edges (Figs. 7-22A and B).

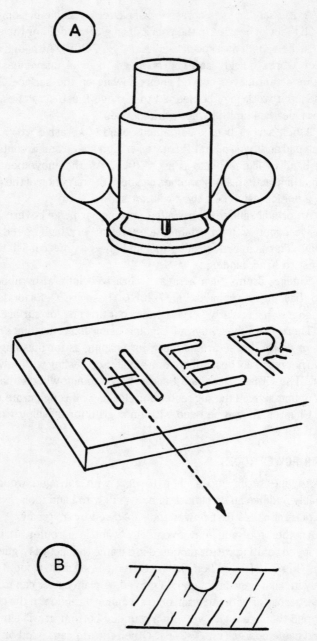

Fig. 7-21. A power router is a versatile tool. One popular use is making routed signs.

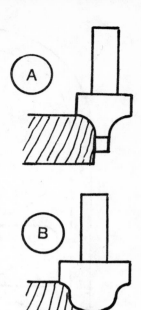

Fig. 7-22. Router cutters are available in many shapes.

A hand router is used only to level the bottoms of grooves that have been cut with a saw or chisel. Its basic form uses a chisel wedged through a block of wood (Fig. 7-23A). A more scientific design has the blade bent (Fig. 7-23B).

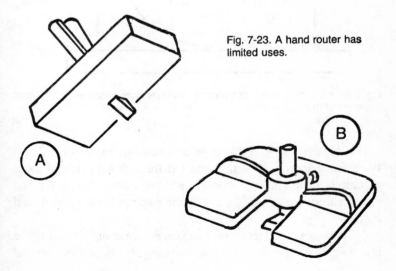

Fig. 7-23. A hand router has limited uses.

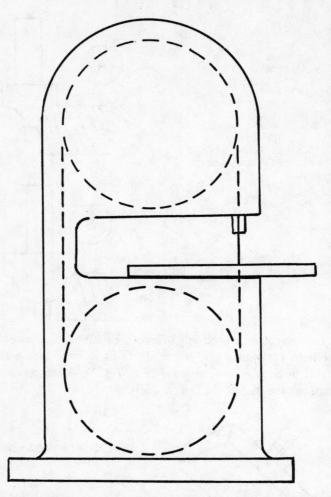

Fig. 7-24. A bandsaw is good for cutting curves, is more accurate, and handles larger wood than a jigsaw.

A bandsaw (Fig. 7-24) uses a continuous blade around two (sometimes three) wheels. Wood fed through it is shaped more accurately than with a jigsaw. It will cut thicker wood, but the distance from one edge is limited by the distance between blade and frame.

There are combination machines in great variety. If your space is limited, they have the advantage of being able to perform several functions in a small space. There is also economy of power, as one motor may drive all parts. In most shops it is the table saw that gets most use, followed by the planer.

In many combination machines it is possible to do only one operation at a time. If there is much labor and time involved in changing operations, the combination may be too much trouble compared to single-purpose machines.

Chapter 8

Tool Handling

A knowledge of wood structure helps in getting the best out of it. If you understand grain and how the wood was formed in the tree, tool operations can be directed to give a good finish and avoid splits.

The grain in wood is due to the annual rings. As a tree grows it adds a ring each year (Fig. 8-1A). In some woods there are alternate light and dark rings, which make identification easy. In others there is little difference in color, but the lines can be detected. The inner, older wood (the heartwood) becomes hard and tough (Fig. 8-2B). Outside that is the sapwood (Fig. 8-2B), which is softer and much less durable. In some trees there is a definite difference in color between heartwood and sapwood. The sapwood of many trees can be used, but it cannot be expected to last as long in outdoor and damp conditions. It is probable that much crate wood will be sapwood, as the better heartwood is usually kept for more important work. Crate wood used outside should be treated with preservative to provide reasonable durability.

Boards are usually cut across the trunk. The board cut from the center has the annual rings at right angles to the surface (Fig. 8-1B). Boards farther out will show more curved grain lines across the end of the board (Fig. 8-1C). If a board end is examined, it is possible to see from which part of the tree it came.

When boards are cut from the tree they contain a considerable amount of moisture. Most of this has to be dried out by seasoning,

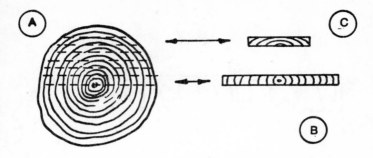

Fig. 8-1. Center- and side-cut boards exhibit different grain.

which may be over a long period (natural seasoning) or by much faster artificial methods. A small amount of moisture is left in the wood after seasoning, but it is in a more stable condition. However, even seasoned wood will take up or give off moisture; both conditions can cause warping.

As wood dries, it shrinks in the direction of the grain lines in cross-section. A board cut across the middle of the trunk gets a little thinner (Fig. 8-3A), but a board farther from the middle develops a curve. This may be thought of as the annual rings trying to straighten out (Fig. 8-3B). A piece of crate wood that has been outdoors and is then taken into a dry, centrally-heated room will tend to warp. If it is tied by being built into a structure with other parts, warping will be prevented, but if it is to be mainly an unsupported board, try to find a piece of center-cut wood.

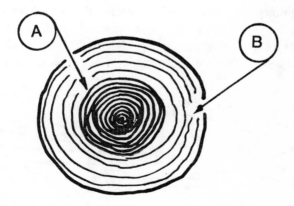

Fig. 8-2. Most crate wood will be sapwood, but heartwood is more durable.

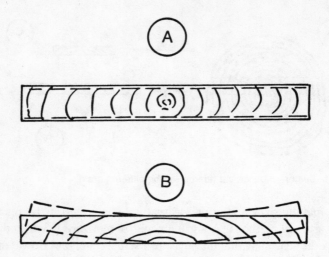

Fig. 8-3. The grain formed as a tree grows affects how wood behaves as it dries and is worked. Strength is greater along the grain than across it.

Grain lines do not form true circles in the cross-section of the log and do not make straight lines in its length. If a board is examined, the grain lines will be seen to be wavy and there will be patterns where they break the cut surface (Fig. 8-4). It is this that gives beauty to wood, but it can also affect tool operations. If the grain lines are considered as loose straws and a diagonal cut is to be made with a chisel, cutting with the grain will be smooth (Fig. 8-5A), but against the grain the straws will tend to turn back instead of be cut (Fig. 8-5B).

This may seem obvious when chiseling the end of a piece, but it also applies to planing the surface of the wood, whether using hand or power tools. If the grain tears up, plane in the opposite direction. Because the grain lines are not straight, it is possible that a sweep of

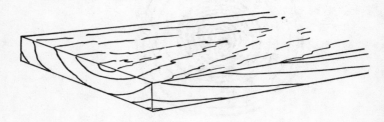

Fig. 8-4. The irregularity of grain is beautiful, but affects tooling operations.

114

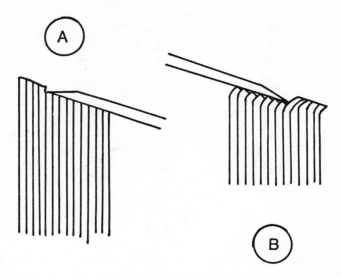

Fig. 8-5. Cutting with and against the grain with a chisel.

the plane along a board may be with the grain at one part and against it at another. With hand planing it may be possible to plane parts in different directions, but with power planing, the direction that gives the least tearing up will have to be used. Some wood with very twisted grain may tear up in both lengthwise directions. The best results on some of these woods are obtained by using a finely-set, very sharp plane at right angles to the grain. In any case, planing is followed by scraping and sanding when a quality finish is to be prepared.

The strength of wood is much greater along the lines of grain than across them. *Short grain* is where the lines are cut across. A curved piece that cuts across grain lines will be weakest there (Fig. 8-6A). Sometimes wood can be selected with grain that will follow the curve (Fig. 8-6B). The modern way to deal with curves is to laminate (see Chapter 11). The grains of several thin pieces are then taken around the curve to give good strength in a stable shape.

During its growth a tree may develop lengthwise cracks between annual rings, due to winds or other causes. They may not affect strength in a board, but beware of shakes that show as zig-zag lines across the grain. Such a line is a weak point. Wood with shakes may have found its way into crates. It will be sound around the

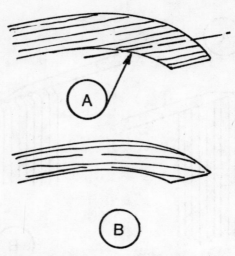

Fig. 8-6. When using solid wood for a curve, select a grain pattern that follows the curve.

shakes, but the wood should be cut to remove the shakes. It would be unwise to make something that has to provide strength if there is a shake within its length.

Plywood is made of several veneers glued together, usually with the grain of the outside veneers matched (Fig. 8-7A). Nearly all plywood is made from veneers cut from a log rotating on a kind of lathe (fig. 8-7B). The opened and flattened veneers have a different, wider grain pattern becasue of this. Obviously, edge planing of plywood will be with the grain of some veneers and against the grain of others. It is usual to plane the edges of plywood in the direction that suits the outer veneers.

Some boards of plywood type may have strips of solid wood as a core between two or more veneers. This *blockboard* or *stripboard* is less common today (Fig. 8-7C), but it makes a very stable thicker board with many construction uses. *Particleboard* is a more recent alternative to thicker plywood. This is made of wood particles bonded with a synthetic resin.

SHARPENING

Working with blunt tools is difficult and frustrating. It can be more dangerous than using sharp tools, as the extra force required against the resistance to cutting may cause accidents. Sharp tools will also produce a better finish than blunt ones. It is unwise to continue with a blunt tool: pause and resharpen it.

Edge tools are sharpened on an oilstone. There are whetstones that can be used with water, but they are just for convenience when working in the field. Better results are obtained with oil. As oil and water do not mix, a stone used for one cannot later be used for the other. The oil used is thin lubricating oil or kerosene. Do not use motor oil, as a thick oil keeps the tool away from the cutting surface of the stone.

At one time oilstones were natural stones. It is possible to buy these, but most modern stones are manufactured. A common size for chisels, plane blades, and similar tools is 8 inches by 2 inches by 1 inch. It is possible to buy one with fine and coarse sides. The coarse side is quick-acting, and the fine side is used to get a better cutting edge.

The stone should be mounted in a box or hollowed piece of wood (Fig. 8-8A). Nail points (Fig. 8-8B) or strips of leather on the bottom (Fig. 8-8C) will prevent the box from slipping. A cover will

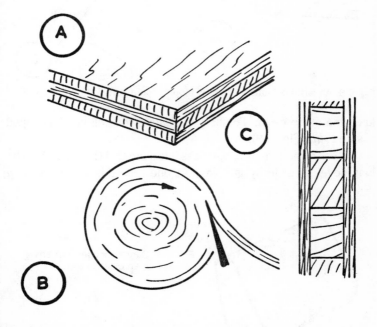

Fig. 8-7. Plywood is made from veneers cut from a rotating log, glued together with grain crossing. Some thicker boards have solid cores.

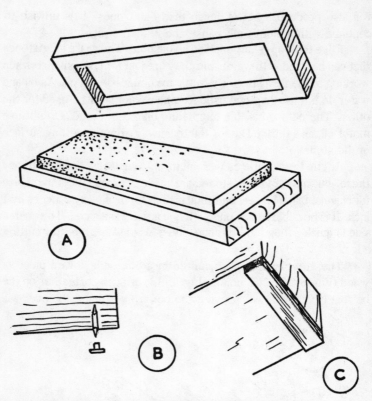

Fig. 8-8. An oilstone is most effective mounted in a non-skid box.

keep the stone clean. To sharpen gouges you will need a shaped oilstone *slip* (Fig. 8-9).

A chisel has two bevels, unless it is quite thin (Fig. 8-10A). The long bevel is made by grinding. At one time this was done on a

Fig. 8-9. Curved gouges are sharpened with an oilstone slip.

slow-moving sandstone, which was kept wet. Today it is more usual to use a high-speed power-driven stone (Fig. 8-10B) and care is needed to avoid overheating. If a steel tool is ground until friction raises the temperature high enough for oxides to appear on the surface, that is a sign that its temper has been drawn. This will have left the tool soft. Have a container of water beside the grinding wheel and dip the tool in it frequently to avoid overheating.

Grinding is needed only at long intervals. The edge is kept sharp by rubbing on the oilstone. When the sharpening bevel has become unduly long, the chisel is ground, so sharpening starts again with a short bevel.

To sharpen on the oilstone, have a little oil on the stone and hold the chisel with one hand on its handle to control it and the fingers of the other hand on the blade to provide pressure (Fig. 8-10C). Rub the chisel backwards and forwards on the stone. Keep the angle the same and move the chisel about on the stone so as to avoid uneven wear on its surface.

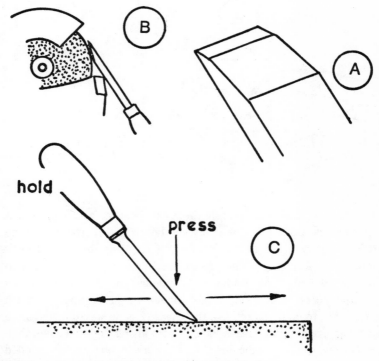

Fig. 8-10. Sharpening a common double-bevel chisel.

Wipe oil off the edge and examine it. If sharpening is thought to be sufficient, wipe a finger gently down the flat side towards the edge. If a roughness is felt at the edge, this is the *wire edge*, turned back after the oilstone has rubbed the bevel as far as the flat side. It is a tiny sliver of steel still clinging to the edge (Fig. 8-11A). This is a sign that the edge has been rubbed enough. Rub the flat side a few times on the stone (Fig. 8-11B), then slice the blade a few times across a piece of scrap wood. This will remove the wire edge and leave the chisel ready for use.

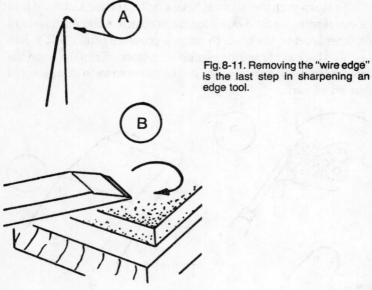

Fig. 8-11. Removing the "wire edge" is the last step in sharpening an edge tool.

A plane iron or blade is sharpened in the same way, except that a thin plane blade may have only one bevel, and sharpening on the oilstone may be all that is needed. If the edge hits a nail or is otherwise damaged, grinding—at the same bevel—is needed to restore the edge line. Both chisels and plane blades may need only sharpening on the fine side of the stone to keep them sharp. If much metal has to be taken off, use the coarse side first. Go through the complete sharpening there, including removing the wire edge, then repeat sharpening on the fine side. Only brief rubbing will be needed there, sufficient to remove the scratches made by the coarse grit.

A chisel is sharpened to a straight edge. Some plane blades are sharpened the same way, but for general use in a plane used on broad surfaces, the corners should be rounded to prevent them from digging in (Fig. 8-12A). For a plane intended to take deep cuts through a rough surface, the edge may be better rounded (Fig. 8-12B).

The method of sharpening a gouge is similar, except that a slip is used on the inner surface—for removing the wire edge of an outside-sharpened tool, or to do the sharpening of an in-cannelled gouge.

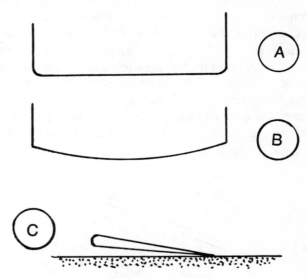

Fig. 8-12. Plane blade profiles and sharpening angle.

A knife is held across the stone, with one hand on the handle maintaining the angle and the fingers of the other hand spread along the blade to provide pressure. Put the blade flat on the stone and lift it until the edge is seen to be in contact (Fig. 8-12C). Rub the knife along the stone, with this angle maintained. If it is a long or curved blade, move it about so all parts of the edge get even wear. When one side is judged to be rubbed enough turn the blade over and do the same on the other side. Check for a wire edge in the same way as with a chisel. Bluntness of any cutting edge can quite often be seen. If you look down on the edge when light shines across it, there will be a line of reflected light on a blunt edge. When it is sharp, there is no reflection.

Saw sharpening by hand requires skill: the teeth have to be bent in opposite directions to provide set and the teeth sharpened with a triangular file. It is better to have a saw sharpened by machine. If a saw has a few teeth blunted from hitting a nail, it may be possible to resharpen them with a file, keeping carefully to the old angles. A saw file is a special triangular file with fine single-cut teeth.

SAWING

The action of sawing is obvious, but it is starting and finishing that may be troublesome. The location of cut with a circular saw is set by a fence (Fig. 8-13A), whether the saw is portable or a table saw. It is unwise and difficult to start a circular saw cut accurately freehand. General hand sawing may be to a pencil line. If the end of the saw is drawn back over the far edge a few times, while the thumb acts as a guide, a deep enough kerf will be made to guide the saw as it starts to cut. For exact cutting to a line, as when making a joint, mark the line across the grain with a knife. For greater accuracy, chisel a slight bevel on the waste side of the line (Fig. 8-13B) to make a hollow to guide the backsaw.

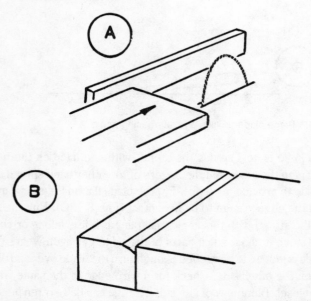

Fig. 8-13. A circular saw with fence, and a beveled cut for hand sawing.

At the end of a cut, support the waste part. Otherwise its weight may break the wood and leave a ragged end. This is as important with light plywood as with heavy boards.

A saw cuts most efficiently when it is going straight across the wood (Fig. 8-14A). This means that a circular saw is better set to a good depth (Fig. 8-14B) than so it only just breaks through the surface (Fig. 8-14C). This also applies to hand sawing, but it is easier to keep a hand saw to the line if it is at a flatter angle, so sawing at about 45 degrees is usual (Fig. 8-15A). Wood can be sawn while upright in a vise, but more power can be applied if the wood is on a trestle and the cut is downwards.

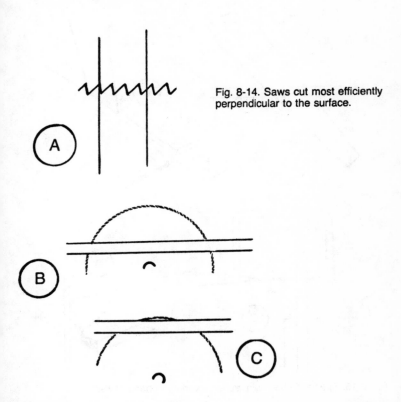

Fig. 8-14. Saws cut most efficiently perpendicular to the surface.

When using a saber saw on thin or springy wood, have the wood supported close to the cut to prevent it from vibrating, which will lead to loss of accuracy and may be dangerous. This may mean moving the support as the cut progresses. Keep the sole of the saber saw tight against the surface at all times. The need for support is particularly important with plywood. For a long cut across a sheet, have support close to the line and hold the cut slightly open to prevent pinching on the saw. This applies to both hand and portable power tools (Fig. 8-15B).

A coping saw or fretsaw can be used with the teeth pointing away from the handle, so the work may be held upright in a vise (Fig. 8-15C). Both hands are on the handle. Experts prefer to have the teeth pointing towards the handle, then sit and use the work over a notched piece of wood (Fig. 8-15D).

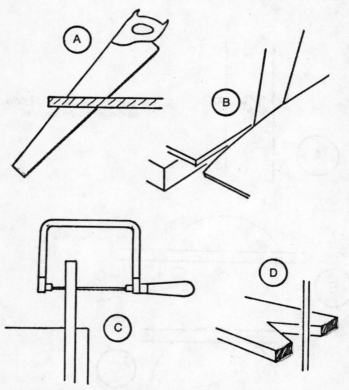

Fig. 8-15. Specialized techniques for a variety of hand saws.

PLANING

A plane has to be set according to its purpose. If it is intended to remove thick shavings from a rough surface, the cap iron is set back from the edge about 1/16 inch or more, and the mouth, if it is adjustable, is opened fairly wide. The blade should be sharpened with a rounded end. It may not leave a very smooth surface, but it will quickly reduce it to a condition ready for final planing. This is also the way to bring a piece of wood down to size when it cannot be machine-planed or sawn.

For finish-planing the blade is sharpened straight across with rounded corners, the mouth is kept narrow and the cap iron is set a short distance from the cutting edge. It is set so only a small amount of the blade projects, so very fine shavings are taken off. The blade needs to be really sharp. For roughing, it may be possible to use a blade that is beginning to blunt, but a finish reflects the sharpness of the plane. A cabinetmaker says that the louder the squeal, the sharper the plane, meaning that if you can hear the plane cutting with a high-pitched shriek, it is doing its job as well as it can be done.

When leveling a piece of wood or straightening an edge, there is an advantage in a plane with a long sole, as it spans the bumps and takes them off first (Fig. 8-16A). A plane with a shorter sole is better for final smoothing after the surface or edge has been made true. A jack plane is the in-between size, and may have the coarse setting and round-edged blade for roughing work.

The top of the bench should be truly flat and kept so. When a piece of wood has to be planed on the surface, it is put on the bench top against the bench stop, which takes the thrust of planing. When an edge has to be planed, the wood is held in the vise, but if it is narrow and may flex under planing, it is better supported on the bench top. A useful device for holding thin wood on edge is a V-shaped block, which can be held with two slip-fit dowels so it can be removed from the bench (Fig. 8-16B).

Power planing reduces labor and should give an accurate result, although light hand planing may follow to improve the quality of the surface. The planing machine may be set to give a coarse cut at first, but a little wood should be left for a fine cut. Feed the wood slowly for the fine cut; the resulting finish should be good enough for many things, and only need light hand planing or power sanding to make a very good finish.

For planing across the grain, have the wood firmly supported and not projecting much above the vise, then plane from both ends (Fig. 8-16C). If the end is trued by planing clear across, the grain at the end of the stroke will break out. For thin pieces of wood a block

Fig. 8-16. A long-soled plane bridges surface irregularities.

plane can be used on its edge to "shoot" the end grain of wood held against the bench hook (Fig. 8-17A).

If a piece of wood has to be prepared to size by planing, it is usual to get one surface true and then plane one edge straight and at right angles to it. These are the *face side* and *face edge*. In all marking-out, measurements are taken from these surfaces, which are traditionally marked as in Fig. 8-17B. Width is gauged across the face side and the underside. That edge is planed to the gauge lines. Thickness is dealt with in the same way.

With a circular saw—with its width fence—and a power planer that controls thickness, sizing is not as painstaking a chore. But it is worthwhile, for the sake of accuracy, to designate surfaces as face side and edge, then work from these to assemble a piece with faces all the same way.

Work should be organized so parts that have to be planed to the same size in one or both dimensions are dealt with at the same time. This introduces less risk of error than dealing with the various dimensions of each piece before moving to the next.

CHISELING

A chisel may be used in the hand, with only hand or body pressure, or it may be held in one hand and hit with a mallet. A chisel used carelessly can be dangerous. The wood should be held in a vise or otherwise prevented from moving. Never depend only on holding by hand and never have one hand in front of the cutting edge.

126

If a chisel is used with its flat side against the wood it will pare the surface. It can be used in this way to remove waste across the grain in a groove (Fig. 8-18A) or for paring a flat or convex surface (Fig. 8-18B). If it is turned with its bevel under, it will shape a hollow (Fig. 8-18C). A gouge sharpened outside will dig out the waste from a bowl shape (Fig. 8-18D), while an in-cannelled gouge will pare inside a circle (Fig. 8-18E).

If a chisel is used for chopping out the waste of a mortise or similar slot, it is used across the grain. It enters like a wedge as it is hit, so allow for this. Do not cut down the end until most of the waste

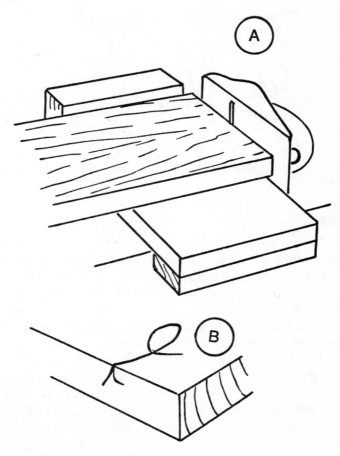

Fig. 8-17. Squaring wood with a plane.

from the rest of the slot has been levered out, otherwise the end of the slot may go further than intended (Fig. 8-18F).

When dealing with a surface, the chisel will cut better if it can be used with a slicing action (Fig. 8-18G) instead of merely being pushed forward. A series of light cuts gives better results than trying to remove a lot with one cut.

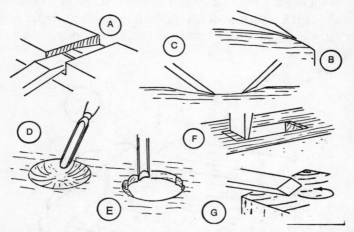

Fig. 8-18. Some chisels and gouges are multi-purpose; others are quite specialized.

DRILLING

The location of holes in wood should be marked by two crossing lines. If there could be confusion with other crossing lines, put a small freehand pencil ring around the place (Fig. 8-19A). If the bit to be used has a spur center, this may be all that is needed, but if there is doubt about the drill entering truly, start the hole with a spike. As far as possible, avoid having holes that go partly through knots; the harder wood in the knot tends to make the drill wander.

If high-speed twist drills bigger than about 3/8 inch are to be used, it helps to first drill a small (1/8 inch or less) *pilot* hole. A pilot hole clears a way for the *dead center* (a non-cutting port of larger twist drills) and keeps the larger drill straight (Fig. 8-19B). Woodworking drills don't have this problem as the central spur centers them; they are also designed to cut cleanly around the circumference, providing another guide.

Any drill taken right through a piece of wood will cause the far side to splinter and break out roughly. This trouble can be reduced by letting the drill continue into a scrap piece of wood (Fig. 8-19C). The scrap must be held tight against the work. An alternative: with a drill having a central spur, watch for the spur to come through, then turn the work over and use this as a guide to drill back the other way (Fig. 8-20A). If holes have to be countersunk, go slowly; the special bit works much better at low speeds.

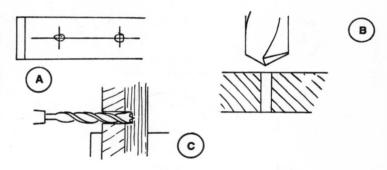

Fig. 8-19. Techniques for accurate drilling.

If holes, particularly large ones, come near the end of a piece of wood, it is advisable to leave a little waste length to be cut off after the hole is drilled (Fig. 8-20B). A certain amount of bursting action is unavoidable when drilling, and this could cause splitting if there was little end grain outside the hole. It is good policy to drill holes after planed wood has been marked out and before other work is done to it.

MARKING OUT

The normal sequence of construction is first, to do all planing, then mark all parts out as far as possible before making joints and cutting to final lengths. In making something where several parts have to carry the same lengths—possibly for only part of their lengths—they should be marked out from each other. A rod is useful for this (see Chapter 7).

A rule can be read more accurately if it is stood on edge (Fig. 8-21A), and it is better to "peck" a position (Fig. 8-21B) than to rely on a single mark. If a line has to be drawn across a piece of wood at a

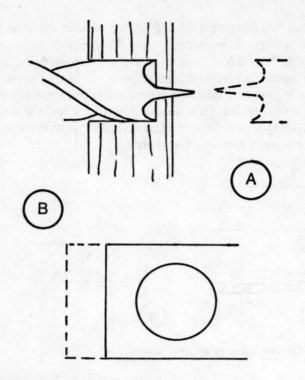

Fig. 8-20. Careful drilling avoids holes splitting out.

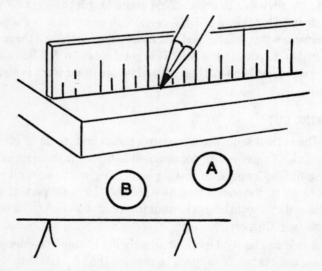

Fig. 8-21. Accurate marking-out is vital to good work.

right angle to the edge, the try square is pushed tight against the edge with the edge of its blade through the point of the peck mark (Fig. 8-22A).

If a line is to be sawn or finished, it should be cut into the surface with a knife. If it is only to mark a position it is better penciled, particularly if it is in a place where a deep knife cut might show on the finished surface. If a line has to go all the way around a piece, use the try square in sequence: first, with the blade across the face side and the stock against the face edge, line the face side; second, line the face edge with the stock on the face side (Fig. 8-22B). Mark the other surfaces so the lines follow around, always with the stock of the square against one of the faces (Fig. 8-22C). If you planed everything perfectly, you would get the same results regardless of what edge you put the try square against, but by working from the faces you ensure uniformity.

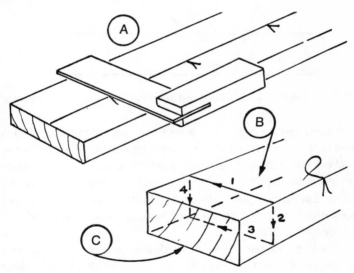

Fig. 8-22. A try square against face edge and face side produces accurate marking and cuts.

A marking gauge needs a little practice to use accurately. Hold around the stock with your first finger, while your thumb presses against the stem behind the cutter. Your other fingers go around the back part of the stem. Place the gauge's stock against the face edge and the cutter on the face surface. Tilt the gauge in the direction it is to go (Fig. 8-23) so its edge as well as the cutter are on the surface. Use your fingers to keep the stock against the edge while your thumb pushes the gauge forward and the cutter makes a scratch parallel with the edge. Be careful that it does not wander with the grain—the fingers pushing against the stock should prevent this.

Other lines, such as those far from an edge or not parallel to it, will have to be marked with a pencil or knife along a rule or straightedge. Mark the points as far apart as possible, even farther than the length you want. There is less risk of error with well-spaced marks than if the marks are close together.

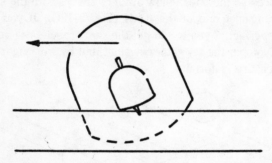

Fig. 8-23. A marking gauge requires both technique and practice for accuracy.

If you must make a series of measurements along a board, it is wisest to total them to get an overall measurement, which will serve as a check when smaller increments are measured. Measuring one short distance after another always seems to result in an overall distance that's larger than it should be. If you need a number of equal spaces it is better to step them off with dividers than to rely on measurements (Fig. 8-24A).

When several parts have to finish the same, as with legs of a table or stool, cut the wood too long and mark all ends, joint positions, and anything else that is common at the same time (Fig. 8-24B). Scribble on the waste parts, but do not cut them off until after the joints and other work has been done. Apart from preventing breaking-out when drilling holes or cutting joints near the ends, the waste pieces take knocks that might otherwise damage finished ends.

If a large assembly has to be laid out, such as the side of a shed, it will be too big to be checked with a try square. Its truth will have to

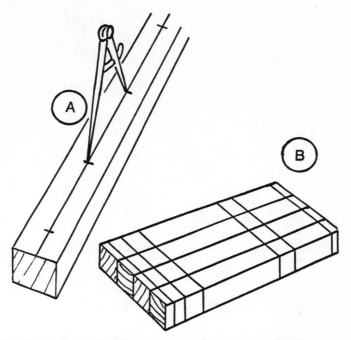

Fig. 8-24. Marking out identical pieces together ensures uniformity.

be ensured geometrically. If it is intended to be symmetrical, its diagonals should be the same length (Fig. 8-25). Corners are usually right angles, but diagonal matching is valid even if the corners aren't 90°, provided the piece is four-sided and symmetrical.

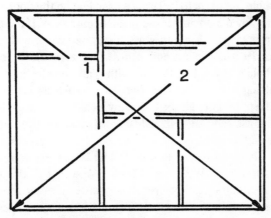

Fig. 8-25. In an accurate rectangle, diagonals (1 & 2) are the same length.

133

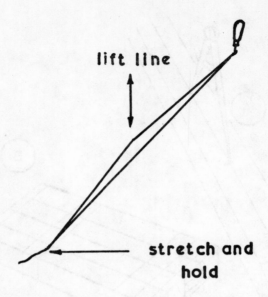

lift line

stretch and hold

Fig. 8-26. A chalk line is valuable for marking long straight lines.

If there is only one right angle to check and no comparable opposite side to permit diagonals, another method is used to check squareness. A good way is the "3:4:5" method. This uses the fact that in a triangle with its sides in that proportion, the angle between the two short sides is a right angle.

It is usually best to set a large right angle down on the shop floor and assemble the parts to it. Draw a base line on the floor, making it longer than any dimension of the piece being made. If the line is too long to draw along a straightedge, it can be struck with chalk and stout cord. Tie a loop in one end to an awl in the shop floor, or have an assistant hold it down. Rub the line with chalk and stretch it along the floor. Holding the end taut on the floor, reach as far as possible towards the other end, lift the line a few inches, and snap it back (Fig. 8-26). This will deposit a straight line of chalk on the floor.

To erect a right angle, mark its point of intersection with the baseline. Choose a convenient unit. The larger the unit, the more accurate the angle. We'll use 3 feet as the unit in this example. Measure four units (12 feet) from the point of intersection along the baseline and make another mark (Fig. 8-27A). Use a tape measure or a strip of wood as a compass to make an arc three units (9 feet) from the first point that is obviously long enough to span a line at right-angles from the first point. From the other point on the baseline measure five units (15 feet) to a point on the arc (Fig. 8-27B). A line drawn or struck through this intersection to the first point will be at right angles to the baseline.

The 3:4:5 method can be used for a right angle anywhere, but for a position away from the end of the baseline it is also possible to use a "compass" method. The compass may be the trammel heads on a length of wood or a piece of wood with an awl as a center. Mark where the right angle is to intersect with the baseline. Measure equal distances along the line each side of the intersection (Fig. 8-28A). Use the compass with the center at each position in turn to draw arcs that will cross (Fig. 8-28B). A line through that crossing and the point on the base line will be at right angles to the base line. Choose distances along the base line and compass lengths that will let the arcs cross at a distance about as far from the base line as the perpendicular should be long. The higher the arc crossing, the more accurate the line will be.

If much large work is to be set out, a permanent right angle can be marked on the shop floor. Pieces of metal can be nailed down with the location of the base and right angle lines marked on them, and lines can be struck through them when needed.

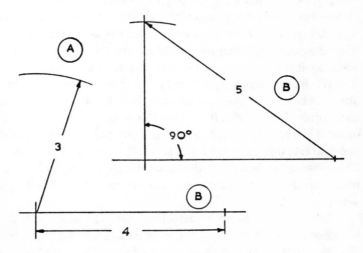

Fig. 8-27. The 3:4:5 method of constructing a right angle.

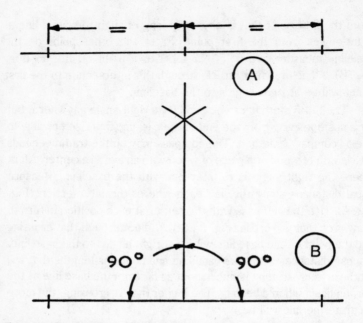

Fig. 8-28. Constructing a perpendicular using a compass or trammel heads.

Associated with marking out is checking the shapes of parts when they are assembled. Most assemblies are variations on the cube, which should have 90-degree corners in all directions. Plywood or other large panels with right-angle corners will keep an assembly true, but if four or more parts have to be joined, they have to be checked in relation to each other and to other parts of the assembly if the finished piece of furniture is to look right.

When four parts are put together to make up a side, check its diagonals before the glue sets or while there is only one fastener at each corner (Fig. 8-29A). If the assembly is longer one way than the other, it is more convenient to assemble the long sides first. Put the opposite side together over the first, so it can be checked to match. If there is any tendency for either assembly to twist out of flat, leave both in position on a flat surface with a weight on top while the glue sets (Fig. 8-29B).

Assemble the parts in the other direction and check their squareness (Fig. 8-29C) and the diagonals as viewed from above (Fig. 8-29D). Do this at the bottom as well as the top. It is possible to get an assembly which is square on all faces, yet is twisted, particularly if it does not stand level or the uprights are not exactly the same length. Although it is possible to check with diagonal measurements from opposite corners if it is an open frame, the best check is to stand back and look at the assembly from a distance. Similar parts on opposite sides should appear parallel. If they do not, push the assembly true, without distorting any of the panels, before the glue has set or the final fasteners are driven. A weight on top until the glue sets will help.

HOLDING AND CLAMPING

Benches, trestles and other holding devices mentioned in Chapter 7 along with clamping devices have fairly obvious uses, but there are some precautions to be taken and some ways of using clamping tools for purposes other than simple squeezing.

It is important that any supports for wood should be firm, particularly when power tools are being used. A portable circular

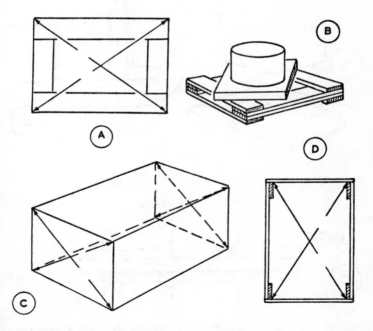

Fig. 8-29. Squareness of three-dimensional objects may also be ensured by checking diagonals.

saw, for instance, could be very dangerous if an improvised support collapsed while cutting. A bench can be braced to a wall or brackets used to fix it to the shop floor. If pieces are fixed to the floor framing the bench's legs (Fig. 8-30A), it can be moved if it is required elsewhere, yet the action of hard planing or other processes will not cause it to move about.

Any clamping device with a screw can exert a considerable pressure, but the area of pressure is quite small, so it may damage wood. It is always good policy to use a piece of scrap wood with a smooth surface under the clamp (Fig. 8-30B). Besides preventing damage to the surface, it spreads the pressure, which will help whether the joint is narrow or broad with many tenons or dovetails. If it is an assembly with several joints, needing several clamps, one long piece of wood under the clamps may be better than individual pads. If parts being clamped are liable to ooze glue out of joints that would stick the scrap wood, paper under the pads will prevent this (Fig. 8-30C) and is easily scraped off later.

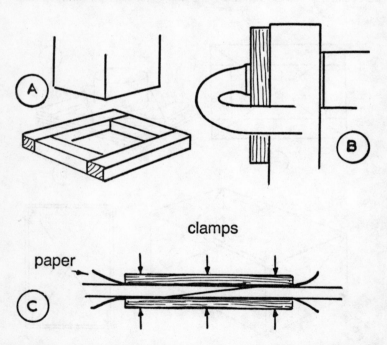

Fig. 8-30. Framing around bench legs (A) prevents movement. Wood scraps (B) spread a clamp's pressure, and paper prevents glued pieces from sticking to the clamps (C).

If an assembly is found to be out of true, a bar clamp used slightly out of true will not only pull a joint together, but force the frame in the direction you want (Fig. 8-31A). This can be done with one or both clamps on a frame. Most bar clamps have feet or pads to rest on. Make sure these are all on the bench top or other flat surface, or the frame may have its glue set with a built-in twist that will be difficult to eradicate.

Wedges can exert plenty of pressure over a short distance. If an improvised clamp is made with a wedge, it can be backed with a packing as progress is made in pushing a joint together (Fig. 8-31B). A single wedge being driven with a hammer has a tendency to push the work aside. This can be cured by using a pair of similar *folding wedges* (Fig. 8-31C), which are driven from opposite sides to give direct pressure. They can be used close to the work or may be quite distant and use a pole to exert pressure, as when lifting a roof beam into place (Fig. 8-31D).

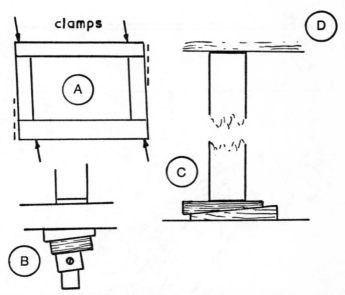

Fig. 8-31. Bar clamps, wedges, and ingenuity are vital woodworking ingredients.

The twisted rope windlass also exerts considerable pressure over a short distance and may damage wood. Use scrap wood (Fig. 8-32A) or wrap the wood with cloth. This *Spanish windlass* works best if made of many strands, rather than one thick one. Like

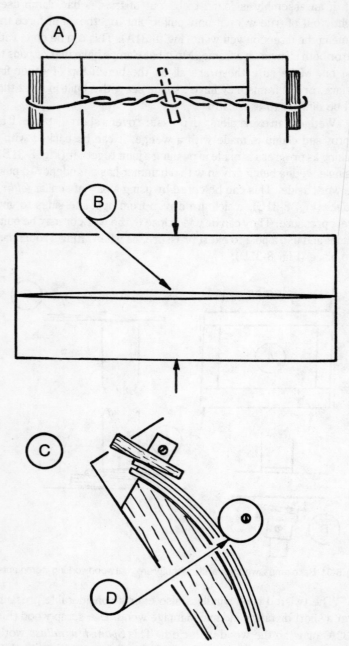

Fig. 8-32. Additional clamping techniques.

wedging, it may be necessary to use a windlass in two steps: first, to pull two pieces solidly together; second, slacken and shorten it to apply clamping pressure.

Modern glues do not require the great pressure on joints that some natural glues did. In fact, excessive pressure may squeeze too much glue out of a joint so it becomes "glue starved" and weak. Meeting surfaces must be in close contact, but not very tightly pressed. When boards are joined edge to edge it is the ends of the joints that tend to open. This can be avoided when preparing the edges for gluing by planing them slightly hollow (Fig. 8-32B, shown exaggerated). When one or more clamps are used near the center, the ends will be pressed tight.

You cannot have too many clamping devices. There will often be occasions when you wish you had more or a different type; lacking them, improvisations can be used, usually incorporating wedges against screwed blocks. Laminations can be held to a form with wedges (Fig. 8-32C). A disc with an off-center screw can be used as a sort of rotating wedge or cam (Fig. 8-32D).

SURFACE FINISHING

Some crate wood may be fit only for rough carpentry, exterior work, or other things that do not require a good surface finish, but much wood that never had a good surface in the crate can be finished with a smooth furniture finish.

If the wood is planed as smooth as possible, there may still be places with slightly torn grain, despite careful use of a sharp plane. Sanding immediately is not the best treatment, because the action tends to bend over some fibers as it removes others. These bent fibers will straighten later and roughness will be apparent. Instead, it is better to use a scraper.

A good finishing scraper is a piece of broken glass. Not every broken edge will cut, but most will. Push the glass forward, adjusting the angle until a cut is made (Fig. 8-33A). The waste should come away like a very fine plane shaving.

Hook scrapers of the type suggested for removing marks from salvaged wood may also be used. They are conveniently pulled with a handle, but the blade should be sharpened and of a type intended for fine finishing. A new blade is better than one that's been filed. A broad scraper that has its replaceable blade sprung to a slight curve is best for a broad surface. Narrow scrapers are intended for recesses or restricted places.

The traditional cabinetmaker's scraper is a flat piece of saw steel (Fig. 8-33B). Its edges are filed or ground square. An edge is sharpened by rubbing with any hard piece of steel, such as a chisel or gouge. This is first done flat on the edge, then tilted slightly each way. The effect is to turn over the edge slightly (Fig. 8-33C, shown exaggerated). This is what cuts.

A filed edge turned over may leave too rough a cutting edge. It is better to rub any file or grinding marks out on an oilstone (Fig. 8-33D) before turning over the edge. The best result is obtained by rubbing the flat of the steel as well as the edge (Fig. 8-33E).

To use the scraper, tilt it forward like a piece of broken glass until an angle is found that will cut (Fig. 8-33F). Hold the scraper with both hands so your thumbs push the steel to a slight curve (Fig. 8-33G): this makes cutting easier and allows better control. Scraping can be in any direction and will have to be in several directions over confused grain, but finish in the general direction of the straighter grain.

There is a Stanley two-handed scraper that uses this type of blade, but holds it at the correct angle with an adjustable curve, in what looks like a spokeshave or a two-handed plane.

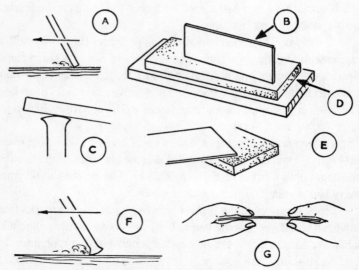

Fig. 8-33. A scraper is sharpened by turning over its edge.

To get the finest results from sanding, whether power or hand, it is necessary to work down through successively finer abrasives, with each grade completely removing the scratches made by the previous ones. So that scratches do not show through a clear polish, do all final sanding in the direction of the grain, where any remaining marks will be disguised by the lines of the grain.

Abrasive paper and cloth will leave particles of grit on the wood. Wipe or brush these off before moving to a finer grade, or you may get coarse scratches mixed with the finer ones. Steel wool can be used to rub a surface smooth, but this is prone to leave little bits of steel. If these are left, they may rust and disfigure the surface. With some woods, such as oak, the steel particles react with chemicals in the wood and cause dark stains.

Before final sanding, it is helpful to wet the surface and let it dry. This will raise any minute fibers that were bent instead of broken, so the next sanding should remove them. Although power sanding is quick and effective, it is better on some woods to do the final work by hand.

Chapter 9
Fasteners

In first-class cabinetwork most wood parts are united by fitted joints and glue. There are few metal fastenings. The quality of wood obtained by salvage often prohibits such joints, but it is worth keeping in mind that where a cut joint is practicable, it is preferable to using nails or screws.

Most salvaged wood is softwood; this is not as adaptable to fitted joints as close-grained hardwood. However, all kinds of wood find their way into packing cases and other containers; with luck, you may find some fine hardwood that would cost quite a lot as new lumber. Of course, your joints depend on what you're making. Rustic furniture, articles to be used on the porch or in the garden, and similar things are satisfactory with rather basic joints reinforced by metal fasteners or by merely putting one piece of wood on another and nailing or screwing it there.

NAILING

Nails are made in a great variety of patterns; many may be accumulated when dismantling crates. Common nails have round wire shanks and round heads (Fig. 9-1A). Points may be round or square. Box nails are similar, but the heads are smaller in diameter. There are nails with larger heads intended for holding shingles, galvanized iron, and other external coverings. There are several nails that are almost headless (Fig. 9-1B); these are used where the head cannot be hidden.

Nearly all nails are made of mild steel. They may be protected from rust by galvanizing (coating with zinc) or by several kinds of plating. Nails are sometimes made of aluminum, brass, copper, and other metals and alloys. They have limited uses; for most work, the mild steel nails (often called iron) are what you need.

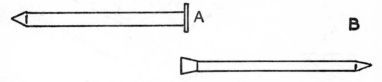

Fig. 9-1. The most frequently used fasteners are common and box nails.

Nails are made in lengths from 1/2 inch or less up to 6 inches or more. The smallest nails may be described as pins. Nail diameters are measured by a gauge number, but there is rarely any choice of gauge in a particular length: what's available will have to be accepted. Up to 1 inch, nails come in 1/8-inch increments; above that the increments are by 1/4, then 1/2 inch. There is a system of "penny" measurements for identifying nails, but it is probably safest to order according to their length. You may know how many you want, but the supplier will charge by weight.

Most people have driven nails; most have also hit their fingers instead of the nail. Use a hammer or a weight that you can manage and hold it by the end of the handle. It is lack of confidence that makes you slide your hand close to the head, or the hammer is too heavy for you. If you hold near the end of the handle, the swing is as much from your elbow as your wrist. This gives better control and more power to the blow when you need it.

What keeps two pieces of wood together with a nail is not tightness in the top piece, just the bottom. A slightly undersize hole can be drilled in the top piece. This reduces the risk of splitting and does not weaken the joint in any way—in fact it may make it stronger as the head squeezes down on the wood against the grip of the nail in the lower piece, without any loss due to grip in the top piece (Fig. 9-2A). Except when using very fine nails or doing rough carpentry, it is always worth the trouble of drilling for the nails. If the nail is to go deep into the lower piece or it is close to an edge where splitting is

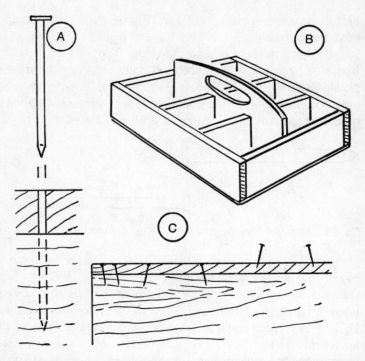

Fig. 9-2. Drilling the top piece and driving nails at angles can add strength to a joint.

probable, you may drill a smaller hole part-depth in the lower piece, but don't make the hole too large. If it is made too easy for the nail to enter that piece, its grip will be impaired.

What length nail to use depends on many factors, but it should go far enough into the lower piece to grip well; this usually means penetrating more than the thickness of the upper piece. If thin plywood is being nailed, the nails should penetrate the wood below at least 1/2 inch. For general constructional work the most common nail lengths are 1 1/2 inch and 2 inch. A stock of these sizes, as well as 3/4 inch, 1 inch, and a few larger sizes should be kept. If much nailing is expected, a box with partitions is useful (Fig. 9-2B). However, if nails are not in frequent use, it is better to keep them in jars with tops to reduce the risk of rust.

For most purposes nails may be driven straight, but if extra strength is required they can be dovetail-nailed (driven at angles) as in (Fig. 9-2C). How close nails are driven depends more on experience than on any set plan. If thin wood is being nailed, the nails need to be fairly close to prevent buckling and even closer at the ends, where there is more likelihood of lifting.

If the head is to be hidden it can be punched below the surface (Fig. 9-3A). If you do this to a nail with an ordinary head, the grain may tear around the hole, so it is neater to use a nail with a small head. When the nail has been punched the head can be covered with filler. There are several fillers; their choice depends on the wood and the intended finish. Although it is possible to make fillers, it is better to buy them ready-made. *Plastic wood* is a good general-purpose filler. It is supplied in a tube or a can. For occasional use the tube is better as there is less risk of the filler hardening in the container. Filler is pressed into the hole and left standing above the surface slightly, so it can be sanded level after it has hardened.

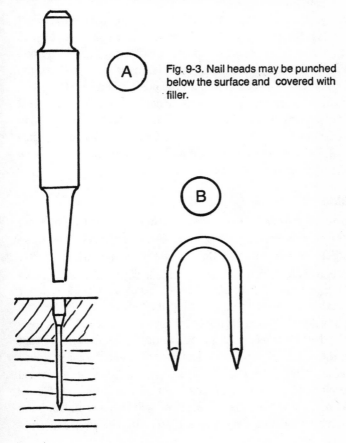

Fig. 9-3. Nail heads may be punched below the surface and covered with filler.

Plastic wood will take stain and it should be possible to finish a surface so the filled nail hole is inconspicuous. Fillers are also obtainable in colors to match several common woods.

Staples (Fig. 9-3B) are really double-ended nails. They are not really construction fasteners, but are used for fastening fencing wire to posts and similar jobs. However, some may be recovered from crates, where they held wire reinforcement or metal straps. Staples can be used for attaching thin plywood in places where the surface does not show, as they hold down thin material better than nails.

If two thin pieces of wood are to be joined by nailing, there is often not enough thickness of wood for a nail to be very secure. The only way to make a safe joint is to drive the nails through and clench them. It is unsatisfactory to merely bend the point over, as this leaves the tip exposed where it could be dangerous, and does not provide maximum strength.

The nail should be chosen so it can be driven through to project 1/4 inch or a little more (Fig. 9-4A). The work is rested with the nail head on an iron block. Then the point is curved over the end of a spike (Fig. 9-4B) and the resulting hook is driven down to bury the point (Fig. 9-4C). It is neatest to bury the point in line with the grain, and this will be satisfactory for many purposes, but for the greatest strength go across or diagonal to the grain. This technique is used to make trellis-work, which gives a diamond pattern for climbing garden plants. With one clenched nail at each crossing, the trellis can be expanded or contracted to suit various spaces.

SCREWING

Screws are generally considered superior to nails. For most parts of furniture where a metal fastener is needed, it is better to use screws. Screws pull parts together and do not loosen when another fastener is driven, which can be a problem with nails: hammering nails at one part may vibrate others loose. Screws are preferable for a joint which may have to be dismantled at a future date, as they can be withdrawn and replaced without damage to the wood. It is very difficult and often impossible to dismantle a nailed joint without marking the wood. Screws may supplement a glued joint in a way that a nail could not. The screw will pull the glued surfaces close and take the place of a clamp in a place where a clamp will not fit.

Like nails, there is a great variety of wood screws made, but a comparatively small range of types will serve for nearly all construc-

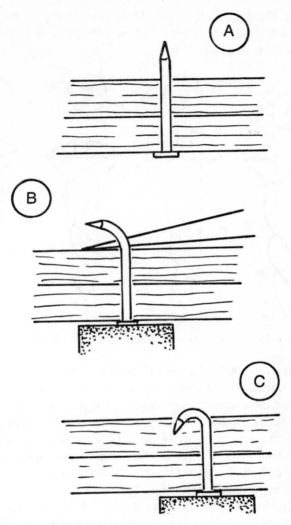

Fig. 9-4. The steps in clenching a nail.

tion needs. The common screw has a flat head (Fig. 9-5A). Round-headed screws (Fig. 9-5B) are used for decoration and for attaching metal fittings. An in-between type has an oval head (Fig. 9-5C) which can be countersunk; the head does not project as much as a round head. Some very large screws (sometimes called *lag bolts*) have a head to take a wrench (Fig. 9-5D). Some smaller combination screw heads have a slot for a driver and a hexagonal outline for a wrench. These are really intended for power driving and are found in some crates. Such screws can be reused, but the head would be ugly in a conspicuous place.

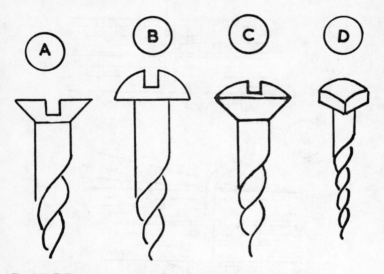

Fig. 9-5. Different screw heads for different purposes and effects.

Screws intended for normal hand driving have slotted heads. Those with X-shaped sockets are intended for power driving, but there are hand screwdrivers to suit them, so any recovered from crates can be used again. The usual range of these screws can be dealt with by a set of three sizes of screwdriver or bits for a combination driver. For slotted heads, the end of the screwdriver should be about as wide as the screw head and a reasonable fit in the slot for easy driving and little risk of damage to the screw head. If the screw head will show in the finished work, a broken or damaged slot will spoil the appearance. If it is a plated screw, a damaged head will admit moisture and cause rusting.

Common screws are made of mild steel, and it's unlikely that screws of any other metal will be found in a crate. They are normally bright, but some very large ones are black. At one time steel screws for outdoor use were galvanized, but that method of applying a protective zinc coating left a rough surface, which helped galvanized nails grip but interfered with driving a screw. Steel screws may be given any of a large number of platings, many of which are intended to match the finish of a head to a metal fitting. They may also be oxidized or treated in other ways to give antique and other finishes to match metalwork. For normal use, the plain steel screws are satisfactory.

Wood screws may also be made of brass, aluminum, stainless steel, and even plastic. Brass was the choice of the traditional cabinetmaker. Most of the other metals are used because of their resistance to corrosion. Except for stainless steel, they are not as strong as steel, and plastic screws have not proved their worth.

Screws are measured by their length from the surface of the wood (dimension L in Fig. 9-6) so any screw with a raised head is longer overall than one with a flat head. Screws are also described by their diameter (gauge). Some length screws are available in several gauges. Small screws come in 1/8-inch length increments; above the 1-inch length the increments are 1/4 inch, and above 3 inches it may be difficult to find other than 1/2-inch increments.

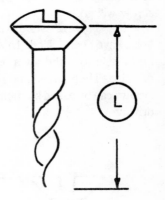

Fig. 9-6. Screw length is measured from the screw tip to the wood's surface.

Higher gauge numbers indicate thicker screws. For the smallest screws, consecutive gauges are available, but from gauge 10 up, only even-number gauges are available. As an approximate indication of size, 8 gauge is about 1/8 inch. Some common screw sizes are 1/2 inch by 4 gauge, 3/4 inch by 6 gauge, 1 inch by 8 gauge, 1 1/2 inch by 10 gauge, 2 inches by 12 gauge. However, any of these lengths are available in other gauges.

It is never satisfactory to drive a screw without first drilling a hole, although this is sometimes done in softwoods. As with nailing, two parts are pulled together by the pressure of the head on the top piece which is generated by the pull of the thread in the lower piece. It is wrong to have the threaded part of a screw gripping the top piece, and a screw forced in without a hole will inevitably grip the top piece of wood. The only exception might be a metal fitting over soft wood, when a screw may be started with a tap from a hammer, then turned tight with a screwdriver.

Normally there should be a clearance hole in the top piece (Fig. 9-7A) and—if the top piece is thin—that clearance hole will extend as far as the unthreaded neck will go into the lower piece. Normally, the clearance hole is the same size as the neck of the screw. What to drill into the lower part depends on the wood. For small screws in soft wood it may be sufficient to start the screw by heavy pressure on the driver, or by making a shallow hole with a bradawl. For larger screws there must be a tapping hole (Fig. 9-7B). For soft woods this hole can be a smaller diameter than the core of the screw threads and need not be as deep as the screw is long. For hard woods the tapping hole should be about the core diameter and almost as deep as the screw will go.

If a screw resists driving, withdraw it and make sure correct holes have been drilled. Thin screws may shear off if forced, and it is impossible to withdraw a broken piece, so the error is difficult to disguise. There should be no trouble driving small screws. Larger screws can be eased by rubbing them with soap or candle wax before driving.

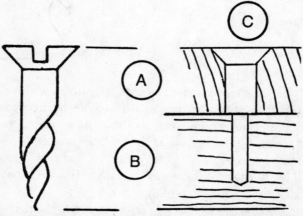

Fig. 9-7. Preparation for a screw may include countersinking and clearance and tapping holes.

A flat-head screw is intended to finish flush with the surface. Even in hard woods it has a tendency to pull in. It is advisable to drive a screw experimentally without countersinking its hole to check how much countersinking is necessary. In many soft woods, the screw head will pull in flush without countersinking. In hard woods it will pull in slightly, so the hole should be countersunk (Fig. 9-7C), but not to the full size of the screw head.

Because of their better holding power, screws can be spaced farther apart than nails. For driving across the grain, most of the threaded part of the screw should be in the lower piece of wood. This means that if the top piece is 1/2 inch thick, the screw should be 1 1/4 or 1 1/2 inches long. Two and a half times the thickness of the top piece is a rough guide to screw length, but soft woods need longer screws than hard woods.

Screws don't hold as well in end grain as in cross grain, so if a joint like the corner of a box is screwed, the screws should be half again as long as for joining the same top piece to cross-grain wood. One way of increasing the strength of a screw in end grain is to drill across the bottom piece and insert a piece of dowel so the screw thread will go through it (Fig. 9-8A). This cannot be used where the dowel would spoil appearance, but in utilitarian construction where strength is more important than appearance, it is a worthwhile trick.

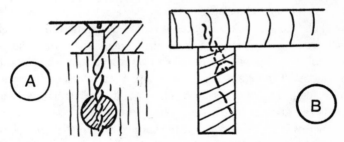

Fig. 9-8. A dowel will add strength to a screwed joint; pocket screwing hides the head.

There are two methods of *slot screwing* that may have applications in making things from salvaged wood. One is used for an edge joint, as when a table top is attached to rails between the legs. A slot or notch is cut for each screw with a chisel or gouge. It should be wide enough to accept the diameter of the screw head with a little to spare, and at a distance from the top edge that will allow the screw to hold the top without going through to the surface (Fig. 9-8B). When attaching a top with a series of these *pocket screws*, tighten each in sequence a little at a time until all screws are tight.

The other method is "secret slot screwing," a way of pulling two edges of boards close while they are glued without the use of clamps. There is no sign of the screws when the joint is finished.

Plane both meeting edges true, so the joint will be close and the boards as flat as one piece when joined. On the two edges mark the positions of screws. Two will be enough on a joint up to 2 feet long, but use three or more on longer joints. Mark the boards together (Fig. 9-9A). On one board put more marks 1/2 inch from the others (Fig. 9-9B). On very thick boards this can be increased to 3/4 inch.

Use fairly stout screws, say 10 or 12 gauge on 3/4-inch wood, but the screws need not be very long—1 inch should be enough. Whatever the length, drive the screws into the board with the single marks so they project about 3/16 inch (Fig. 9-9C). In the other piece drill a clearance hole (as wide as the screw neck) opposite the screws and make a hole that will clear the screw head at each of the other points. Drill these holes a little deeper than the screws project from the other piece. Cut a slot—again, as wide as the screw neck—from each clearance hole to the other (Fig. 9-9D).

Put the boards together dry with the screw heads in the large holes prepared for them. Use a mallet to knock one board along the other so the screw heads will cut their way along to the other ends of the slots. Knock back the other way and dismantle the joint, give each screw a tightening quarter-turn, put glue on the joint and assemble it again. The tightened screws will go along the slots, but with increased pressure (Fig. 9-9E), forcing the glued surfaces close and holding the joint together. They will also contribute strength across the grain in the finished joint.

Screws may be sunk below the surface by *counterboring*. A hole big enough to clear the head is drilled a short distance before the clearance and pilot holes for the screw (Fig. 9-10A). There are combination drills that will drill this hole as well as the clearance and tapping holes for certain sizes of screws, but usually separate drills have to be used. After the screw has been driven, the hole may be filled with plastic wood, but it is also possible to use a wooden plug. This may be a piece of dowel rod glued in, but when that is planed level its end grain will show in contrast to the side grain of the surrounding wood.

154

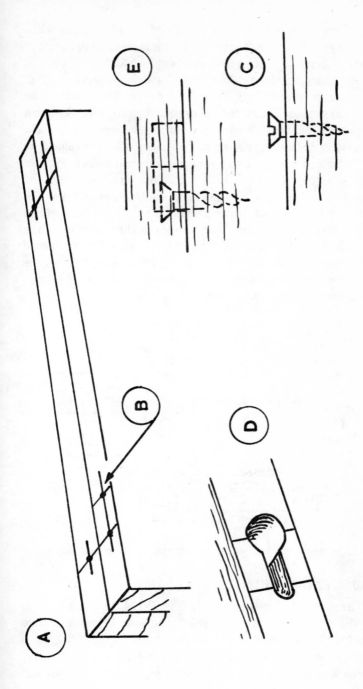

Fig. 9-9. The steps in "secret slot screwing."

In some designs a pattern of dowel ends may be regarded as a design feature, but if you don't want this, it is possible to use plugs with cross grain to match the surrounding wood (Fig. 9-10B). It would not be impossible to make them by hand, but plug cutters (Fig. 9-10C) that fit an electric drill are much easier. The drill must be mounted in a stand. The cutter makes plugs up to 1/2 inch long that can be levered out with a narrow chisel or screwdriver (Fig. 9-10D). If the plug grain is well-selected and matched, it is very difficult to detect a plug after it has been planed and sanded level.

Most screwing has to be done from one side because of the nature of joints, but where two pieces of similar thickness have to be joined over an area that requires many screws, the joint will be stronger if screws are driven from both sides, alternating in zig-zag fashion. Screws look neater in straight lines, but if they're aligned with the grain they can split the wood. The risk of splitting along the grain can be reduced by staggering the screws. If staggered evenly, the pattern may look better than a straight line.

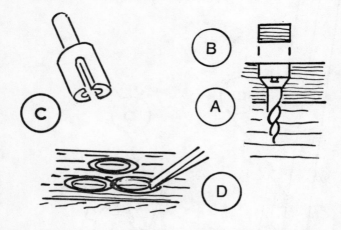

Fig. 9-10. Holes may be filled with plugs that match the work's grain.

CORRUGATED FASTENERS

The corrugated fastener or nail (Fig. 9-11A) has limited uses. One edge of the corrugations is sharpened to make teeth to drive into wood. The corrugations of some fasteners are parallel, but a better type has them sloping slightly on each side toward the center, so as the fastener is driven in, the boards are pulled closer together.

The usual corrugated fastener is about 1 inch wide with five corrugations and may be obtained 3/8 inch, 1/2 inch, and 5/8 inch deep. It is easy to drive directly with a hammer, but a set can be bought to use as a punch. Fasteners are made of untreated steel. Once fully driven, they cannot be withdrawn without damage to the wood.

Corrugated fasteners are used in rough woodwork to keep adjoining boards in line (Fig. 9-11B). This is how they are likely to have been used in a light crate. This application breaks grain lines and is only suitable for softer woods. In more important work it is possible to use a fastener in a hidden place, where it may be more

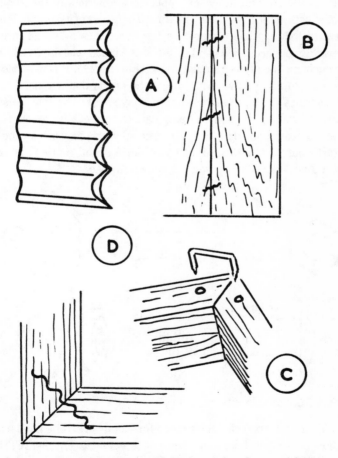

Fig. 9-11. Corrugated fasteners and staples are used across joints.

suitable than any other method. An example is under a mitered *plinth*, made up of strips. A corrugated fastener across the bottom will pull the glued joint together (Fig. 9-11C). A possible alternative is a long nail with its head cut off or a piece of wire. The ends are bent and pointed, then driven across the joint hard enough to bury the top part (Fig. 9-11D).

NUTS, BOLTS AND WASHERS

Nuts and bolts are mainly engineering fasteners and are not much used in woodwork. However, they are useful for large construction and have applications where parts pivot, as in a folding chair. The word "bolt" is loosely applied in a general way, but a bolt is more exactly defined as having its thread only part of its length. If it is threaded full length, or almost to the head, it is a "metal thread screw." Engineering bolts and screws have hexagonal heads to take a wrench and the nut is a similar shape (Fig. 9-12A). It is possible to get metal thread screws with any of the heads that are used with wood screws. In the smaller sizes it is convenient to be able to use a screwdriver. Nuts are sometimes square instead of hexagonal. If the nut and bolt are to be dismantled occasionally, you may use a wing or butterfly nut (Fig. 9-12B) to turn by hand. A round knurled nut may be used on a small screw for the same purpose.

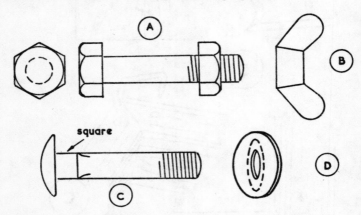

Fig. 9-12. Bolt and nut patterns.

There are coach bolts intended for woodwork. The head has a shallow curve and there is a square neck below it (Fig. 9-12C) that pulls into the wood and resists turning, eliminating the need for a wrench on the head. These may be black steel, which has some resistance to rust.

Engineering bolts and nuts are usually bright mild steel, but they may be plated in many ways and can have antique and other finishes. They are also made from many other metals and alloys, particularly for marine purposes where resistance to rust and corrosion is important.

In woodwork, nuts and bolts are normally used with washers. The washers provided with many engineering nuts and bolts do not have a diameter much bigger than the nuts. For woodwork it is better to have larger washers with the same size hole (Fig. 9-12D): they spread the pressure over a greater area and resist pulling into the wood. Where several bolts go through wood close together, it may be better to use a piece of sheet metal with holes in the right places to spread the pressure.

If a screw will have to be withdrawn occasionally, it may go through a plain washer to reduce wear on the wood, but for flat-head or oval-head wood or metal thread screws, cup washers give a neat finish (Fig. 9-13A) and allow many removals without marking the wood. These are useful for lift-off plywood panels and similar applications.

Bolts and metal thread screws may have several sizes of thread on the same diameter shank. These are important in engineering applications, but for woodwork anything available can be used, with a preference for coarse threads. Normally, a close clearance hole is drilled right through all parts. If it would be useful for a screw to be retained in the wood at its head end, it is possible to drill a slightly undersize hole and screw the threads into that part (Fig. 9-13B), while using a clearance hole in the other part. This way, if the parts are dismantled there is no risk of the screw being lost. One type of coarse thread screw with slotted flat or round heads is sold as *stove bolts*, in diameters up to 1/4 inch and lengths up to 3 inches. They may be zinc plated, and are a convenient small bolt for woodwork.

If thin plywood or other sheet material salvaged from crates is used for wall paneling, it may be too thin for fasteners to grip. In this situation you can use several devices that expand behind the panel to provide a grip. A Molly Jack Nut is an example. A hole is made to pass the neck of the nut on the screw (Fig. 9-13C). As the screw is tightened, it pulls the nut back and expands it behind the panel (Fig. 9-13D). Some of these expanding nuts need a greater depth behind the panel than others. Some become fixtures, so a screw can be removed and replaced without the nut coming away. Most are metal, but there are plastic and neoprene versions, which seal and dampen vibration as well as providing attachment.

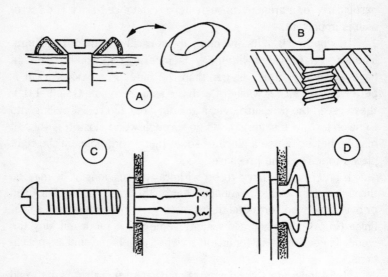

Fig. 9-13. Special-purpose bolts and fittings.

SELF-TAPPING SCREWS

There are several types of screw made from hardened steel which cut their own threads in metal. They are mostly used in the quantity production of cars, domestic appliances and similar things, but some may be recovered from crates. Some types of these screws are not much use, but one sheet metal screw has a thread very similar to a wood screw, but taken to the head (Fig. 9-14A). It can be used in wood.

Heads may be similar to wood screws, although countersinks are steeper, or they may be slotted hexagonal heads for power driving. A common form is a pan head (Fig. 9-14B), which spreads pressure on sheet metal without a washer, but is not very attractive on wood. If these screws are used on sheet metal, the size of the tapping hole depends on the thickness and type of metal. With soft thin metal, the tapping hole can be the same size as the core diameter of the screw, but for thicker and harder metal it must be a little bigger. It is possible to use small pieces of sheet metal as nuts on these screws, so they are suitable to use behind thin panels of plywood. If the other side will not be accessible after assembly, the metal "nut" can be held to the back with a spot of glue until the screw enters from the front.

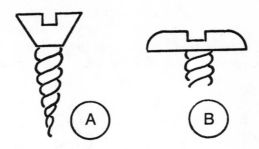

Fig. 9-14. Some sheet-metal screws have uses in wood.

LOCKNUTS AND RIVETS

If nuts and bolts are used as fixed fasteners, they are tightened down once and for all. If the joint is one that has to move—as in the crossing legs of a folding stool—an ordinary nut on a bolt will soon work loose. There are two ways of dealing with this: use a locknut or substitute a rivet.

The simplest locknut arrangement is to use two thin nuts (Fig. 9-15A). The two nuts are driven and, using two wrenches, the lower nut is turned back against the top one. With a single nut it is possible to burr the end of the bolt so the nut cannot come off. This can be done with a cross or ball-peen hammer (Fig. 9-15B), or several center punch dots can be driven into the thread above the nut—both while the head is supported by an iron block.

There are nuts which incorporate a spring section so they resist unscrewing. Others have a ring of fiber or other stiff material included; the bolt cutting into it makes a tight joint (Fig. 9-15C). Another way of making the nut grip is to smear epoxy glue on the thread or to put epoxy around the tightened nut and projecting bolt thread. The metal must be free of grease for this to be successful.

In a small folding wood joint, it may be better to use a rivet. This can be bought with a head already formed or it can be a piece of iron, copper or other malleable metal. Use large washers between as well as outside the wooden parts (Fig. 9-15D). Cut off the rod so it stands up a distance slightly less than its diameter. If there is already a head at one end, support this with an iron block or another hammer, then use a ball-peen hammer to spread the top end over the washer. Work all around, not too heavily, but gradually turn the edge onto the washer to make a reasonably uniform rounded head. If it is a plain rod without a preformed head, rivet a little at each end in turn so both ends eventually butt onto their washers with rounded heads (Fig. 9-15E). Well-formed rivet heads cannot come apart; if it is expected that the joint will have to be separated later, locknuts on bolts are preferable, as they may be released.

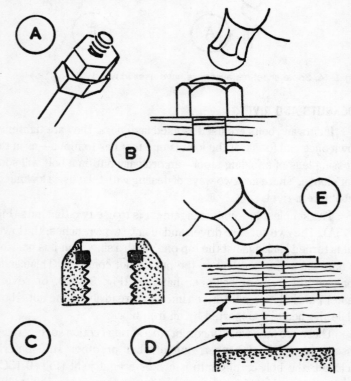

Fig. 9-15. Techniques for locking nuts and riveting.

GLUES

At one time, wood glue was made from animal hooves, fish bones and animal hides, and some of the resulting mixtures had a powerful smell. Later versions were in a more refined state and the odor was much less objectionable. This type of glue has not been completely superseded. It is still used for repairs to antiques, but does not have much application for new work.

This glue may be supplied ready to use, but it may have to be heated in a double boiler to prevent overheating. An advantage is its slow setting time, so it is possible to spread glue over a large surface and deal with it in an unhurried way. The solvent in this glue is water and the set glue is not water-resistant. If it becomes damp, it will weaken, although it will recover strength as it dries out again. Of course, by then it may have lost its hold and parts may have moved. However, some traditional furniture has survived for centuries without its glue weakening.

Modern glues are mostly the result of the plastics revolution since World War II. Most glues are supplied under trade names and it is not always easy to decide which is the most suitable glue for a purpose. The strongest wood glues are mostly described as for wood, without reference to other materials. If a glue is described as suitable for paper, cloth, leather, and other materials as well as wood, it is probably only suitable for light handicraft woodwork and not for furniture or similar heavier construction.

In this group are polyvinyl glues, often described as "white" glues. They are in plastic containers that also serve as applicators. If this glue is used for general woodwork, the joints should also be screwed or nailed and should then be satisfactory for such things as drawer rails or framing to stiffen plywood. It is not the best glue to use for heavily loaded dowel or mortise-and-tenon joints.

Plastics development is an ongoing process, so there are new glues developing that are used like white glue, but have greater strength. Franklin Titebond aliphatic resin is one of these glues. Anything described as a contact cement is not a wood glue for general purposes, although it may have a very secure grip.

Some contact cements give off dangerous fumes and have to be used outdoors or in a well-ventilated place. More recent contact cements do not have this drawback. As the name implies, two surfaces coated according to the instructions will bond immediately when placed in contact. In some cases they cannot be moved, so it is important that the parts are in correct alignment as they touch. For woodworking, contact cement is suitable for veneering and fixing synthetic table tops to wood. It has other uses with leather, linoleum and plastics.

Most of the strong construction glues for woodwork are two-agent synthetic resins. If the glue is described as suitable for wooden boat building, it is one of the strong waterproof wood glues. This is a safe choice for any type of wood construction. Some glues stain, leaving a reddish glue line. This may not matter for some work, but other glues leave a clear glue line.

In one type of two-agent glue, the resin is applied to one surface and a liquid hardener (accelerator or catalyst) to the other. Nothing happens until the two surfaces come into contact with each other; then a chemical reaction takes place and the resin sets. The resin has a life of several months and the hardener keeps indefinitely, providing the two are not brought together. Setting time depends on temperature. Only pressure sufficient to keep the surfaces in contact is necessary. Clamps can probably be removed in an hour or so, but joint strength builds up for a day or more.

In another type, the resin and catalyst are mixed together in the recommended proportions just before use. Since setting begins as soon as the agents are mixed, the parts being joined have to be coated and brought into final contact within a specified time. This depends on temperature, but may be as much as an hour, so there is plenty of time to adjust and clamp joints.

Another version of this type of glue has both the resin and catalyst in powder form together in one container. As long as they remain dry they have a life of several months. When needed, the powder is mixed to a resin consistency with a little water. Like the other version, any left over will set and is wasted, so requirements have to be estimated with reasonable accuracy.

The strongest of the two-part glues is epoxy. It is also the most costly—epoxy comes in small containers (usually tubes)—and it is unusual to use epoxy extensively for woodwork. Besides giving the strongest bond between wood surfaces, it will also stick almost every material, including metal, fabrics, porcelain, and plastics to themselves or to each other. This is the only glue that can be trusted to join metal to wood. It can be used in wood joints, but because of its cost it is better kept for special applications, such as joints with other materials.

The two semi-liquid parts of epoxy glue should be mixed together just before use. There is a reasonable time for application and adjustment of the joint. The normal epoxy glue takes a long time to set and has to be left for as much as a day. There are quicker-setting versions, but they lack some of the strength of the standard glue.

All of the plastic-based glues may be regarded as water resistant and the two-part ones are waterproof for all practical purposes. None of them can be softened again once they are set. The setting action cannot be reversed. Epoxy and resorcinol will hold even when submerged in water.

No glue has much gap-filling quality. This means that for greatest strength the glued surfaces must be in close contact if the strongest joint is to result. Machine-planed wood sometimes has a "case hardened" surface, due to the pounding of blunt cutters. This has a resistance to glue penetration and it should be coarsely sanded before gluing. Another way to prepare a surface is to draw a fine saw, such as a backsaw, sideways across the wood in several directions to break the surface fibers and give the glue an opportunity to penetrate.

If glue is used on surfaces that do not fit very well and there are gaps of perhaps only 25 thousandths of an inch, the glue there will craze when it hardens, producing a pattern of tiny lines in the glue. This is weakness. If glue is mixed with sawdust before applying to an open joint, the glue will bond to the wood in the sawdust as well as to the wood surfaces and will not craze, so the joint will be stronger.

This idea can also be used for filling holes or cracks. Ordinary filler may fill the space, but it does not provide strength. If an old screw hole or a crack in a piece of crate wood is filled with glue-and-sawdust mixture, this can be leveled off and the wood should be almost as strong as it was originally. When sanded level with the surrounding wood, the glue and sawdust mixture should take stain or varnish and not be very obvious.

Chapter 10
Simple Joints

Most construction woodwork consists of joining pieces of wood together. The number of possible ways of doing this seem to be infinite—there are large books on woodwork joints alone. The number required by most woodworkers is comparatively small, and for most projects are simple. However, a knowledge of joints helps in deciding the method of construction to use. It is often possible to adapt a feature of a more advanced joint.

One of the most interesting parts of woodworking is devising ways of assembling parts. Sometimes no joint in its basic form is suitable and the craftsman's ingenuity and experience will produce a joint for the circumstances. This is where knowledge of many joints is valuable, even if they are rarely or never used.

Nailed joints are the obvious simple ones and are perfectly satisfactory for many purposes. Box construction—sides nailed to the ends and a bottom nailed on (Fig. 10-1A)—is often used. In the simplest form the nails are driven straight in. Strength at each corner then depends on friction between the sides of the nails and the wood fibers. This is often adequate. Many crates are assembled this way and a direct hit outwards dismantles a joint.

For greater strength the nails can be driven dovetail fashion, and if it is an open-topped box the nails can be closely spaced near the top. If the wood is not very thick, it is advisable to drill the top piece for each nail to prevent splitting.

A similar construction can be made with screws (Fig. 10-1B). The screw threads have a better grip than the smooth nail surfaces, so a screwed corner is stronger. For greater strength the top screw in an open box may be driven into a dowel (Fig. 10-1C). The bottom can also be screwed, but it may be sufficient to screw the corners and nail the bottom. In this type of box construction the corners do not benefit much from glue, since one surface is end grain, but the bottom has two side-grain surfaces, so glue can be used there as well as nails.

If the sides of a box are fairly thin, direct nailing or screwing in a corner may not produce a very strong joint. It may be better to reinforce the corner with a block inside. This may be square, beveled, or rounded. It should be nailed flush with one end before the other piece is nailed to it (Fig. 10-1D).

Another simple method of corner jointing is to use dowels instead of nails or screws (Fig. 10-1E). Temporary nails can be partly driven to hold the parts in register while dowel holes are drilled and dowels glued in. Let the dowels project slightly and plane them level after the glue has set. For most purposes choose dowels with a diameter between 1/3 and 1/2 the thickness of the wood.

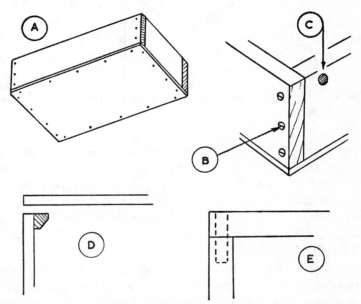

Fig. 10-1. Boxes may be constructed using nails, screws, dowels, and internal glued reinforcement.

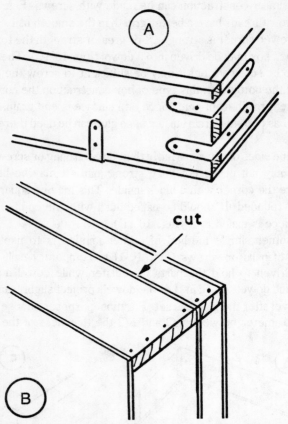

Fig. 10-2. A box may be made in one piece, with the top separated later; corners may be reinforced with metal strips.

For a box intended for rough treatment, metal strapping salvaged from crates can be used to make reinforcing bands or brackets. They can be simple angle pieces with enough overlap each way to take two nails or screws (Fig. 10-2A). Trim the corners round and hammer them down after attaching. Nail holes can be started with a pointed punch. The burred steel edge left by the punch will help grip the wood.

A convenient way to construct a lid is to make both body and lid together and then saw them apart. This will ensure a match and is much less trouble than making them separately. The fasteners, whether nails, screws, or dowels, should be kept away from the line of cut. Mark the cut around the sides and ends, with double lines to allow for planing the edges after sawing, and make sure there are fastenings close enough to the new edges to provide strength when the parts are separated (Fig. 10-2B).

If a table saw or a portable circular saw is available, separating the parts is a simple matter of setting the fence correctly and cutting all around. A large box on a small saw table may be a little unwieldy, so get help to handle it while you concentrate on keeping the edge tight against the fence. Be careful of one part dropping and causing a split as the fourth corner is reached.

The box can be given a lining of plywood that stands up (Fig. 10-3A), with the lid fit over it. Another way is to put strips in the corners of the box and let the lid fit over them (Fig. 10-3B). If the box and lid are of light construction it is better to line all around, as corner pieces alone do nothing to prevent the panels from warping or flexing when the box is loaded.

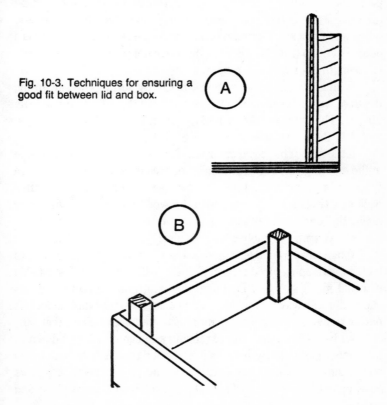

Fig. 10-3. Techniques for ensuring a good fit between lid and box.

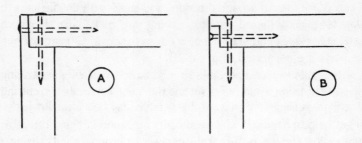

Fig. 10-4. Cross-nailing produces a strong corner.

A simple overlap at a corner depends only on fasteners in one direction. To strengthen it, cut the wood so fasteners can be driven in both directions; such a corner cannot come apart without breaking the wood. The simplest way to do this is to *rabbet* (cut back) one piece for the other to fit into (Fig. 10-4A). Nails or screws can be driven first through the plain end to bring it into the rabbet, then the other way to lock it. Sometimes both ends are rabbeted so there is a double overlap (Fig. 10-4B), but this does not produce any increase in strength over a single rabbet.

With a table saw the rabbets are cut by setting the saw to the depth of cut required and controlling the width with the fence (Fig. 10-5A). The wood is then turned the other way, with new settings, to cut in the other direction (Fig. 10-5B).

If the rabbet has to be cut by hand, mark it out with a little waste at the end (Fig. 10-5C). Use a knife for the cut across the grain and a gauge for the line around the end. Saw across the grain first with a back saw (Fig. 10-5D), then, with the wood on edge in a vise, saw down the ends before sawing straight to remove the waste. If necessary, trim the rabbet with a chisel.

When any sort of overlapping corner joint is made, it is wisest to let the overlapping piece project slightly. With perfect craftsmanship it would make an exact fit, but if this is attempted and it finishes short, the only way to disguise it is to plane down the whole side. It is better to aim at a slight projection of the end, and plane that off.

With a belt sander, the extending end can be sanded down to match the side. Otherwise use a plane, but if there are any nail heads on the surface, punch them out of the way, and make sure screws have pulled below the surface. Have a finely-set sharp plane and work diagonally towards the side (Fig. 10-6A). Final strokes can plane the side as well as the ends. For a good finish, sand all around with power or by hand, using the abrasive paper over a block.

It is advisable to make a bottom slightly oversized and plane its edges, either with the corners of the box or after they have been trued. Watch squareness of the box when fitting the bottom. Measure diagonals if it is a large box, or use a try square on the corner of a small one. The safest method is to get the box frame true, then fix the bottom with temporary nails partly driven near opposite corners (Fig. 10-6B). Check squareness again. If still square, drive the temporary nails fully and continue nailing all around. If there is an error, lift one nail and adjust the frame.

STIFFENING PLYWOOD

At one time pieces of solid wood had to be joined edge to edge to make large panels. Today various forms of manufactured board are used; plywood is the most likely to be salvaged from crates. The usual maximum size of a panel is 8 feet by 4 feet. Plywood has plenty of strength in a thin panel, but it lacks stiffness. If it is to be used as a base or backing, or made into a shelf as a substitute for solid wood, it has to be stiffened by battens.

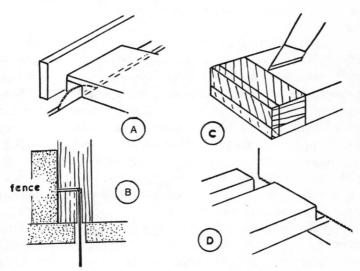

Fig. 10-5. Lap joints are cut by careful work with saw and chisel.

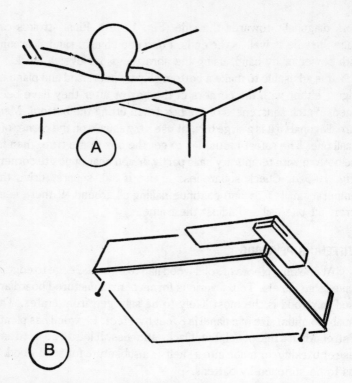

Fig. 10-6. Check squareness before attaching the bottom of a box.

For a shelf edge it can be merely nailed or glued to a strip (Fig. 10-7A). This leaves the plywood edge exposed, which may not matter for some purposes, but for more important work it looks better covered. A strip may be glued along the edge (Fig. 10-7B) and its edges rounded. If the edge of the shelf should match wood used elsewhere, this piece can be of matching wood. Another way is to cut a rabbet in the stiffening strip so it covers the plywood (Fig. 10-7C).

In good-quality work this joint can be glued. If clamped while the glue sets there will be no need for nails or screws. Let the wood overlapping the plywood edge stand a little high so it can be planed or sanded level after the glue has set.

The simplest way to build up the thickness of plywood is to put framing battens all around (Fig. 10-7D). End grain showing at a corner may not matter, but if it does, the pieces can be mitered (Fig. 10-7E). A large panel may need other battens across the body to stiffen it.

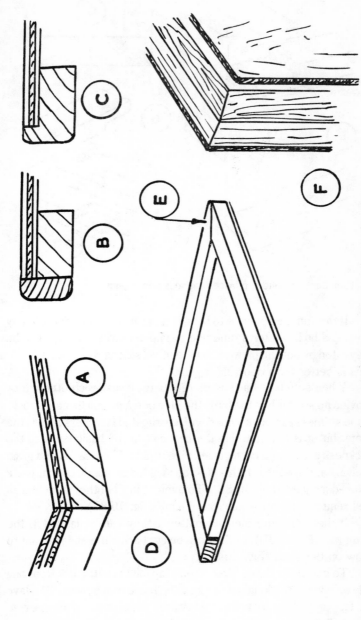

Fig. 10-7. Thin plywood panels are stiffened with strips which may have lap joints at the corners.

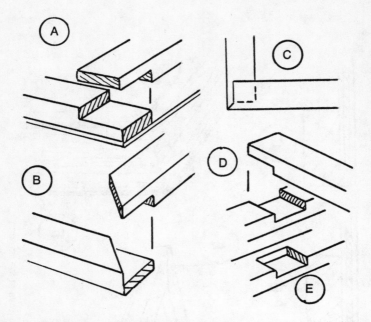

Fig. 10-8. Lapping battens provides stiffness and strength.

If the stiffened panel is to hang free, as it would in a door, it may develop a hollow after a time due to uneven stresses. This can be prevented by putting plywood on the other side as well (Fig. 10-7F). This is better for a door, in any case.

When stiffening battens merely butt against each other, they provide no strength at the butt: the plywood may still flex and crack. Some stiffness can be provided with corrugated fasteners across the joints, but it is better to lap the battens. In the basic lap, half the thickness is cut from each piece (Fig. 10-8A). This leaves end grain showing at the edges. If this is to be avoided in one direction, use a mitered lap joint (Fig. 10-8B). To avoid it in the other direction as well requires a more complicated joint (Fig. 10-8C).

If there are intermediate battens, they can be lapped in the same way (Fig.10-8D), or they can be cut back if the ends are not to show on the sides (Fig. 10-8E).

To get the surfaces level when a lap joint is cut, work from one side only when marking out or using the fence on a power tool. Have the face side of the batten wood towards the plywood. Any unevenness will stand up and can be planed level after assembly.

To mark out a simple lap joint, gauge both pieces from the same side, but pencil on the waste parts (Fig. 10-9A). Use knife cuts across the grain. Allow a little excess at the ends for trimming level after assembly. Saw across with a back saw, if working by hand tools (Fig. 10-9B), then put the wood in the vise and saw in three steps: diagonally one way, then the other, and finally straight through (Fig. 10-9C). Keep the saw kerf on the waste side of the gauged line. Trim any roughness with a chisel, but be careful not to cut the joint too far.

If the joint is to be cut with a table saw, cut across the grain first (Fig. 10-9D), then down the end, keeping the face side towards the fence and adjusting the fence position to allow for the width of the kerf (Fig. 19-9E).

For an intermediate position one part is cut in the same way as for a corner, but the other piece has the cuts marked with knife and gauge. The knife cuts must be the same as the width of the other piece; use it for gauging, rather than measuring. To remove the waste, cut down (with the saw kerfs on the waste side of the line as in Fig. 10-10A) with a backsaw or power saw. A few more cuts across the waste part may help in its removal (Fig. 10-10B).

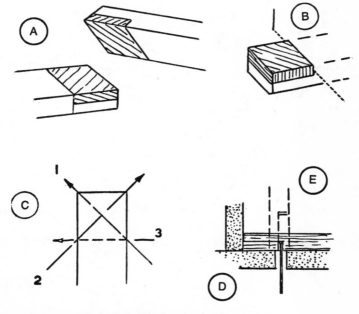

Fig. 10-9. Lap cuts must be marked and cut with care.

175

If the waste is to be removed by hand, hold the wood in the vise or to the bench and use a broad chisel, by hand or with a mallet. Do not try to cut straight across, but work upwards from both sides at first (Fig. 10-10C). This avoids breaking-out. Continue at flatter angles and finally cut straight across. A power router can be used to remove the waste cleanly.

If the part cut out is "stopped" (not clear across), make your saw cuts diagonally (Fig. 10-10D). Chisel out between the saw cuts, then chop down across the grain with a wide chisel and less heavily along the grain, so the remainder of the waste can be removed (Fig. 10-10E). Finally trim back to the lines so the other piece will fit. Again, a router will remove the waste efficiently.

Even the most experienced craftsman will sometimes cut a joint too deep, so one part goes too far into the other and the surfaces are not level. This can be cured by putting a wood shaving or a piece of cardboard or paper in the joint before gluing.

If there are intermediate stiffeners in both directions behind a plywood panel, they are both cut in the same way where they lap each other (Fig. 10-10F).

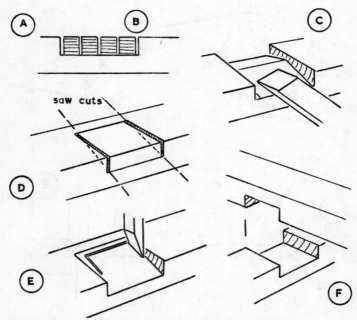

Fig. 10-10. The steps in cutting a lap joint with hand tools.

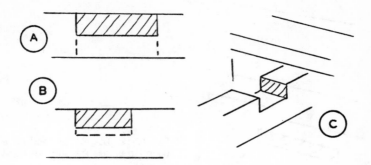

Fig. 10-11. The depth of the lap depends on the dimensions of the wood.

LAPPED JOINTS

Lapped joints are used in many types of construction and are often preferable to mortise-and-tenon or other more complicated joints. If both parts are the same thickness and the surfaces are to finish flush, the lapped surfaces meet in the middle of the wood (Fig. 10-11A). If the pieces are of different thickness, it is stronger to cut less from the thinner piece (Fig. 10-11B). If the difference is considerable, there may be nothing cut from the thin piece (Fig. 10-11C).

Crossings are not always at right-angles. In that case the cuts are marked with the aid of an adjustable bevel instead of a try square. After marking out, try one piece over the other, as it is possible to get bevels in the wrong direction. If there are opposite diagonal joints, as in the sides of some chairs, make sure that they are cut so they make a pair and are not both cut the same way. Try one marked-out assembly over the other and make pencil marks on the parts that have to be cut away, to avoid confusion.

Crossings need not always be cut deep enough to bring surfaces flush. It is obviously stronger not to cut away any more wood than is necessary, so in chair sides, where strength is important, the cut-outs need to be no more than one-third the thickness of the members. This gives rigidity to the joint, while weakening the parts no more than necessary (Fig. 10-12).

Another variation of the lap joint is used when parts cross on edge, as with divisions in a box (Fig. 10-13A). For neatness it is important that the joints are cut accurately. A fine-toothed circular saw can cut each side of a slot. This will leave a small amount to be

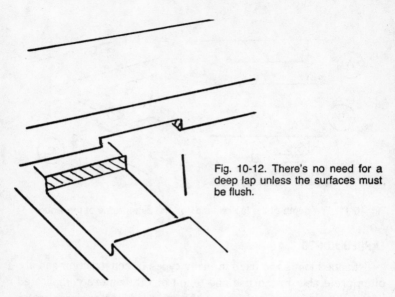

Fig. 10-12. There's no need for a deep lap unless the surfaces must be flush.

cut with a hand saw (Fig. 10-13B). If a band saw or jig saw is used, its blade will cut right into the corner, but is not as easy to keep straight. If a back saw is used, it can be kept at a low angle to follow the line (Fig. 10-14A) then brought perpendicular to the wood for the last few strokes (Fig. 10-14B). This makes a more accurate slot than if the cut is made perpendicular all the way. The end of the slot is chopped out with a suitable chisel.

Such a joint is suitable for box divisions and other places where little strength is needed. If plywood or other thin wood has to cross in this way and will be under much load, glue reinforcing pieces in the angles, either on two (Fig. 10-14C) or all four sides.

Lapped joints are suitable for any wood of square or rectangular section; any lapped joint of reasonable fit will have adequate strength. However, when joining molded or round pieces, lap joints will not look neat, nor have sufficient strength. It may be possible to notch a molded piece into a square-edged piece, but designs should be arranged to avoid having two shaped pieces crossing at the same level. In turned work, it is usual to arrange a pattern with a square part at any point where a crossing joint has to be cut.

DADO JOINTS

There are many places where one flat piece meets another, usually at a right angle. Shelves in a bookcase are an obvious example, but there are many other applications.

178

The simplest treatment is to nail or screw through (Fig. 10-15A), but there is not much strength in such a joint. If it is part of a structure with other components that will share the load, it may be satisfactory, but it would not do for a shelf or similar construction where the screwed or nailed piece has to carry a sideways thrust.

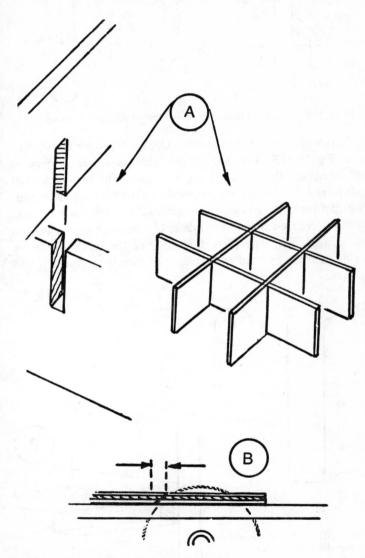

Fig. 10-13. Notching is a variety of lap joint.

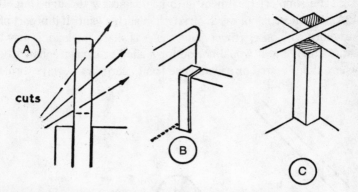

Fig. 10-14. Notched crosspieces may be reinforced with glued blocks.

A stronger method is to attach a block of wood for the shelf to rest on (Fig. 10-15B). For shop and shed shelves, where appearance is not important, this is a good and easy joint. The blocks of wood should be glued and nailed or screwed first, then the shelf put on top. Its attachment to the blocks can be quite light, particularly if it may have to be removed at some later date: two thin screws driven from above are enough. The projecting edge of the block should be rounded, and the forward end beveled or rounded to make it less obtrusive.

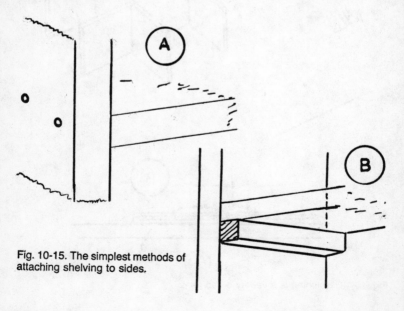

Fig. 10-15. The simplest methods of attaching shelving to sides.

The more acceptable joint in better construction is the *dado* or housing joint (Fig. 10-16A). There are a few variations, but the basic joint suits many purposes. Except for cutting its end carefully square, there is no preparation for the male piece. In a structure where there are other parts, be careful about length or the sides may bow out or in (Fig. 10-16B).

Mark the joint with knife lines and use the male part to get the width of the dado (Fig. 10-16C). Gauge the depth, but if appearance is important, be careful not to let the gauge marks run outside the cut marks on an edge that will be visible in the finished article.

A router is a convenient tool for making dado joints. With careful setting it may be possible to rout a dado without preliminary marking-out, but guide lines are usually advisable. A piece of wood can be clamped across the wood at a suitable distance to act as a guide for the router (Fig. 10-16D). If the cutter is not full-width, you may need a second, overlapping pass to make the other side of the slot.

If the dado is to be cut by hand, it helps to chisel inside the cut line to provide a guide (Fig. 10-17A). Hold the wood on a bench hook and saw across the full width for a little depth, then slant the saw

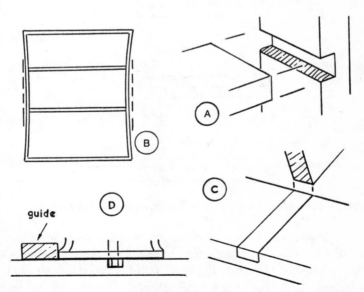

Fig. 10-16. For shelves and similar constructions, the dado joint is the best choice.

forward while you watch the far side and stop when you reach the full depth. Slant the saw the other way and cut to the full depth on the near side. Resume sawing straight through, but watch both ends of the cut to avoid going too deep (Fig. 10-17B). Do this on both sides, keeping the saw kerf on the waste side of the lines.

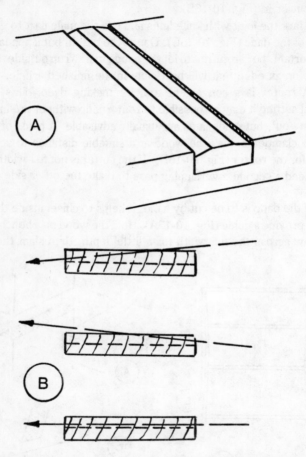

Fig. 10-17. Chiseling inside the dado line provides a guide for the saw.

Remove the waste wood in the same way as for a lap joint. Use a chisel almost as wide as the slot and slope upwards from each side at first, then straight across. If a hand router is available, that can be used to level the bottom after the bulk of the waste wood has been removed with a chisel. Ideally, the bottom of the joint should be absolutely straight across, but it is better to err towards a slight hollow in the middle than to have a high spot somewhere. With a hollow the outside edges of the joint will come tight. A high spot in the middle would prevent this or distort the outside piece if the joint were forced right with clamps.

In furniture and better construction, the edge of a plain dado joint has to be disguised; this is done by making a *stopped dado* (Fig. 10-18A). Normally, only one edge needs this treatment as the other is hidden at the back. The piece that projects forward is unsupported so it should be kept reasonably narrow. In most assemblies, cutting back 1/4 inch is enough.

Mark out the dado the same way as for a plain one, but do not take the knife cuts right to the front edge, and gauge back the end of the dado (Fig. 10-18B). With the same gauge setting, mark the distance to be cut from the shelf, and use a knife to mark the cut in the other direction (Fig. 10-18C). Saw down both directions on the waste side of the line. If necessary, use a chisel to cut the edge that will be at the front.

If a router is available, the dado may be cut to the front line, then the slot squared with a chisel (Fig. 10-18D).

If the dado is to be cut by hand, a hole must be cut from the forward end of the slot to allow a saw to be used. With the slot marked out, use a chisel at least 1 inch wide to chop across the grain close to the limit of the dado, but not right up to the line (Fig. 10-18E). Lever out the waste to the full depth. Use the chisel again across the grain to pare down exactly to the line, but leave a little waste at what will be the end of the slot.

Saw across, tilting the back saw to cut the near side first, then let the front end of the saw work in the space that has been chopped (Fig. 10-18F) until the full depth has been reached. Do this along the other line as well. The saw will almost certainly hit the end of the slot a few times, but this will not matter since the waste wood you've left there will take the blow. Chisel away the waste between the saw cuts or use a hand router if you have one. Finally, trim the end of the slot to the line. The two parts should now fit. Joints fit best on first assembly, so trust your workmanship and do not make trial assemblies if you can avoid it. Multiple trial assemblies loosen the joint.

In an assembly like a tier of shelves with a top and bottom and a plywood back, the ordinary or stopped dado joint has plenty of

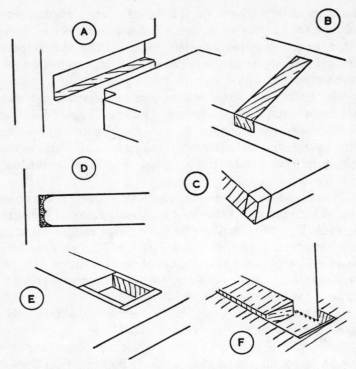

Fig. 10-18. If the front edge is to be hidden, a stopped dado joint is used.

strength. If it does not get much help from other parts of the assembly, it may be advisable to reinforce the glue with screws or some other way. The glue bond in a dado joint is mostly between side and end grain. The end grain component of the joint does not provide a very good bond, so if an unreinforced dado joint is subject to a wracking strain, the glued surfaces may fail.

If the outside surface will not show or its appearance does not matter, you may drive screws from the outside (Fig. 10-19A), but usually the outside appearance is important. The appearance of the shelf top may also be important. Screws may be driven diagonally from below (Fig. 10-19B). Drill quite close into the angle and be careful not to angle the drill too much towards the outside or the screw end may go through or crack the outside. Do not drill too upright, or the hole may show through the angle of the top shelf surface. It may be necessary to countersink the holes, but in most cases the heads will pull in. In an average shelf joint, one screw near the back and another towards the front (but not so far forward as to be obvious) will be sufficient reinforcement.

Another reinforcing method is to glue in a block, but this need not be as big or as long as in a shelf without a dado joint (Fig. 10-20A). There are ways to cut a dovetail dado joint that has considerable strength, but this is only really suitable for close-grained hardwood—not the usual salvaged woods.

For rougher work there is a simpler version of the dado joint. Instead of cutting top and bottom of the slot, only the bottom is cut, then the waste chiseled towards it (Fig. 10-20B). The end of the other piece is sawn to a matching bevel. Providing the joint is part of an assembly that keeps it pushed together, this will take as much downward thrust as a full dado joint. The joint may be reinforced with screws from outside or below, or it may be adequate to nail upwards (Fig. 10-20C).

DOWEL JOINTS

Although the idea of making joints with wooden pegs is something that goes a long way back into history, dowel joints as we know them are more the product of the mechanical age. The Egyptians used wooden pegs. The Vikings held the planks of their boats

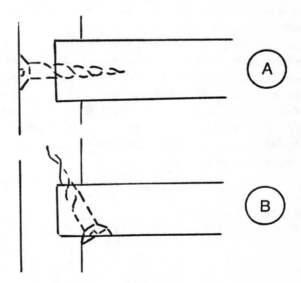

Fig. 10-19. A dado joint can be reinforced with screws or nails.

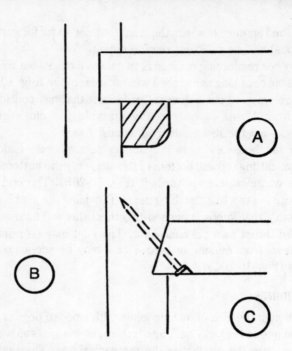

Fig. 10-20. A full dado isn't necessary in some construction.

together with wooden pegs. Even as late as the 19th century, sailing ships had as many wooden fasteners as metal.

There are occasions when that type of doweling has applications. One variation used often in outdoor woodwork uses round holes and roughly shaped pegs with a light taper. The pegs are driven in without glue. If joints have to be pulled together, the holes can be drilled slightly out of true (Fig. 10-21); then as a tapered peg is driven in, they are forced into line and the joint tightens. The projecting pegs may be left as a design feature, although they may all be cut to the same length.

Fig. 10-21. Dowel holes slightly offset can pull joints together.

A variation on this is to use a wedge. Much medieval furniture was made this way, both for indoor and outdoor use. Modern furniture based on these designs is still made with wedges as design features. Of course, a wedged joint can be taken apart, so the method can be used for take-down chairs, stools, and tables.

One piece fits through a slot in another, but the slot for the wedge is cut back within the thickness of the first piece (Fig. 10-22A). This allows the wedge to pull the parts tightly together. The wedge may be a simple tapered piece, or one or both ends may be decorated by shaping (Fig. 10-22B).

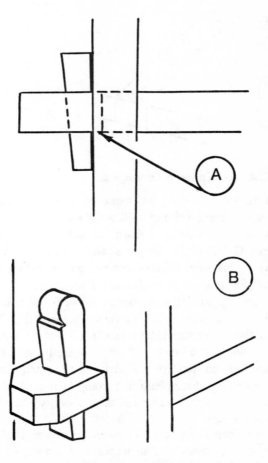

Fig. 10-22. The slot in the tongue extends into the vertical piece.

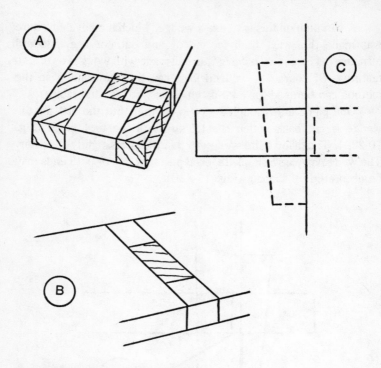

Fig. 10-23. The steps in marking the wedge slot.

When marking out the joint, make the projecting piece wide enough to have a good width of solid wood each side of the wedge slot. Mark this all around, and mark the slot on the other piece similarly (Fig. 10-23A & B): this gives lines as a guide on both sides of both pieces. This is not so important with power cutting, but even then it is helpful to have these checks for accuracy.

Before cutting, mark the position of the wedge slot. It will help to make a full-size drawing of the side view of the joint (Fig. 10-23C). The taper of the wedge should be between 1 in 6 and 1 in 8: if it is 3 inches long, it will be 3/8 inch to 1/2 inch thinner at one end than the other. Mark the top and bottom surfaces to match the wedge dimensions when it is driven halfway through, but cut back enough on the inside to allow it to drive further than halfway without jamming the wedge in the slot.

Cut the outline of the part that takes the wedge. Drill through the wedge slot to remove some waste, but remember that the underside of the hole will finish narrower than the top. Trim the hole to shape with a chisel, making cross-grain cuts before those with the grain. Make sure the taper is smooth on the side where the wedge will bear.

The hole in the other part can be cut in a similar way: drill holes to remove the bulk of the waste wood, then remove the rest with a chisel. Work from both sides towards the center to avoid the possibility of the grain breaking out. Plane the wedge to the bevel marked on your full-size drawing. Make a trial assembly and adjust the bevel of the wedge or pare the hole until the result is satisfactory.

A variation on this uses a piece of dowel rod instead of a wedge. The two parts fit in the same way, but a round hole is drilled in the tongue at a slight angle. The dowel rod is planed to a taper and driven in as a wedge (Fig. 10-24).

For most modern doweled construction, dowel rods are bought. They are accurately machined from close-grained hardwood and may be bought in diameters to fit many sizes of hole. Traditional dowels were made by driving roughly-shaped pieces of wood through a hole in a steel plate, preferably tapered from below to

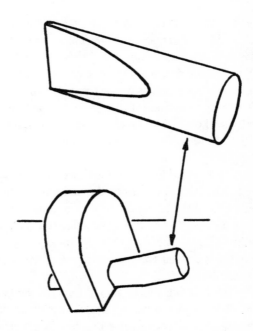

Fig. 10-24. A tapered dowel can perform the same function as a wedge.

provide cutting edges at the top (Fig. 10-25). Untapered holes will work. Such a dowel plate may be used when you want the wood of the dowels to match the wood they are driven into. Or, if a lathe is available, you can turn them.

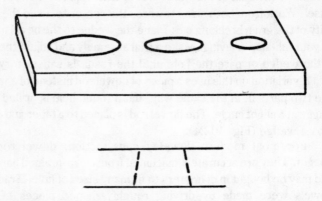

Fig. 10-25. Dowels can be made by driving roughly-shaped wood through a steel plate with tapered holes.

Success with modern dowel joints depends on accuracy. Freehand, it is difficult to maintain sufficient accuracy for a series of dowels. It is important that holes are at right angles to the meeting surfaces. If an electric drill in a stand is used, the holes can be drilled with precision, but some pieces will be too wide to fit into a drill stand or press. In this case use one of the guides or jigs available. Attached to the wood, they keep a drill at right angles to the surface, and most of them also act as templates to ensure that holes in mating surfaces will match exactly.

In a typical doweled joint there are two dowels in a rail which engage a leg (Fig. 10-26A). Besides the need for the holes to be at right angles to the surface, the distance between them must be the same on both pieces. If you don't have a jig, you can mark the two parts together (Fig. 10-26B). Centers should be marked with a spike. If the drill is started accurately, the two pairs of holes should mate together properly.

Usually the dowel diameter should be between one-third and one-half the thickness of the thinner wood in a joint. How far they go into the wood depends on several factors, but the greater the depth, the greater the glue area and the strength. It is reasonable to dowel into a piece of wood about four times the diameter of the dowel, but in thinner wood you may have to settle for less.

Dowel ends should be chamfered (tapered) with a chisel or a sander to help in entering a hole. When a closely-fitting dowel enters a hole, it compresses air like a piston going into a cylinder. To reduce the bursting effect, something should be done to let the air out. Special dowels are made with a helical groove pressed in them, but in the home shop it is usual to saw a shallow groove in the length (Fig. 10-26C). Dowel joints should be completed while the glue is still soft. Glue the meeting surfaces as well as the dowels, and squeeze joints together until glue oozes out.

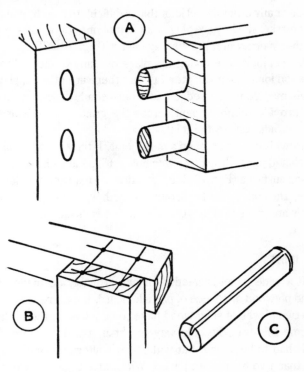

Fig. 10-26. A typical doweled joint, joint marking, and grooved dowel.

A joint made with a single dowel allows one part to turn on the other. This may have to be accepted, but whenever possible use at least two dowels in any joint. In a small joint the alternative to a single dowel may be two smaller ones arranged diagonally (Fig. 10-27A).

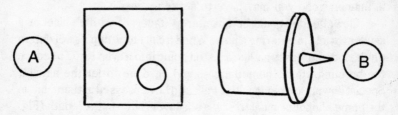

Fig. 10-27. In a tight joint, dowels can be arranged diagonally (A). A dowel marker simplifies marking (B).

For this or any other dowel joint that is difficult to match, you can use dowel markers. They are plugs that fit into one set of holes and mark the other piece when pressed against it (Fig. 10-27B).

Dowel joints are taking the place of many traditional mortise-and-tenon joints (see Chapter 11), but there are other applications. Dowels may be used in edge joints between boards (Fig. 10-28A). They provide reinforcement across the grain, where board fibers are weak adjacent to the joint.

Dowels can strengthen a miter joint. If they are to be hidden in the finished joint, they can enter holes drilled at right angles to the meeting surfaces (Fig. 10-28B). If it doesn't matter if the dowels are visible, the miter can be brought together, then drilled through. Dowels are glued in (Fig. 10-28C) and the ends cut off after the glue has set.

EDGE JOINTS

If a wide panel is needed, it will probably be made up from framed plywood or a piece of particle board, but there are occasions when two pieces of solid wood have to be joined at their edges. At one time this was the only way to obtain a wide panel and many boards had to be joined, but with today's alternatives it's rare that more than two boards are joined. With modern glues a close-fitting glued joint is all that is needed for adequate strength. Dowels across the joint or secret slot screwing can also be used (see Chapter 9).

Flatness is important (Fig. 10-29A). Hand planing should be checked at several points with a try square (Fig. 10-29B). Any deviation from squareness can be offset by turning one board over on the other (Fig. 10-29C). If the board was power-planed with anything other than exceptionally sharp blades, it is advisable to finish each edge with a hand plane to give the glue a better bite.

When clamping an edge joint, make sure it is resting on a flat surface or a pair of bar clamps that are on a flat surface. Before leaving the assembly for the glue to set, stand back and sight over the boards from a distance to see that there is no twist. Besides using scrap wood under the jaws of the clamps, you may need parallel pieces under the work to keep the boards level and in line with each other. Use paper to prevent these pieces from being stuck with glue that oozes out (Fig. 10-29D).

Boards expand and contract in their width according to the amount of water they take up or give out, and may also warp. If a

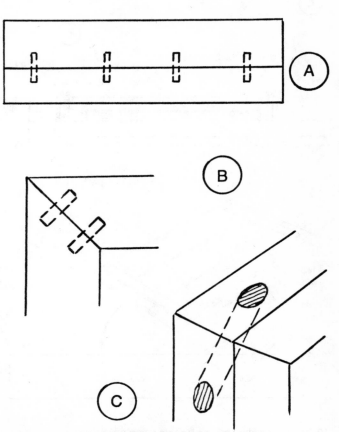

Fig. 10-28. Dowels may be used on edge joints and corners.

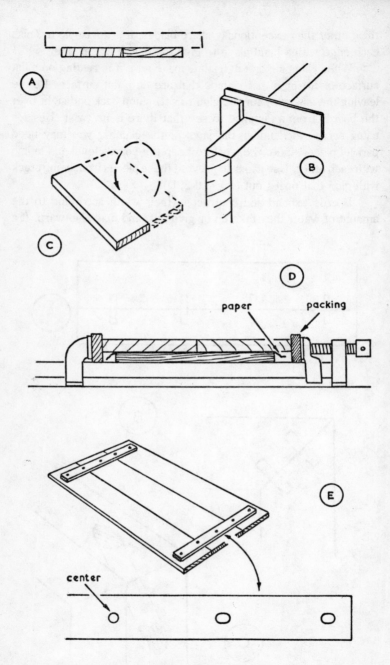

Fig. 10-29. Large widths can be built up using edge joints.

wide built-up board will not be strengthened by forming part of a bigger assembly, it may be stiffened and made warp-resistant by affixing battens across its back. Do not glue them or something will break if the wood expands or shrinks. Use screws. The center screws can go through round holes, but expansion and contraction will be greater toward the ends of the battens; use slots here (Fig. 10-29E).

Chapter 11

Advanced Joints

The joints described in Chapter 10 serve for most woodwork, but sometimes special circumstances or the quality of the work demand other joints, which are usually more complicated. Modern glues have much greater strength than those used even as recently as the 1930s. Some older joints depended heavily on interlocking parts so failure of the glue would not cause parting. With glues that are unlikely to fail, it is safer to rely on the glue line. Although this has made some of the more complicated joints unnecessary, there are others that are still worth using. Modern glues have made new joints that take advantage of the increased strength possible. An example is laminating—not unknown before modern glues, but now used in many more applications.

LAMINATING

Several pieces of wood glued together to make up a particular thickness are *laminated*. Plywood is laminated from several layers of veneer glued together with their grain running in several directions. This gives a uniform strength in all directions that is considerably greater than a solid piece of wood of the same thickness. In addition, the fact that veneers are peeled from a rotating log enables the manufacture of sheets much larger than would be possible from solid wood.

Sometimes wooden parts are built up from pieces with the grain crossing, as in plywood, to get the same strength in all directions. However, laminating is used more often to make shaped parts that have uniform strength despite their curves. Because of the relatively straight grain of most wood, any curve cut will usually cross grain lines, resulting in a weak area (Fig. 11-1A). At one time wheelwrights, boat builders, and others who had to make curved parts would set wood with curved grain aside, using it only for curves, and matching the grain lines to the desired curve as closely as possible. Today the same result is obtained by laminating many thin pieces (Fig. 11-1B). With all grain lines following the shape, there is greater strength and a lighter section is often possible. A further advantage of laminating is in holding the shape. A solid piece of curved wood, even with well-matched grain lines, may warp as it takes up or gives off moisture.

Laminated assemblies are valuable wherever curves and strength are needed: chair parts, table parts, boats, etc. Even a simple thing like a shelf bracket can have a modern laminated form (Fig. 11-1C). An interesting effect can be obtained by laminating with contrasting woods: dark and light woods alternating are very effective under clear polish (Fig. 11-1D).

The number of laminations needed for a particular shape depends on the degree of curvature needed and flexibility of the chosen wood. Never use fewer than three layers. A stiff wood will have to be cut thinner to go around a curve than a more flexible one. Almost any wood can be laminated providing it is cut thin enough, but making a large number of laminations can be tedius, although the result will be satisfactory and strong.

You will need a mold or former around which to bend the laminations. It can be made of any available material that is stiff enough. For a typical moderate double curvature lamination of about 1 1/2 inch section—as might be used for a chair back and leg—the mold can be made from pieces of 2 × 4. If the curve is cut on a band saw, it will be square to the edge and should be smooth enough without further treatment. If the curve has to be made with hand tools, check squareness across; otherwise the lamination may finish with an unwanted twist. If necessary, cut away the mold to admit available C clamps (Fig. 11-2).

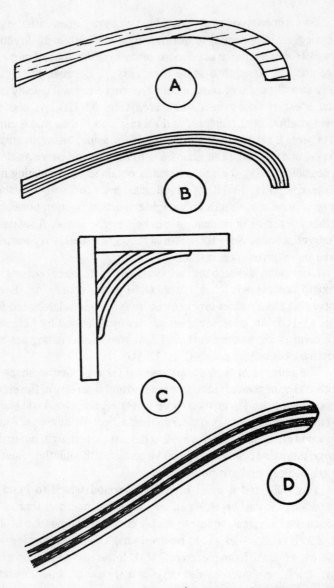

Fig. 11-1. Solid wood is weak where it is cross-grained. Thin strips can be laminated to build up strong curved parts.

In this case four laminations 3/8 inch thick should be satisfactory. Cut them slightly too wide, to allow for planing level later. If sawn with a fine circular saw, it may be possible to use the wood as it is, but a thinner glue line and a better joint will result from planing. Paper can be put around the mold to prevent it from sticking to the first lamination if any glue gets on the surface. Make the pieces longer than they will be finally to allow for trimming the ends. In some laminations the extreme ends may not glue as well as the main part of the assembly, so an inch or so extra will allow the doubtful parts to be cut off.

Have the laminations ready, and sufficient glue prepared. Assemble enough C clamps and blocks of wood to go under them against the laminations. If there is considerable curvature at a particular clamping point, a shaped block may be necessary, but in most places flat pieces of scrap wood will do. Apply the glue to all pieces and start assembling them at one end of the mold. Tighten the clamps only enough to prevent much movement at first. When all the clamps are on, push or knock the parts into place. See that edges are level and tighten the clamps. Make sure the strips are set properly; it is inadvisable to tighten, slacken to move, and tighten again, as this may lead to glue being squeezed out of the edges and weakness from glue starvation. Leave the clamps on for at least as long as the specified glue setting time. When released, the joints are under stress: incompletely set glue may allow them to part.

When the laminated part is removed, it can be treated in the same way as solid wood. Surfaces are best planed parallel first, to give true surfaces to work from, even if the finished piece will be curved in cross-section.

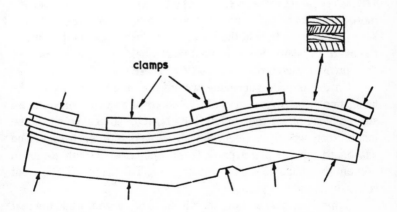

Fig. 11-2. Laminating a double curve using a form or mold.

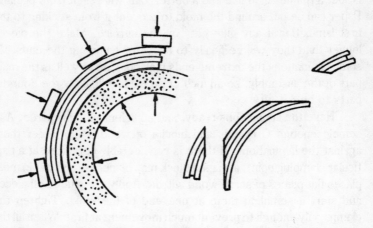

Fig. 11-3. Curved laminations should be extra-long, with waste cut off after the glue has set.

It is sometimes possible to use existing items as molds. A light lamination for a shelf bracket can be pulled around a stout can, a piece of concrete pipe, or other item of the right size and curvature. Make such a lamination extra-long (Fig. 11-3) so part can be cut through to fit the outside of the bracket.

There are other ways of clamping, particularly light laminations of intricate shape. Consider a bracket for a hanging lamp that has considerable double curvature, made of several pieces of 1 inch by 1/8 inch section that bend easily. The mold is made of wood slightly more than 1 inch thick on a thick plywood baseboard (Fig. 11-4A). Wedges are used to hold the laminations close to each other and to the mold. Pressure comes against blocks held by single screws, so they pivot to match the wedges (Fig. 11-4B).

On the outside curve the wedge may press directly on the lamination or be over a scrap of plywood. For an inside curve, use a shaped block under the wedge (Fig. 11-4C). The curve should be longer than what you need. Locate a wedge at each end. The baseboard will keep the parts level, but cover it with paper to prevent the laminations from sticking to it. The paper will stick, but is easily scraped or planed off.

Sometimes only part of a length has to be curved, while the rest of the piece of wood is straight. If the straight part is short in relation

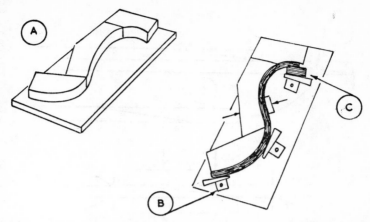

Fig. 11-4. Wedges and blocks provide clamping action on compound curves.

to the curved part, it is usually simplest to laminate the straight part as well as the curve. One method of semi-laminating can be used if a fine circular saw is available. Make several cuts for the length of the curve, dividing the thickness into smaller, equal thicknesses. The thickness of each sub-thickness depends on the severity of the curve. Spring the cuts open, bend the cut parts around a form, and glue (Fig. 11-5). Leave until set, and treat as a normal lamination. Of course, the finished curved part will be narrower than the solid part by the amount removed in the saw kerfs. This may not matter. If it does, use the method described next.

If wood has to be joined to make up a length, as when joining a laminated part to a solid part, the joint used with modern glues is a simple *scarf* or splice. Make the laminated part with enough straight end to more than make the splice. This is better than trying to cut a splice into a curve. Glue does not make a good bond to end grain, but

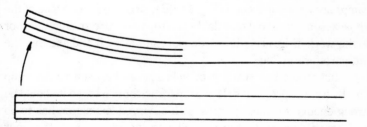

Fig. 11-5. Slicing the end of a piece allows a curved lamination.

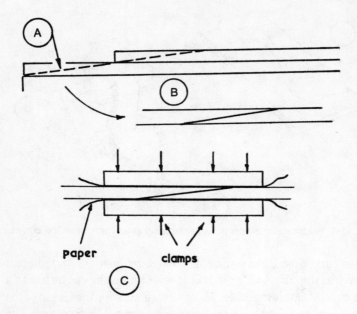

Fig. 11-6. Cutting and gluing a scarf joint or splice.

is best with side grain. If the bevel of the splice is long enough, the meeting surfaces are mostly side grain and a good joint results.

The usual minimum angle is 1 in 7, i.e., the bevel is 7 inches long if the wood is 1 inch thick. A more gradual angle may be even better. For two flat pieces, one can be set back on the other by the amount of the bevel and the two clamped farther back to the bench (Fig. 11-6A). If the two are planed together until their ends are feather edges, the bevels will be the same and the right length (Fig. 11-6B). Clamp the scarf joint between two boards, with paper to prevent sticking, letting the boards extend past the joint, so two of the clamps are over solid wood (Fig. 11-6C). Arrange for one side of the whole assembly to rest on a flat bench top to ensure straightness, or do the work in a place where you can sight along it and see that the two parts are in line.

This method of scarfing or splicing can be used to make up lengths from short pieces. It is used for yacht masts, so it should be strong enough for most purposes. If a curved lamination has to be made up with pieces that are not all long enough, some of the inner pieces may be short and merely butt against each other. A few such joints will not affect strength, but if there are many, they may be scarfed before being built into the laminations. The same method can be used for building up a thick and long piece from odd lengths taken from crates. The result will have ample strength, as can be seen from the substantial roof beams built up this way.

RABBETS AND GROOVES

A piece of wood may be given a rabbet so it can take a piece of glass, held in with *points* (little headless nails) and putty (Fig. 11-7A). It may form a picture frame, or it could take a glass panel held in with a fillet of wood (Fig. 11-7B) which can be levered out if the glass has to be replaced. Grooves may take a plywood panel (Fig. 11-7C), sliding doors, photographs or many other inserts.

The rabbet may be cut with two passes over a circular saw. The piece removed may then make a fillet. It can be worked with a wood shaper or spindle molder. If it has to be made by hand, the tool is a rabbet plane or a fillister. A groove may be cut with several passes of a circular saw. If a wobble saw (dado saw—with washers that allow the saw to run out of true to an adjustable amount) is available, it can be worked with one cut. Or it may be made with a router, using a suitable guide. By hand, it is cut with a plow plane.

If pieces of wood with rabbets or grooves have to be joined, the shaping causes complications, except in the case of a plain miter. A miter is a simple joint, but any error is obvious, so accuracy is important. The angle can be marked with a 45-degree square, such

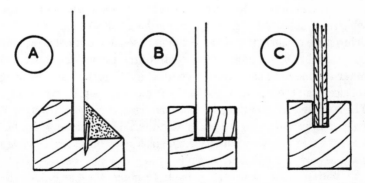

Fig. 11-7. Rabbetted (A, B) and grooved (C) methods of retaining glass or a panel.

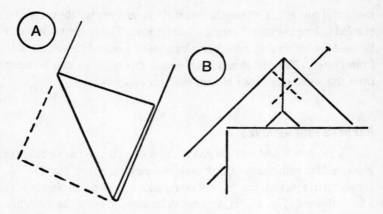

Fig. 11-8. Folding a rectangular piece of paper as shown gives an accurate 45° angle.

as is found on a combination square, or an adjustable bevel can be used set to a protractor, but a simple and accurate way to obtain 45 degrees is to fold the corner of a piece of paper (Fig. 11-8A). There are special tools for truing the edge after sawing, but for occasional use the angle can be sawn with a fine back saw and the surface trued with a block plane.

Most picture frames use corners made with plain miters, glued, with a fine nail driven in each direction. Miter clamps are available which bring the parts tightly together and have spaces to allow the nails to be driven. They simplify the assembly of picture frames, but for occasional work the parts can be held in a vise and nailed (Fig. 11-8D). It helps to predrill part way for each nail.

Picture-frame miters are not used for framed panels or doors, which are rabbetted or grooved. Something still stronger is needed in furniture construction. One technique uses dowels: cut down one part (usually the upright) to the depth of the rabbet or groove and miter the meeting parts to this depth (Fig. 11-9A). The remaining surfaces can then be doweled in the same way as plain wood (Fig. 11-9B). Use care in cutting the small miters to ensure they will come tight as the main joints are pulled together. They can be sawn, but leave a little to remove with a chisel, so all stray fibers are removed and the surfaces will meet cleanly.

With a rabbet it is also possible to notch one piece over the other (Fig. 11-9C). In frame furniture it always looks best if upright lines follow through, so the horizontal member should be notched into the upright to give a long vertical line in the joint. If the wood is thick enough the dowels can come behind the rabbet edge (Fig. 11-9D). This is fairly easy to drill accurately, but if the wood is thin and the dowels extend onto the standing edge (Fig. 11-9E), holes must be drilled with the aid of a jig, or there is risk of slipping and an inaccurate joint.

If grooves are used, one piece may have the end of its groove filled with a piece of wood glued in. Allow enough room for the panel that will be in the main part of the groove. The glue should be allowed to set, then drill holes for dowels in the same way as in solid wood

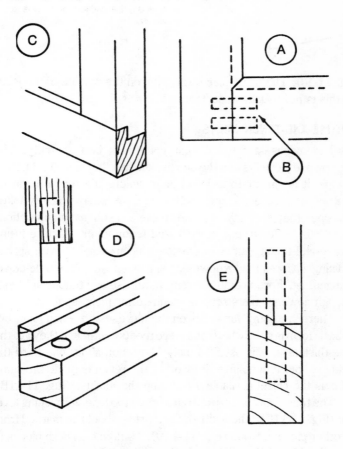

Fig. 11-9. Rabbets and grooves must be adapted at corners.

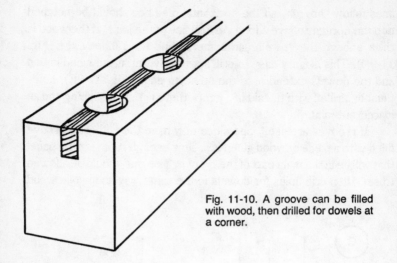

Fig. 11-10. A groove can be filled with wood, then drilled for dowels at a corner.

(Fig. 11-10). The filling piece will show on the outside of the joint, but this is not usually important.

MORTISE-AND-TENON JOINTS

The mortise-and-tenon joint goes back into antiquity. The tenon on one piece fits into the mortise on the other (Fig. 11-11A). In principle it is similar to a dowel joint, where the tenon might be regarded as a square dowel. Although dowels have mostly taken over since they are easy to make, there are still many applications where it is better to use mortise-and-tenon joints. A close-fitting mortise-and-tenon joint gives a better glue area and a better spread of joining surfaces than a doweled joint, even with a multiple dowel arrangement. For maximum strength mortise and tenons are best, although dowels have strength adequate for many applications.

There are many variations on the mortise-and-tenon joint, but the basic form is used where one piece meets another. If they are the same thickness, it is usual to make the tenon about one-third the thickness, but it simplifies the work if the tenon is made the same width as the chisel available for cutting the mortise (Fig. 11-11B).

The tenon may be marked out slightly too long, for planing level later (Fig. 11-11C). The width of the mortise should be marked from the other piece of wood (Fig. 11-11D). Markings on both pieces of wood should be taken all around. Gauge the widths of the tenon and mortise with the same setting of the gauge: an ordinary marking gauge will have to be set twice and used both times from the face sides. If a mortise gauge is available, set the two points to the width of the chisel (Fig. 11-11E), then set the stock to give the correct distance from the edge. If the tenon is to be cut on a table saw, its thickness can be controlled by setting the fence, but gauging the width provides a check.

Hand sawing a tenon is similar to the method described in Chapter 10 for lap joints, but work is from both sides. Be careful not to go too deep when cutting across the grain, as any excess cut into the tenon will weaken it. Cut down the end in three stages, with the wood held in the vise (Fig. 11-12A). Aim to complete the cut by sawing but, if necessary, level surfaces with a chisel.

Most of the waste wood can be removed from the mortise by drilling. It is possible to do this freehand, but it helps to have the drill mounted in a stand. In any case there is less risk of breaking-out if

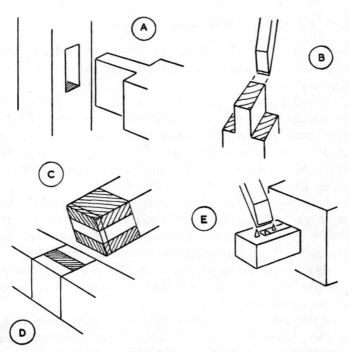

Fig. 11-11. The mortise and tenon is the most common joint in traditional woodwork.

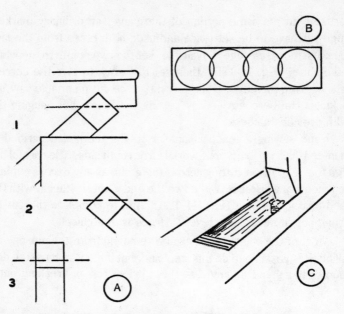

Fig. 11-12. Hand techniques for cutting a mortise and tenon.

the drill is taken only a little more than halfway from each side. Holes can be drilled to overlap so there is little work for the chisel later (Fig. 11-12B).

It is also possible to use a router or special drill jig to make a clean cut that only needs the rounded ends squared with a chisel. A router cutter can be used in a drill on a stand, and the wood slid along a guide under it. The old method was to chop out the waste with a chisel used across the grain. This often had a bursting action that cracked the wood. It is much better to drill first.

When the end of a mortise is trimmed with a chisel, it is very easy to get the slot too long. Make final cuts lightly and use several, rather than a heavy chop on the line, which will force the cut back over the line if there is much wood in front of it (Fig. 11-12C).

As with other joints, you get a better fit if you do not make trial assemblies, so trust your workmanship and make only the one assembly, with glue.

A tenon should be drawn closely into its mortise by clamping, but beware of forcing it so tight that the end grain presses a dent into the more resilient cross grain. In the basic mortise-and-tenon joint, the projecting tenon is planed level to complete the joint.

Further security can be obtained by wedging. There are two ways of doing this. The outer side of the mortised piece can have the ends opened to admit wedges, which are driven outside the tenon (Fig. 11-13A). Another way is to make one or two saw cuts across the tenon before driving it, then enter wedges into these cuts (Fig. 11-13B). The mortise may be opened slightly to allow the tenon to spread, but don't open it much or the tenon may split through to the other side. If the tenon is nearly square, the wedge may enter diagonally, but do not drive wedges in line with the grain; this will apply a bursting load to the mortised part, which may split.

A dowel may be arranged across a tenon. This is often done with outside woodwork and in places where it is impossible to pull the joint together with clamps. If a hole is drilled through the

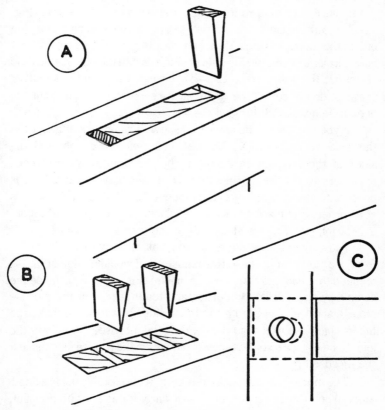

Fig. 11-13. Mortise joints may be tightened with wedges or dowels.

mortised part, then another through the tenon slightly offset toward its shoulder (Fig. 11-13C), a dowel with a tapered end can be driven through which will draw the joints tight. Make the dowel long enough

The ordinary mortise-and-tenon is used for joints away from the end of the mortised piece. At corners a similar joint called a *bridle joint* can be used (Fig. 11-14A). Another alternative at an end is a haunched mortise-and-tenon joint (Fig. 11-14B). The tenon is cut back in width to allow some solid wood in the other piece, and there is a small haunch carried through. If there is a groove in the wood for a panel, the tenon is cut thicker than the groove, so if the haunch is cut as deep as the groove, the groove disappears at the joint.

This tenon is cut in the usual way, then the part to be removed to make the haunch is marked and cut (Fig. 11-14C). When marking the mortise it is wise to leave some spare wood at the end (Fig. 11-14D); otherwise there is a risk of the narrow end part breaking out as the mortise is cut. Mark and cut the part of the mortise that goes through, then saw in the sides of the part to take the haunch and chisel out the waste (Fig. 11-14E). Unless it's essential for other reasons, do not cut off the waste at the end until after the joint has been assembled and the glue has set.

If you don't want the haunch to show, it can be cut at a taper to the surface (Fig. 11-14F). If the parts being joined are rabbetted, the sides of the tenoned part have to be stepped. It is sometimes necessary to cut the mortise into the higher part, but usually it is possible to get it entirely into the rabbet (Fig. 11-14G). If the joint is at a corner, it is made the same as a haunched mortise and tenon, except for stepping the shoulders of the tenon.

You may not want the tenon to go all the way through; on the front of a piece of furniture, the exposed end would not look right. A stopped (or blind) mortise-and-tenon joint (Fig. 11-15A) is made the same way as an ordinary mortise-and-tenon joint, but the mortise stops a short distance from the other side. It is usual to make the tenon slightly shorter than the depth of the mortise. This allows the joint to be clamped so the tenon shoulders make a close joint against the mortised piece.

The mortise should be drilled carefully, preferably using a depth stop. When the chisel is used, particularly if it is hit with a mallet,

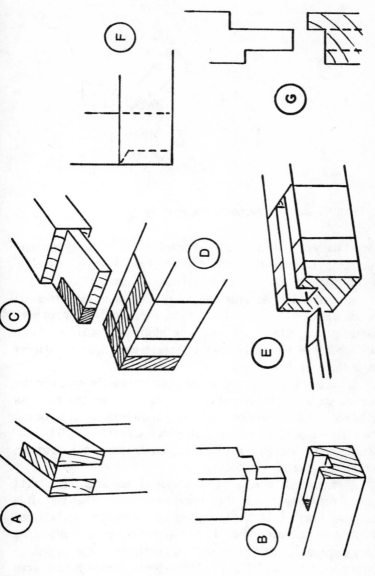

Fig. 11-14. A haunched tenon is used on corners where open joints aren't wanted.

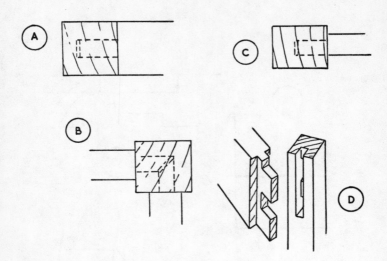

Fig. 11-15. Variations on the mortise and tenon for corners.

support the wood on the bench top or the grain may break through underneath. Lever all the waste wood out before paring the end to size or it may be damaged getting the waste out.

In many assemblies, rails tenon into posts or legs at corners on the same level. Tenons should not be too short, or they will not have enough glue area to provide strength. Mortises should be cut into each other, then the ends of the tenons mitered so they almost meet inside the post (Fig. 11-15B).

If the part to be tenoned is much thinner than the part with the mortise, the tenon may be made thicker than one-third the thickness of the rail. For a thin-sectioned rail going into a stout upright, you can use a "bare-faced" tenon—cut back on one side only (Fig. 11-15C). Retaining one shoulder is advisable to provide control of penetration depth if the mortise is too deep.

If a rail is wide in relation to its thickness, one large tenon might mean a very long mortise that would weaken the other part. It is better to use a variation on the haunched tenon and cut back between two or more narrow tenons. If the rail comes near the end of the other piece, as it would with a rail into a leg under a table top, there can be a haunch as well (Fig. 11-15D). A tenon of even thickness can be cut accurately with a table saw, but if you use a back saw you'll probably have to finish with a chisel to get the size exact.

212

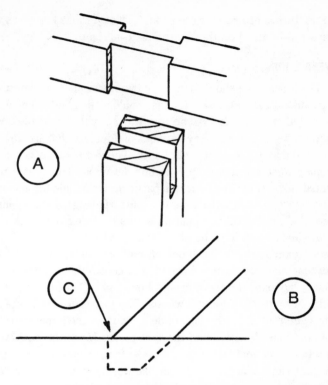

Fig. 11-16. Mortise and tenon can be reversed, and need not join at a right angle.

Occasionally it is conveneint to reverse the role of mortise and tenon, as where a top rail crosses an intermediate leg. The rail is marked as it would be for a mortise, but the outsides are cut away and the center left, and the leg is notched to match (Fig. 11-16A). Except where necessary for the sake of appearance, as in this case, use a mortise-and-tenon joint: it's stronger than this version of the bridle joint.

Mortise-and-tenon joints do not have to be at right-angles. If one piece approaches another at an angle, keep the cuts in line with the angle (Fig. 11-16B) and not perpendicular to the mortised part, although the far end of a blind joint may be perpendicular (Fig. 11-16C).

Sometimes a joint is needed mainly to provide location and resist movement, without having to provide much strength. An example is a series of light upright rails under a hand rail—strength in the structure is provided at the ends. Shallow tenons known as stub tenons can be used on the intermediate uprights.

DOVETAIL JOINTS

Dovetails have about them a certain mystique associated with the traidtional cabinetmaker. If a man could make good dovetails, he was skilled at his trade. Maybe that was so with handmade secret dovetails, but there are many versions of dovetails that are no more difficult to make than most other joints. The virtue of any dovetail is its ability to resist pulling apart in one direction. This is due to its dovetail shape (Fig. 11-17A). It is particularly suitable for any application where the method of assembly puts a pulling load on a joint, or where the usage load is a pull, as with a drawer front.

A simple version is the dovetail lap joint (Fig. 11-17B). This is sometimes made with the taper on one side only, but both sides tapered is more usual. It is marked out in much the same way as an ordinary lap joint, but the taper is about 1 in 8 (1/4 inch in a 2-inch width), or up to 1 in 6 for soft woods. The tapers are sawn after the lap has been cut. It is advisable to delay marking the female part until it can be done directly from the first piece. Mark the cuts with a knife. If a full dovetail would weaken the female piece too much, the male part can be tapered to about half thickness at the shouldered

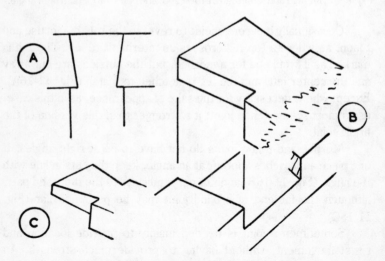

Fig. 11-17. A dovetail joint resists pulling apart in one direction.

214

end (Fig. 11-17C). Do not taper it too much, or the male piece will be weakened.

The dovetail is most often used as a corner joint. The simplest version is a single dovetail, as when a frame is built up from 2-inch-by-1-inch strips (Fig. 11-18A). A reasonable shape for a dovetail in such a frame is shown in Fig. 11-18B.

It is advisable to make a small allowance for cleaning off after the joint is assembled, then mark the width of each piece on the other (Fig. 11-18C). Use a try square to mark these lines all around. Some craftsmen favor marking the socket first, but it is probably simpler for the beginner to mark the dovetail itself first. Use a knife to mark the cross-grain parts that will be sawn and pencil on the waste parts. Use a fine backsaw to cut away the waste, keeping the kerf on the waste side of the lines.

Put the dovetail in position on the other piece. Sharpen a pencil to a long thin point or use a thin spike to mark each side of the dovetail closely (Fig. 11-18D). Remove the dovetail and mark these lines more clearly if necessary, then carry them down to the other line parallel to the sides of the piece (Fig. 11-18E). Again, pencil on the waste part.

Saw down the sides of the socket, but keep the saw kerf on the waste side (inside) of the lines. Be careful not to go below the line and watch both sides. Some of the waste can be removed by diagonal saw cuts (Fig. 11-18F), but remember the gap is narrower on one side and be careful not to cut too far into the pins at the sides. A few saw cuts into the remaining waste will help break it up so it can be easily cut out with a chisel. It may be possible to remove more of the waste with a jigsaw, but for hand work, support the wood on a piece of scrap wood on the bench top, preferably over a leg to prevent bounce.

Chop away the waste from both sides a little at a time. When chopping from the wide side, angle the chisel to avoid cutting into the pins (Fig. 11-18G). It will be necessary to use a mallet for the first chopping, but as the line is approached, hand-pare with a sharp chisel.

The dovetail should be a close fit in its socket so it will pull the shoulders close as it goes in. Avoid excessive tightness as this might cause cracking at the base of the pins. If force has to be used to get the glued joint together, lay a piece of scrap wood just behind the dovetail and hammer on that.

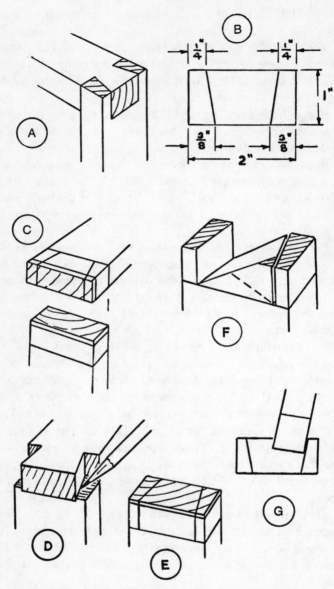

Fig. 11-18. Cutting a dovetail. One part is used to mark the other.

A more complex joint is a series of dovetails which might occur at the corner of a box. A box with dovetailed corners is superior to any nailed or screwed box. The size and number of dovetails is as much a matter of personal preference as of design. The old-time cabinet-maker favored extremely narrow pins, but that was probably to show his skill, as wider pins would have been stronger. With a limited tool kit, the dovetails and pins should be arranged to match the available chisels. A chisel will conveniently cut sockets for pins about 1/8 inch wider than itself, so a 1/4-inch chisel suits pins about 3/8 inch. Similarly, a 3/4-inch chisel will suit dovetail sockets that are about 7/8 inch on the narrow sides. In any case the pins and dovetails have to be spaced to suit the width of wood (Fig. 11-19A).

Bevels can be marked with an adjustable bevel, but it is useful to make a little template with bevels of 1 in 8 on one side for hard woods, and 1 in 6 on the other side for soft woods (Fig. 11-19B).

Mark the widths of the wood on each piece, with a little to spare for cleaning off after assembly, then mark out the dovetails. Fix the wood in the vise, with a little projecting, then saw down the sides of the dovetails on the waste side of the lines. Saw away the pieces at the sides. It may be possible to saw away some of the waste between

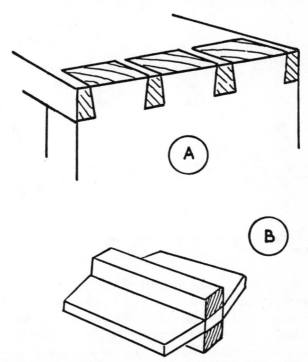

Fig. 11-19. A bevel template is useful for making multiple dovetails.

the dovetails, but there is not much room so this usually has to be done with a chisel. Hold the wood flat over scrap wood on the bench top and chop downwards, working to the center from each side (Fig. 11-20A). Pare by hand close to the line. Make sure the final cut is straight through and does not leave a bump near the middle.

When you are satisfied with the dovetail piece, put it in position on the other part and use the long-pointed pencil to mark each dovetail on the end grain. Square these lines down to the other line on each side and pencil on the waste parts. Saw down the lines, keeping to the waste sides. Saw away some of the waste with diagonal cuts, or remove more wood with a jigsaw. Chop out the remainder of the waste with a chisel, working from both sides (Fig. 11-20B). Make sure the bottoms of the sockets follow across in a straight line. A common fault is to let some of the sockets go below the line.

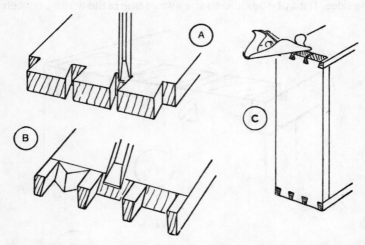

Fig. 11-20. Saw and chisel will remove dovetail waste. Plane in the direction that will not break grain.

See that there are no particles of wood in angles that would prevent tight assembly of the joint. Make sure lines are cut cleanly, but be careful to avoid taking off too much and creating a loose joint. Use a piece of scrap wood to spread the effect of hammer blows when finally assembling. When the glue has set, plane off projecting wood, always working towards the solid part (Fig. 11-20C)—never

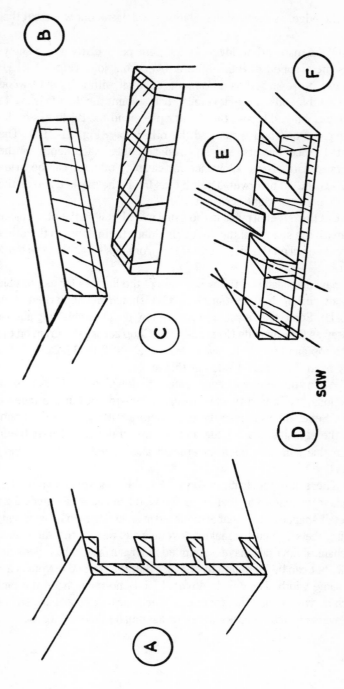

Fig. 11-21. A stopped dovetail hides the joint on one surface, but it has to be carefully cut with a chisel.

219

over the edge, as parts of the dovetails will break out when cut that way.

Of the many other dovetail joints, one particularly worth knowing is the stopped dovetail—the drawer-front joint (Fig. 11-21A). This can be regarded as a common dovetail with a layer of wood covering the ends of the dovetails. The amount the dovetails are to overlap is gauged across the thicker piece and the thickness of the other piece of wood is marked the other way (Fig. 11-21B). The dovetail piece has its end squared and the exact depth of the dovetails marked—no allowance for cleaning off later can be made (Fig. 11-21C). The dovetail depth is as far as the marked line on the other piece; not right across it.

Cut the dovetail piece in the usual way. Put it on the other piece and mark the shapes of the dovetails. Mark them down to the other line and pencil on the waste parts. It is from this stage that the work differs.

Saw diagonally on the waste side of the lines as far as possible without cutting into the surfaces that should be unmarked (Fig. 11-21D). Some waste can be removed by diagonal chiseling almost as deep as the saw cuts (Fig. 11-21E). Chop across the grain on the bench top and lift out the waste from the end (Fig. 11-21F). Keep away from the tapered sides at this stage.

When the center of each socket is down to the lines in both directions, use a narrow chisel—carefully—to get out the tapered parts. Sever fibers across the grain before cutting along the grain. Use the saw lines as a guide and be careful not to cut past them. When this joint has been assembled and planed flush, it is very attractive.

There are mechanical ways of making dovetail joints. The simplest tool uses a jig that holds the wood and acts as a guide for a dovetail-shaped cutter that is mounted in an electric drill. By moving the jig, the same cutter makes dovetails and pins of the same size. Mechanical dovetails have a rounded inner surface, which does not show, but can be identified by the fact that the pin and dovetails are the same width. Handmade dovetail joints normally have the pins much narrower than the dovetails. Mechanical dovetails are strong and are satisfactory alternatives to handmade dovetail joints.

Chapter 12

Covered Wood

Much modern furniture is not made from solid wood, but has an outer covering that simulates wood or some other finish, with a backing of manufactured board or cheap wood. The outer surface may be genuine wood veneer or it may be a plastic with a wood-grain effect. It may even be paper printed with wood grain and protected by varnish or lacquer. It may be Formica or a similar hard plastic that makes a tough, smooth working surface, or a softer plastic or tile. Most of these coverings have possibilities on things made from salvaged wood.

Ideally, a surface to be covered should be absolutely stable, with no risk of expansion and contraction. This is why much new construction that's covered is made of manufactured board: it—and plywood—is very stable and most coverings can be safely applied to it.

Antique furniture is commonly constructed of veneers over a seasoned hardwood base. Although natural wood may be expected to expand and contract with changes in the moisture content of the surrounding air, most of these old pieces still have good veneered surfaces, showing that furniture made from seasoned wood does not alter much. There may be occasional cracks in veneer due to movement of the base, but many hardwoods are excellent for veneering. Softwoods are not as suitable since they expand and contract more.

It is not advisable to veneer the soft woods and much of the hardwood that comes from crates. Wood obtained as offcuts from factories and lumber yards may have possibilities, but avoid any that's not well-seasoned. Almost any plywood is suitable unless it has a very coarse grain marking on the surface that would show through a thin covering. It may be sanded level, but if the plies are thin there may be little to sand away. Particle board, chip board and similar salvaged panels are very suitable for covering, providing the surface is not damaged.

Most covering material is thin, so it follows any undulations and imperfections in the surface below. Thicker materials may bridge joints or small imperfections, but even with them there is a risk of puckering or air pockets where the glue does not make a good bond; these blemishes will show on the surface, particularly if it's a glossy surface and is looked across towards a light.

Make sure there is nothing on the surface of old lumber or manufactured board that will interfere with the bond of the adhesive. Paint and grease must be removed. Use of chemical paint stripper may cause some paint to be washed into the grain. This will prevent adhesive from penetrating, so scraping or coarse sanding may be a better way of removing paint. If oil has penetrated the grain, it is probably best to not consider covering that piece of wood, as it's almost impossible to remove it all.

As the surface is to be covered, its appearance is not important. If holes or cracks have to be filled, the filler need not match the wood color. All that is important is that the surface will sand level.

Check overall levels. Use a straightedge, on edge, and look towards a light. Try it diagonally as well as parallel with edges (Fig. 12-1). Any slight bending or twisting can be pulled out when the panel is built into something or framed, but if there are more local uneven parts, you will either have to fill to level or forget covering the wood.

It is very unlikely that you will be able to get large pieces of covering material from surplus or salvage sources but, like plywood, small offcuts may be found in a factory's scrap pile. Even if you have to buy the covering material, its cost will only be a small part of the total, so your product will still be made mostly of salvaged material and its total cost well below its value.

Quality furniture is covered with wood veneer, with either a plain wood effect or a geometric pattern or picture using several different woods (marquetry). Plastic veneer with simulated wood grain is used similarly but more usually to make an overall covering so the effect is of solid wood. Close inspection by anyone who knows wood will show that it is not solid wood, but to the casual observer it has an acceptable appearance of solidity.

Some plastic veneer is patterned and doesn't attempt to look like wood. There are pictorial and patterned plastics in bright colors that can be used for bedroom and nursery items.

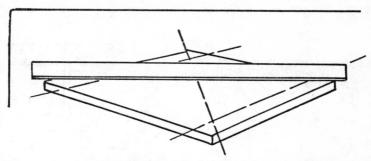

Fig. 12-1. Use a straightedge to check for twisting or warping in all directions.

The thicker plastic panel with a hard surface (Formica is a well-known brand) is used as kitchen working surfaces, table tops, bar and counter tops, splash backs and similar things. These are stouter than the veneerlike plastics and have some rigidity in and of themselves. It is possible to lay them on surfaces that would not be good enough for most other coverings, such as several softwood boards side by side.

There are tiles, both plastic and earthenware, that can be fixed to wood. They have some tolerance of slight movement of the backing and are not so likely to show minor unevenness, but a reasonably flat backing is still advisable.

Masonite or other hardboard can sometimes be used as an intermediate backing (Fig. 12-2A). The hardboard is then the true base, but it can be laid, for example, over a complete crate side used as a table top. It will accomodate the expansion and contraction of the softwood boards of the crate. It should be glued down, but not with one of the synthetic resin glues that sets very rigidly. A glue with elasticity is needed to allow slight movement of the softwood relative to the hardboard. If fasteners are used to attach the hardboard, they should be small brads or nearly headless finishing nails, punched and covered with filler (Fig. 12-2B). Any metal fasteners on a base surface must be punched below the surface and covered with filler. If metal is left on the surface it will show through eventually, even if it's not obvious at first.

Some new hardboard has a very hard shiny surface that resists the adhesion of some glues. Salvaged hardboard will probably have lost much of this, but any hardboard that is to be veneered or otherwise covered should be sanded in several directions to leave a matte, but not necessarily rough, surface.

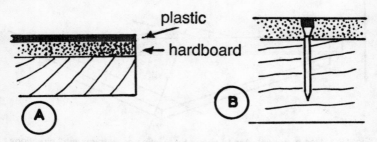

Fig. 12-2. Fastener heads must be below the hardboard surface before covering uphill.

HARD PLASTIC

Formica, Melamine, and other smooth-surfaced hard plastic sheet will make a strong hygienic surface for a table or other top that may be in contact with food or liquids. It can be cut with a fine back saw held at a fairly flat angle, with support close to the cut (Fig. 12-3A). Some of the material is brittle enough to crack if flexed accidentally or allowed to twist as the saw cut progresses.

The wood surface should be level and smooth, without too fine a finish. It should not be contaminated with paint, grease, old blobs of glue or anything else that might prevent close contact or interfere with the adhesion of the glue. If the surface is very finely sanded it may not hold glue as well as if coarsely sanded. One way of increasing the grip of a smooth surface is to scrape a fine-toothed saw across the wood to make a checker pattern diagonal to the grain (Fig. 12-3B).

Check the size of the plastic on the wood. If it goes better one way than the other, mark the two surfaces so they will be brought together the better way.

The makers either provide their own glue or recommend certain types. Usually the adhesive is a contact type, which means that the plastic cannot be moved once it is brought into contact. To ensure correct register it is helpful to nail strips lightly along one edge (Fig. 12-3C) and along the adjoining corner. Instructions with the adhesive should be followed; typical instructions call for both surfaces to be coated using a metal spreader provided with the adhesive. After drying partially or completely they are brought together.

Use extreme care to avoid placing the sheet out of register or causing air bubbles. Put the plastic sheet against the temporary strips, while holding it curved so only the edge meets the adhesive on the wood at first (Fig. 12-3D). Lower the rest of the sheet, following the curve with your other hand so as to bring the surfaces together progressively without trapping air pockets. Press down all over with your hand, a cloth pad, or a roller from the center toward the edges, paying particular attention to achieving close contact at the edges.

The edges can be trued with a finely-set steel plane, using it diagonally so the cut is a slice towards the wood (Fig. 12-3E). A Surform tool or a file can be used in a similar way. A router cutter with a guide along the wood surface will also make a good edge. If the wood edge is to remain visible, bevel the plastic edge slightly (Fig. 12-3F). Do not try to round the edge as this will make a blurred edge to any pattern in the plastic) a plain bevel gives a clean edge line.

The edge also may be covered with hard plastic. When leveling the edge, be careful not to round it. Use a strip of plastic slightly too wide, attaching it the same way as the surface material (Fig. 12-3G). When its adhesive has set, finish the meeting edges by first reducing the overhand with a plane, then making a bevel that extends over both pieces (Fig. 12-3H).

SOFT PLASTIC

Many decorative patterns of flexible plastic sheet are available, some of which are applied with a brushed adhesive, and some of which are self-adhesive, with their surface protected by paper which is peeled off immediately before use. Some of these plastic materials (one brand is Contac) are intended for shelf coverings or other

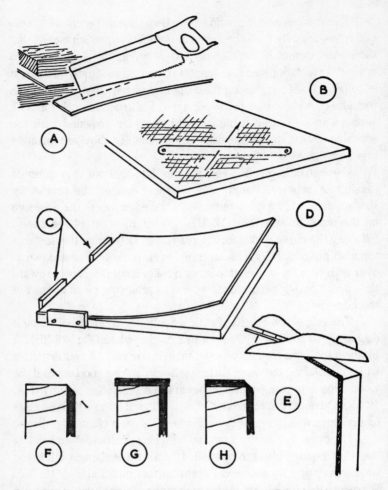

Fig. 12-3. Avoid cracking and trapped air bubbles when fitting laminated plastic sheet. Edges look best beveled.

temporary coverings, but they may also be used to cover rough wood for certain uses.

The main problem is fitting the material so it covers properly, without creases or air bubbles. Do not place edges of the material too near a fold; allow a generous overlap (Fig. 12-4A) so there is no tendency for the fold to spring the edge away from the wood (Fig. 12-4B). If possible, make one strip go all around a box; locate the joint along one side away from a corner (Fig. 12-4C). Allow enough to go underneath with mitered corners and finish the bottom piece a short distance back from the edge (Fig. 12-4D). Around the top edges, allow enough to turn inside, miter the corners, and use a lining to overlap inside (Fig. 12-4E). The top miters may be cut so one overlaps the other slightly, to avoid a gap showing wood through the joint.

Deal with one surface at a time. Some of these plastics will stretch. Although it is necessary to get them taut over a surface, be careful of stretching so much that the surface pattern is distorted. With self-adhesive sheet, peel off the paper far enough to cover one surface, then get one edge right while holding the remainder away from the wood. Use one hand to stroke down the plastic as it is lowered. Press out air bubbles. If a wrinkle or crease occurs, gently

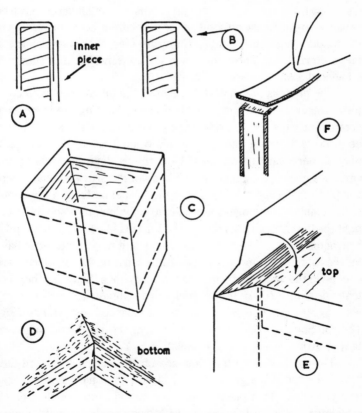

Fig. 12-4. Soft plastic can be wrapped over edges of a box. Some self-adhesive material has to be ironed on.

lift the sheet and stroke it out. Avoid lifting and repositioning as much as possible, as this weakens the adhesion.

If it is the type of plastic without self-adhesive backing, use the recommended adhesive. These adhesives are as strong as the contact adhesives for hard plastic, and allow some movement as the plastic is positioned. Soft plastic shows through details of the surface it covers, so for the best results it should be used only on a smooth surface.

A similar plastic covering uses a heat-activated glue. It is ironed on, much like a pants patch (Fig. 12-4F).

TILES

Hard-surfaced plastic laminates are an excellent choice for damp locations like kitchens or bathrooms. Their appearance can be enhanced by using tile on some of the vertical surfaces. In addition to the traiditonal porcelain and earthenware tiles, there are plastic and metal alternatives. These may have self-adhesive backs or they may be affixed with a separate adhesive.

The process is simplest if the area can be covered with complete, uncut tiles. This is possible if you're building the piece from scratch and can plan the surfaces to suit the tiles. If the article has to be made to a certain size, as it would when it has to fit a recess, it may be necessary to cut tiles. How this is done depends on the circumstances but, in general, the body of the article should accept complete tiles (Fig. 12-5A). If the tiled panel rests on a horizontal surface and the top edge is more in the sight line, tiles should be cut to fit the bottom, with full tiles at the top (Fig. 12-5B). If the panel is high and the bottom edge is more obvious, it may be better to have full tiles at the bottom and cut tiles at the top (Fig. 12-5C). If cuts are needed in the width and one side is less obvious than the other, cut that side (Fig. 12-5D). If the panel is in a symmetrical situation, you will have to cut both sides to give a balanced appearance (Fig. 12-5E). Some makes of tile can be obtained in precut widths or border strips, which eases installation.

The method of cutting depends on the material. Glazed tiles have to be cut with a glass cutter; a plaster *grout* fills any roughness of a cut edge. Thin plastic tiles may be cut with a knife along a straightedge. Some may be cut with scissors, but a knife gives a cleaner edge. Some soft aluminum tiles can be scored with a knife

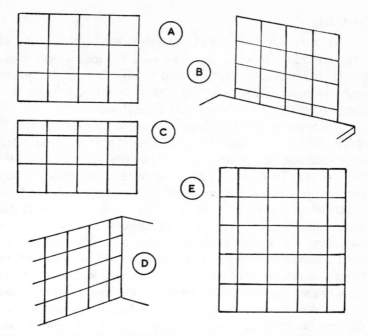

Fig. 12-5. Tiles should be cut so their unequal size will be least obvious.

and snapped off. Others have to be cut with a fine saw and the edge filed smooth.

It is important that tiles are laid parallel; normally this means with truly vertical and horizontal joints. The sides of a panel may be sufficient guides, but it is helpful to draw guide lines at right angles to each other across the panel before starting covering. In many places the center of the panel is the most obvious; in such cases it's best to work from near-center guide lines measured from the edges. Lay tiles on these lines first, then progress toward the edges. Tiles should butt against each other evenly. Be careful to avoid setting one tile slightly askew: this can affect further rows of tiles and give an uneven appearance.

Follow the adhesive instructions carefully. Some tiles require only a spot of adhesive at each corner; some must be covered with a special grooved trowel; others must be covered to the point that when the tile is pressed on, adhesive is forced out between the joints. In any case, be careful: improper adhesive application can ruin a job's appearance or cause it to fall apart in short order.

Veneering

Veneers may be made of many decorative woods, some of which are unsuitable for use as solid woods. This means veneers can provide beautiful effects not obtained by any other means. Veneer suppliers issue catalogs showing what is available, although it is always better to select from stock at the store.

There are several thicknesses of veneer; the most common is about 1/25 inch thick (about 1mm). Obviously, if several veneers are to be combined on a panel they should be the same thickness, for there is very little wood in a veneer to level by sanding. Many veneers are made in the same way as the plies for plywood, by cutting off a revolving log. Not all veneer woods are suited to this method of cutting, and some do not give the best grain effect cut this way. Some are cut straight across with a knife. Some can only be sawn, meaning more wood is removed as sawdust than is left as veneer, so saw-cut veneers may be expensive. Widths depend on the way the veneer was cut, the size of the tree and many other factors. Most veneers are not much more than 1 foot wide, although they may be quite long; designs using veneers should allow for this.

Many veneers can be cut with a sharp knife along a straightedge, but veneer saws are better. They have very fine teeth on curved edges, with an offset handle so the tool can be used either way against a straightedge (Fig. 12-6A). A knife may be deflected from a straight line by diverging grain, but this is not much of a problem with a saw. The fine saws in some combination knife sets are suitable for veneer.

Veneer must be pressed tight on its backing; hand pressure can accomplish this to a limited extent, but special tools help. A small hardwood roller is a good pressing tool, particularly along joints (Fig. 12-6B), but the traditional pressing tool is a veneer hammer. This is better than a wide roller for large areas.

A veneer hammer is not swung like a hammer, although there are some that are made like hammers. A simple type can be made or bought (Fig. 12-6C). The key part is a strip of almost any metal, about 1/8 inch thick and 4 inches or more across, fit into a slot in the wooden part. The lower edge is well rounded and the corners are rounded to prevent them from digging in. The edge is smoothed with fine abrasive paper to almost a polish.

A veneer hammer is used with one hand on the handle and the other pressing over the head. It is pulled or pushed with a slightly zig-zag movement across the laid veneer (Fig. 12-6D), so the adhesive surfaces are pushed tightly together and any trapped air is worked towards an edge.

Traditionally, veneer was laid with an animal or fish glue. This had the advantage of being slow setting, so the veneer could be positioned and pressure on the surface leveled only uneven glue. It could also be softened by heat: an iron over the veneer would soften the glue and allow an air pocket to be closed or a weakened joint to be brought together again. The disadvantages were that subsequent heat might soften the glue and moisture would weaken it. However, much of the antique furniture veneered with this type of glue is still in good condition.

These glues can still be used, but modern veneer glues give better results. With one type, glue is applied to the veneer and the

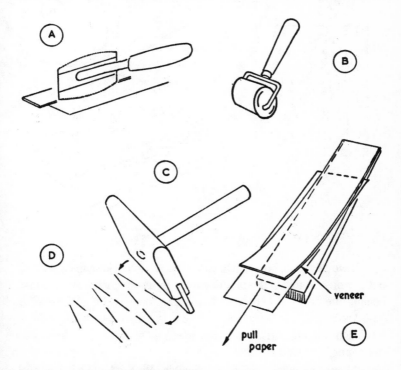

Fig. 12-6. Wood veneer may be cut with a special saw and pressed down with a roller or hammer. Paper is used with some adhesives.

231

backing and allowed to dry. Paper is then put over the backing and the veneer is positioned over it; when the position is exact, the paper is withdrawn and the veneer pressed down following the moving paper edge (Fig. 12-6E).

The simplest veneering job is covering a panel with a single veneer sheet. If you must, or want to, join veneers, you may either match their grain or—an interesting effect—bring two together so each is a mirror-image of the other (Fig. 12-7A).

For this sort of cut, both edges may be cut straight independently, or one may overlap the other and both cut simultaneously (Fig. 12-7B). A small block plane is useful for truing veneer edges. It is helpful to have a *shooting board*; the veneer projects slightly over its edge and is held down tightly as the plane runs on its side along the edge (Fig. 12-7C).

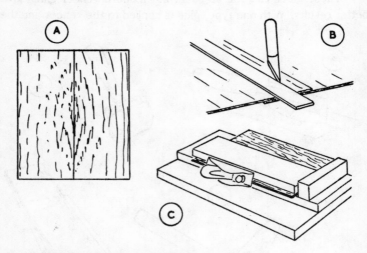

Fig. 12-7. Joined veneers produce interesting effects.

It would not be impossible to lay such a simple joint in two parts, but it is best to follow the practice used for more complicated joints, holding the edges together with masking tape on the surface (Fig. 12-8A). Adhesive is applied according to instructions and the assembly laid as one unit. After rolling or pressing with a veneer hammer, the paper is peeled off.

There are many variations possible. Pieces laid with diagonal joints are effective on a table top (Fig. 12-8B). Use a full-size drawing (which may be just diagonal lines on the backing piece) to get the shapes of the parts. Allow some surplus around the edges to allow for truing meeting edges and for trimming after the veneer is affixed. Assemble the four parts with masking tape and lay them as one piece.

If old furniture is examined it will be seen that many panels use veneer to form a frame. The center is one piece of veneer and the framing veneers are cut so their grain runs across their width (Fig. 12-8C). Some panels feature a narrow band inside the frame (Fig. 12-8D). The inside panel may be veneered in various patterns (Fig. 12-8E).

A design feature should be noted. If the panel will be horizontal in the finished piece, any border may be the same width all around (Fig. 12-8C); if this is done with an upright panel, the bottom border will appear narrow, so it is usual to make it deeper (Fig. 12-8F).

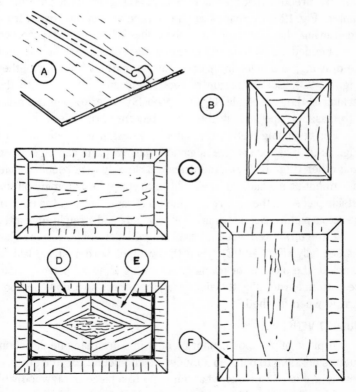

Fig. 12-8. Veneered panels can be arranged in several decorative ways.

MARQUETRY

The intricate veneered geometric patterns on antique furniture were called marquetry, but today the word refers to making pictures from veneers. With the large variety of woods available and their many colors and grain patterns, it is possible to select woods to suit certain features of a picture. The result is very effective. Some workers dye veneers or shade them chemically or by charring them, but this is not always considered good practice.

Smaller offcuts of plywood and hardboard make good backings for marquetry pictures. Kits can be bought that include a drawing and a supply of suitable veneers, so it's not necessary to be artistic to make marquetry pictures, although after a little practice it's easy to use a picture or photograph as a basis for marquetry.

Use veneer thin enough to be cut with a knife. A knife with interchangeable fine blades is invaluable. Be careful to cut from an edge in a direction that does not break out the grain of the part that is wanted (Fig. 12-9A). Shapes can be marked with carbon paper from the drawing, then cut freehand with a knife. Where utmost precision is not needed, as with a rural scene, some shapes may be cut over the drawing, and adjoining pieces can be marked from each other (Fig. 12-9B). Some marquetry craftsmen affix cut pieces to the backing as they are made, but it is probably wiser to joint the parts with masking tape and lay the whole picture in one piece.

For beginning marquetry, choose a design with bold outlines (Fig. 12-9C); as experience is gained, narrow parts can be cut into each other (Fig. 12-9D). An intricate assembly may require slight adjustment as it's laid, so leave a little to spare for trimming on the outside pieces. If the picture is to have a straight border, the edge of the actual picture can be trimmed with a knife and straightedge after laying, the unwanted wood levered off with a chisel before the glue has set fully (Fig. 12-9E), then the straight border strips laid to complete the picture for framing. As with geometric panels, make the bottom border slightly wider than the others so it does not look narrow when finished.

MOLDED VENEER

A piece of plywood cannot be bent in more than one direction, but it is possible to build up a moderate compound curve if strips of veneer are used to make what amounts to a piece of plywood with the desired shape. This technique is used for boat hulls, but is

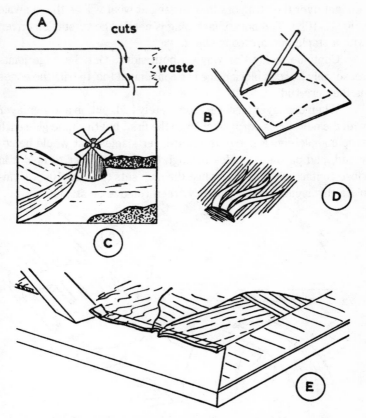

Fig. 12-9. Marquetry pictures are built up with different wood veneers.

adaptable to other things. It is particularly suitable for the offcuts of veneer obtained from a plywood factory.

A simple form or mold has to be made in the intended shape. In the case of a canoe (Fig. 12-10A) there are frames at intervals with stringers laid lengthwise. A hollow is left for a central *hog*, and there may be provision for stems at the ends. The stringers need not fit closely, but the overall shape must be a fair curve.

The veneers are cut into rectangular strips. For a canoe they may be about 3 inches wide, but for anything with greater compound curvature they would have to be narrower. The first layer is put on at about 45 degrees to the hog, starting near the middle of the canoe. Place plastic sheeting over the mold to prevent glue going through and sticking to the stringers. Each strip is glued to the hog and brought over the stringers to overhang at what will be the gunwale (Fig. 12-10B). Temporary fastening is needed here: staples driven with a staple gun are convenient.

Continue to lay this way on both sides. Get the edge joints reasonably close; a block plane is a convenient tool to trim the edges as they are laid.

When one layer has been completely laid, put on another layer with the new strips perpendicular to the first, but this time glue each strip completely. Remove the first-layer staples that would be covered, and put new staples through the second layer to hold it in close contact with the first while the glue sets (Fig. 12-10C). Complete this layer, let the glue dry, then remove all staples.

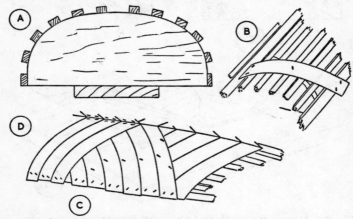

Fig. 12-10. A canoe hull can be built up by gluing three layers of veneer.

For some things, two layers of veneer may be enough, but for a canoe it is better to put on a third layer. This has been done with the outside layer going lengthwise, but it is easier, and probably stronger, to lay the third layer in the same direction as the first. The second layer is cleaned off by scraping or sanding away any blobs of glue or other unevenness, then the outside layer is glued and stapled on (Fig. 12-10D). When that glue has set, the outside is sanded true after all staples have been removed. The holes left by the staples can be closed by wiping the wood with a cloth soaked in hot water.

When the molded hull is lifted off the mold, it will keep its shape and is ready for the gunwale strips to be fitted, the edges trimmed, and internal fitting-out. There is no need for framing inside to hold the shape, as the hull itself provides strength and rigidity.

Chapter 13
Turning and Carving

Both wood turning and carving are regarded as specialized activities, but they are part of general woodworking. They provide a way of using unusual woods to the best advantage and can make use of even the smallest piece of salvaged wood. Many items can be improved by turning or carving, and some constructions are possible only with turning and carving.

Basically, wood turning makes things round. Any salvaged wood that can yield enough material to make a round thing has possibilities. This usually means wood of square section or wood that can be cut to square section. *Spindle turning* refers to making such items as tool handles and stool legs. *Faceplate turning* usually means turning a bowl shape, and can use grain which goes across the square. Offcuts from the end of a board may be suitable: for instance, a piece 6 inches square and 1 1/2 inches thick that might otherwise be thrown away would turn into quite a good bowl.

Carving can use wood of almost any size. If it has to be part of something else, it will obviously have to be a certain size, but many carvers get a lot of satisfaction out of whittling tiny pieces of wood that would be no use for anything else.

Almost any wood can be turned or carved, but close-grained hardwoods are best for the finest work in both disciplines. The harder woods may mean harder work, but also finer detail with less risk of breaking. However, softwood with milder grain can be used; its ease of working allows bolder patterns to be worked successfully.

When salvaging wood, it is worthwhile keeping aside anything that seems appropriate to carving or turning, particularly wood which has interesting grain markings. For turning, it is possible to use logs straight from the tree. If a branch is pruned from a fruit tree, straight parts may be cut out for turning. If it is newly cut, it must be seasoned, but it can be roughly turned to a size larger than what it will be eventually, left to dry naturally, then finish-turned. Logs may also suggest ideas for carving. Another source is driftwood picked up on the shore: its shape may suggest something to carve. Twigs and small branches may make a perch for a carved bird.

WOOD TURNING

Turning requires some special tools, the most important of which is a lathe. This is a machine tool, with the accent on "tool": it is powered, but it is your skill in handling it that produces results. Lathes vary in size and complication, but considerable work can be done on the simplest, which is powered by an electric drill. A larger lathe (Fig. 13-1A) has an independent motor and is altogether more substantial, but the principle is the same.

The powered part—to the left of the operator—is called the *headstock*. This may consist of the electric drill clamped to a stand or it may be a spindle mounted in bearings with a stepped pulley to give variable speeds from a matching pulley at the motor. For small wood turning high speeds are needed, so the usual electric drill is satisfactory driving directly. For larger diameters a slower speed is better. The *mandrel* (spindle) is threaded and may be hollow, to take various fittings to drive the wood. On an electric-drill lathe, these fittings go in the drill chuck.

The bed provides a mounting for the parts; its size limits the length of wood which can be turned. Sliding on this is the *tailstock*, which can be locked in any position on the bed and is centered on the same axis as the headstock spindle. Also sliding on the bed and capable of being locked at any point is the tool rest. This has a long edge on which hand tools can rest and be moved over the work, and it may have height and swivel adjustments.

Those are the essentials for spindle turning. The lathe may also have a faceplate (Fig. 13-1B) that screws on the spindle nose. This

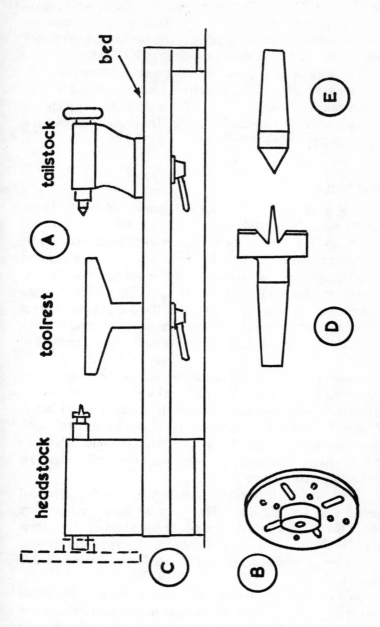

Fig. 13-1. The basic parts of any wood-turning lathe.

239

drives large-diameter shallow work, such as bowls. Work diameter is limited by the clearance above the bed. Some lathes have a gap in the bed to allow large shallow work to be turned. Large-diameter work is accomodated on some lathes by another faceplate with a left hand thread at the other end of the headstock (Fig. 13-1C).

The simplest turning uses a *driving center* to drive the work. There are several forms, but most have a central spur and teeth to grip and turn the wood (Fig. 13-1D). This is usually held by friction in a tapered socket in the headstock spindle. The tailstock spindle has a similar taper and takes a plain center (Fig. 13-1E).

LATHE TOOLS

Most work on a lathe is done with gouges and chisels. Those used for heavy lathe work are much longer than those used for ordinary woodwork, but some standard woodworking tools may be adapted for use with an electric drill lathe. A turning gouge is ground on the outside; for most work it has a rounded end (Fig. 13-2A), although for some work it is better straight (Fig. 13-2B). A gouge 1/2 inch wide is a good first choice, but there are places where a narrower one is more use. For a large lathe, a broader gouge (up to 1 1/2 inches) is convenient for quickly removing large amounts of wood.

Some turners use gouges for almost all their work, but a chisel is better for getting a smooth surface on long curves. The end of a turning chisel is skewed and beveled on both sides (Fig. 13-2C). A 1/2-inch chisel is likely to get the most use, with a 1- or 1 1/2-inch a close second. A parting tool (Fig. 13-2D) is also useful. This goes straight into the wood and is narrow behind the cutting edge so it does not bind on the cut.

Bowls and other faceplate work is started with gouges and finished with scraping tools. These can be made from ordinary chisels, but for large work they have to be much heavier. The edge is ground to a broad cutting angle (Fig. 13-2E). It may be straight—for flat surfaces or outside curves—or rounded—to go inside a hollow (Fig. 13-2F).

You'll need calipers for measuring across curves. The precision engineering type are best, but simple friction-joint calipers are satisfactory (Fig. 13-2G). Outside calipers are usually all that's

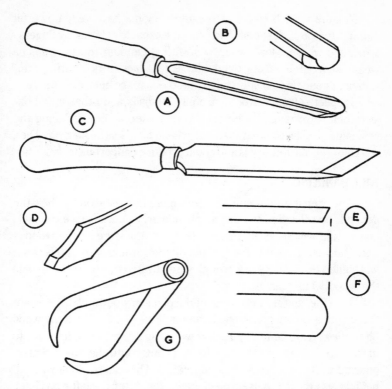

Fig. 13-2. Turning is done with gouges, chisels and scraper tools. Calipers measure diameters.

needed, but inside calipers are sometimes useful; friction-joint outside calipers can be used inside by overlapping the points.

LATHE SAFETY

Most tools are dangerous if used carelessly, and this is particularly true of power tools. The danger of some is obvious: one look at a circular saw tells you it can easily take fingers off. Some are not so obvious. A file looks substantial enough to pry with or, lacking the proper punch, to drive a stuck bolt free with. But a file is tempered to extreme hardness to resist dulling and, as a result, is brittle: if used to pry it can snap suddenly into sharp-edged pieces; struck with a hammer, it may shatter or chip, sending fragments flying. A power drill doesn't look menacing, but a key left in the chuck accidentally will fly out with considerable speed when the drill is turned on.

A lathe must be used with caution. Some have very powerful motors, turn at high speed, and are quite capable of breaking fingers, arms, and worse. Don't wear loose-fitting clothing. Button cuffs or wear a short-sleeved shirt and, above all, *never* work wearing a tie. Catching your tie in a lathe might be the last accident in your life.

Inspect salvaged wood carefully for nails and other metal objects before turning. Probe any holes to see if they're hiding the remnants of a nail or other fastener whose head has broken off. They will chip and dull your tools and could produce dangerous fragments.

TOOL HANDLING

The preparation required before mounting the wood in the lathe depends on the lathe. If it has ample power, a square piece can go in square and will be easily turned. If it is a drill lathe or the wood is exceptionally large, it helps to plane off the corners. A rough octagon will suffice (Fig. 13-3A). A trough (Fig. 13-3B) can be made to hold the wood while planing.

Find the center of each end of the piece of wood and make a dent there with a center punch and hammer (Fig. 13-3C). Push the wood on to the driving center, possibly with a light tap from a hammer to make sure it grips. Push the tailstock center into the other center-punch dot. Its point should be lubricated. This can be done with oil, but it is less messy to use a piece of candle. After the lathe has been

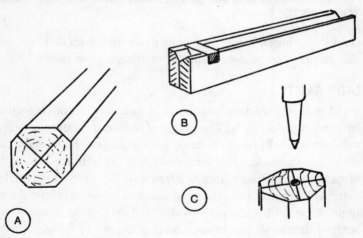

Fig. 13-3. A trough will hold wood while being planed to roughly octagonal section in preparation for turning.

running for a short time, tighten the tailstock; the center usually wears its way into the wood slightly, causing the wood to vibrate.

Adjust the tool rest so it is at or just below center height. Bring it fairly close to the wood. Spin the wood by hand to make sure it misses the tool rest. Switch on the lathe; the wood will revolve with its top coming toward you (Fig. 13-4A). One hand should be on the end of the tool handle and the other pressing down on the tool over the tool rest (Fig. 13-4B). For light work it is easier to see what the tool is doing if only your thumb is on top; for heavier work you should hold the tool with your whole fist.

Advance the tool to the wood so it starts taking off shavings (Fig. 13-4C): this is a scraping action. Lower the handle so the tool points up more, and the cut will be more of a slice (Fig. 13-4D). This is the normal angle for the tool.

The first aim is to make the piece of wood round. To do this the round-nosed gouge can be moved along the work at an angle (Fig. 13-4E), or a wider square-nosed gouge can be moved in a series of rocking actions (Fig. 13-4F). Stop the lathe and examine the wood. What looked so smooth while rotating quickly will be found to be quite rough yet; parts of the surface may not have even been touched. Continue turning until all flats have been removed. The roughness of the surface does not matter and is to be expected at this stage.

Suppose the shape wanted is a rounded point (Fig. 13-4G). Use the gouge to approximate this shape, but don't cut down to the final size (Fig. 13-4H).

Change to a chisel. Cuts with a chisel are always made towards the smaller diameter with the lower edge of the chisel leading (Fig. 13-4J), whereas the gouge roughed to shape by pushing directly in. The chisel cuts by slicing. Rest the chisel over the rotating wood with the long point clear and the under bevel resting on the wood. Hold firmly as you roll the chisel on the tool rest until the short corner of the edge begins to cut. Move or swing the tool as it cuts toward the smaller diameter (Fig. 13-4K). Continue until you have reached the bottom of the hollow. Turn the tool over and slice down from the other high part into the hollow and the two cuts meet. Stop the lathe and examine the wood. You will find a smooth surface such as would be obtained on flat wood with a plane.

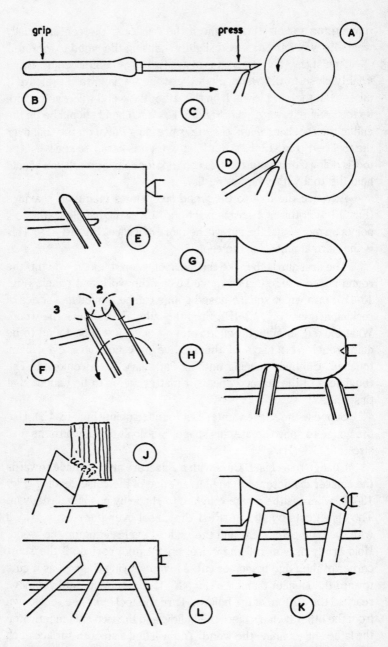

Fig. 13-4. Wood is roughed to shape on a lathe with a gouge and smoothed with a chisel.

Parallel parts can be turned in either direction by slicing with the chisel. A wide chisel is less likely to dig in: the long point must always be clear of the wood, and it is easier to ensure this if the cutting edge is wide. Angles of approach (Fig. 13-4L) will vary according to the wood and the grain.

If a gouge is turned on edge and used with a slicing action the effect is very similar to using a skew chisel. In some deep hollows this may be the only way of turning, but where a chisel can be used, it is preferable.

Usually, the sawn end is not true. This does not matter if the end is to be cut away, but if it should be true, the long point of a chisel can be used to square it (Fig. 13-5A). Hold the chisel firmly on the tool rest with the long point downwards and turn it sideways until the bevel facing the wood is perpendicular to the turning axis (Fig. 13-5B). Push it straight in as far as the center. If necessary, use several cuts. A parting tool will also true an end, but it does not leave as smooth an end.

The center hollow is not wanted in most finished work, so it has to be cut off. Mark where the final end will be by pushing the parting tool straight in (Fig. 13-5C). Do not cut so deep that the wood is weakened and may break when other work is being done. When all of the other turning has been done, complete cutting the end. You may turn down the waste part a little as the end is shaped (Fig. 13-5D) to give you more room to manipulate the shaping tool. If the wood is cut completely with the parting tool, the last bit may break under the pressure, leaving an end that cannot be finished smooth. It is usually better to lathe-cut down to about 1/8-inch diameter, take the wood out of the lathe, and finish it by hand.

Much turned wood features decorative lines (Fig. 13-5E) or *beads* (Fig. 13-6A). Lines are easily made by pointing the chisel downwards on the tool rest and advancing it into the wood (Fig. 13-6B). These, and the limits for beads or other turning divisions, can be marked on the wood by holding a pencil on the tool rest so it lightly touches the revolving wood.

To make a bead, mark it and cut in with the point of the chisel. Put the chisel on the tool rest as if to turn it towards one of these cuts with the short point leading (Fig. 13-6C). Roll the chisel so the short point cuts. After a little practice the cut will roll from the center of the bead until the chisel is nearly upright on the toolrest with the short

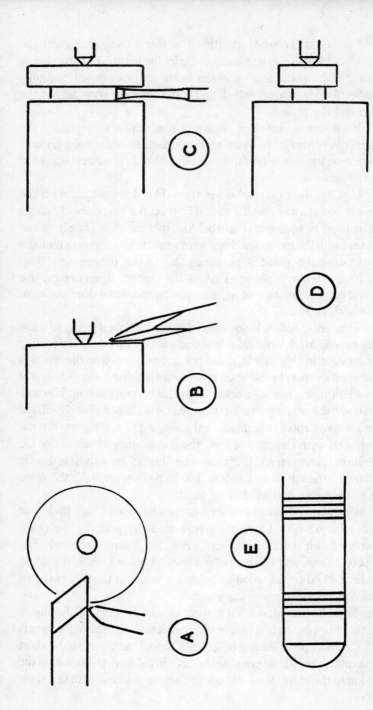

Fig. 13-5. Ends are cut on a lathe with a chisel or parting tool. Lines and beads are worked with a chisel.

point at the bottom of the cut (Fig. 13-6D). Do this on each side of the bead and the parts beside it (Fig. 13-6E). There may be several beads alongside each other, but the method of making them is the same.

If part of the wood being turned has to remain square, as in some table and stool legs, care is needed to avoid damaging the corners of the square part. Revolve the wood by hand to make sure it will not hit the tool rest. Reduce the part that is to be rounded with a gouge, tilting it as you reach the shoulder so the bottom of its curve

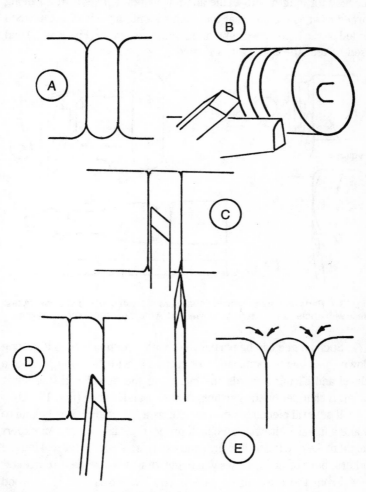

Fig. 13-6. Decorating turned work with beads.

is towards the square (Fig. 13-7A). This will cut into the sharp angle with the least risk of splintering. Although an expert might turn the end of the square with the short point of the chisel leading, it is safer to lead with the long point downwards (Fig. 13-7B). It might be possible to cut in with the parting tool, but there is a risk of it catching the grain and breaking a corner of the square. This sort of cut is commonly followed by a bead and a more sweeping curve, all of which are done with a chisel after roughing to shape with a gouge.

If the piece being turned need not match anything else it can be checked for length with a rule and for diameter by eye. If it's being turned to fit a hole and is at the tailstock end, a piece of scrap wood drilled to the hole size can be hung over the center (Fig. 13-7C) and used to test the end as it is turned.

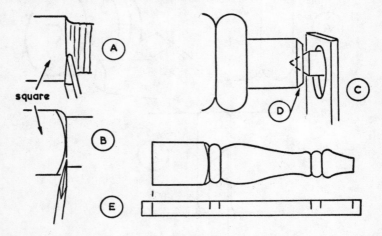

Fig. 13-7. Parts that are to remain square are cut with gouge and chisel. A test piece with a hole can be used on a dowel end. A rod is used to compare lengths.

Such an end can be partially cut with a parting tool, but getting down to size is a combination of cutting in with the long point of a chisel and slicing towards the cut along the dowel with the short point. A chamfer on the end helps in fitting and testing (Fig. 13-7D).

If several pieces have to match, as a set of legs, it is helpful to make a full-size drawing to check proportions as you go. An expert might make one leg by eye first and use this as a guide for making the others, but a drawing allows you to get vital measurements correct.

From the drawing prepare a 'rod,' which is a strip of wood showing the position and diameter of vital cuts on the turning (Fig.

13-7E). Turn the larger diameters first, using the rod to pencil the rotating wood. Cut in with the parting tool where there will be hollows and turn key diameters to size before doing much shaping.

A skilled wood turner is proud of getting a good finish from his tools with little or no sanding, but your early efforts at turning will have to be finished by sanding on the lathe. Use hand-held, folded abrasive paper. Using a hard backing or too much pressure may cause the paper to get too hot, even to the extent of charring the surface of the wood. This is more likely to happen with fine grit. Because the wood is turning at high speed, a coarse grit will have a finer effect than on a flat piece of wood.

Of course, sanding revolving wood in this way puts scratches across the grain, so you will have to use a series of finer and finer abrasives to remove scratches, particularly the deeper ones caused by hard sanding. Experts often finish the surface with a handful of shavings held under the wood. Whether this really does anything much to the surface is debatable, but many good turners do it.

FACEPLATE TURNING

Turning anything that is larger in diameter than it is long requires a different technique. Even if it is turned over the bed, the tailstock is not usually used, and if it is turned on the left of the headstock, the tailstock cannot be used. A faceplate is provided with many holes and slots, so screws can be driven through. These may go directly into the work, but a more common method is to screw a piece of wood to the faceplate and join the work to it. The work may be joined by screws (Fig. 13-8A) or by glue with paper in the joint (Fig. 13-8B). Glue and paper holds well enough for turning, but the paper can be split by levering with a chisel, then sanded level. Even if the work is screwed directly on, it is advisable to have a piece of plywood or other thin wood between the work and the faceplate, so the tools will not hit the faceplate (Fig. 13-8C).

The work should be cut to a circle before mounting on the faceplate. A circle the size of the faceplate can be drawn on it so the faceplate is accurately centered. For a bowl with a flat base, the first step is to set the tool rest outside and use the gouge to scrape the circumference to size (Fig. 13-8D). With most woods cut across the grain it is unwise to tilt the gouge upwards as in spindle turning, as it

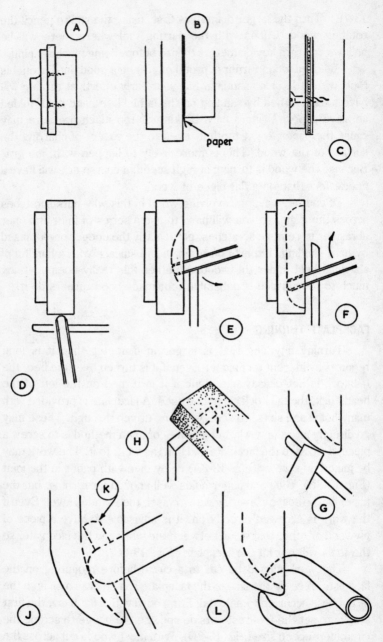

Fig. 13-8. Wood mounted on a lathe faceplate is turned with gouges and scraper tools.

might catch in the grain. The alternative to the gouge is a scrapping tool.

Move the toolrest to the inside surface of the wood and use the gouge to start removing waste wood. For this it can be tilted up slightly, but the best angle must be found by experiment. Some turners favor working from the center outwards (Fig. 13-8E). Others prefer to work from the rim in (Fig. 13-8F). At this stage do not try to get the wood anywhere near the exact size; the object is just to reduce the bulk of the wood.

Return to the outside and shape it with a scraper tool (Fig. 13-8G). Keep the scraper sharp by frequent rubbing with an oilstone used on the edge like a file (Fig. 13-8H).

When the outside is satisfactory, work on the inside using a scraper with a rounded end (Fig. 13-8J). If the whole width of the tool rest will not go inside the bowl, turn a corner in (Fig. 13-8K). A scraper must be supported fairly close to its edge or it may vibrate and cause chatter marks on the surface.

From time to time check the thickness of the bowl with calipers (Fig. 13-8L). The minimum thickness depends on the wood, but a very thin bowl is liable to warp, crack, or break. Round the rim carefully with light scraper cuts and sand the whole bowl. When the bowl is taken off the faceplate any screw holes may be plugged, but a good finish for a bowl is to glue a disc of cloth under it; this will also hide the screw holes.

If the underside of a bowl has to be turned as well as the top, the work is done in two stages. The wood, cut to a circle, is mounted with the base outwards using screws into the waste wood inside the bowl (Fig. 13-9A). The base is turned and much of the outside can be shaped (Fig. 13-9B). When this has been completed, it is removed from the faceplate and a piece of scrap wood turned to make a pad to fit into the bottom of the bowl (Fig. 13-9C). The pad is attached with glued paper or screws (Fig. 13-9D) and the hollow, rim and the rest of the outside are turned in the usual way (Fig. 13-9E).

Another type of faceplate turning is a base for a table lamp or candlestick. If there is a recess in the base, it can be made in the same way as described for the bowl in Fig. 13-9. If flat, the base may be screwed directly to the faceplate if it is larger than the faceplate (Fig. 13-10A and B). It can go on a plywood pad if it is smaller. Shaping is done with scraping tools.

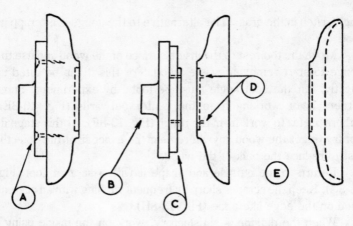

Fig. 13-9. Bottom and top of a bowl can be turned in two stages.

If the work is being done over the lathe bed, a drill can be used to make the hole. Bring the tailstock up so its center makes a dent in the revolving base, then put a chuck and drill in the tailstock and drill the base (Fig. 13-10B). If the hole must be larger than your largest bit, put the tool rest across the wood and use a narrow chisel to cut straight in (Fig. 13-10C) progressively until the hole is the right size. When drilling and chiseling, make sure you cut clear through, but not so far that the tool hits the faceplate.

Another useful device for holding small work that has to be hollowed on the end is a *screw center*. Some types hold a wood screw, but the basic form has a screw projecting from a pad (Fig. 13-10D). The wood to be turned is screwed onto this.

For the early turning, the tailstock center can be brought up and the outside shaped (Fig. 13-10E). Then move the tailstock out of the way and position the tool rest across the end. Scrape away the interior with a gouge, working outward towards the front of the lathe (Fig. 13-10F).

Interesting effects can be obtained by building up wood for turning with many pieces glued together. Modern synthetic resin glues produce strong bonds that will not break during turning or in subsequent use. Several boards of the same wood can be glued together with their grains crossing, then turned into a warp-resistant bowl of unusual appearance (Fig. 13-11A). Woods of different color can be joined together in segments (Fig. 13-11B) and give an unusual effect.

252

Similar ideas can be used for spindle turning. Four pieces can be glued together (Fig. 13-11C) or one color can be glued around another (Fig. 13-11D). When a shaped spindle is turned so the cuts break through the different colors, interesting effects are obtained.

Wood can be polished while rotating in the lathe. Any of the friction polishes can be used (see Chapter 14), but it is usually best to apply a brush coat to seal the grain first. Leave the waste parts that connect to the lathe attached to work that will be polished this way, so it can be taken out and replaced. The actual polishing is done with the wax or other polish on a cloth held against the wood while it is

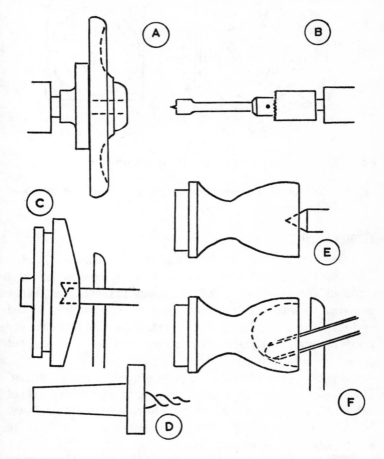

Fig. 13-10. Drilling can be done in a lathe with a drill or chisel. Small items can be mounted on a screw center.

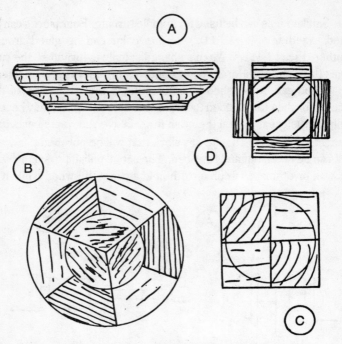

Fig. 13-11. Laminated wood gives beautiful effects when turned.

turning. Be gentle: excess pressure may take off the polish or heat-mark the work.

WOOD CARVING

There are many types of wood carving. The simplest is whittling, which many workers do with a knife while the wood is held in the hand. With some artistic skill it is possible to fashion many things from small pieces of wood this way. Whittling can certainly be applied to the smallest pieces of salvaged wood. Softer and less splintery woods are preferred. Hardwoods may make attractive objects, but the work can be laborious.

A pocket knife with a curved point is good for most whittling. The edge of the blade does normal cutting, the curved end will get into restricted places, and the point can be rotated to make hollows. Sets with interchangeable blades are available that give a variety of knives, saws, and other tool blades.

The skill needed for whittling is mainly artistic. The practical part is mainly patience and care. The knife must be kept sharp: it will do better work than a blunt blade and will be safer as it requires less force. An appreciation of the behavior of grain when cut will help to avoid spoiled work. A cut across the grain is unlikely to go wrong, but a cut along the grain may develop into a split. Sometimes a cut will try to go deeper than you intend; sometimes it will tend to pull towards the surface. The grain lines may give a clue as to what to expect, but a light preliminary cut is advisable to sense how a cut will go.

A cut may be stopped by a first cut across the grain (Fig. 13-12A). If you are working into a hollow, cut into the middle first and taper each side of it (Fig. 13-12B). If it is a deep hollow, taper as deep as the first cross-grain cut, then cut cross-grain again and repeat the tapering.

If you are working all around a stick, a pencil guide line can be drawn using a piece of wrapped paper (Fig. 13-12C). This line is cut in and whittling cuts are made towards it (Fig. 13-12D). The same idea can be used to make a spiral: draw it freehand or along a wrapped string. Cut the spiral straight in, then taper each side of it (Fig. 13-12E).

ROUTER CARVING

A traditional carver did almost everything with gouges and chisels and a mallet. This often meant a lot of labor just to remove surplus wood before getting down to the more artistic work. With modern machine tools it is possible to remove scrap wood safely and accurately with little effort. One of the more useful machine tools for this purpose is a router. With suitable cutters it can go into hollows, leaving little to be removed with carving tools. It is not considered good practice to leave an obviously routed surface adjoining surfaces cut with gouges, but the router can be taken almost to the intended surface, with just enough tool cutting to follow to give an overall tooled effect.

One type of routing gives an effect sufficiently close to carving to be accepted as such for things like name boards. Driftwood and weathered salvaged boards can be made into effective routed signs.

A cutter with a rounded end (Fig. 13-13A) is used freehand or with a special guide. The guide controls the cutter to get precise lines, but freehand control following penciled lines will produce accurate work with the handmade touch. Freehand work also allows

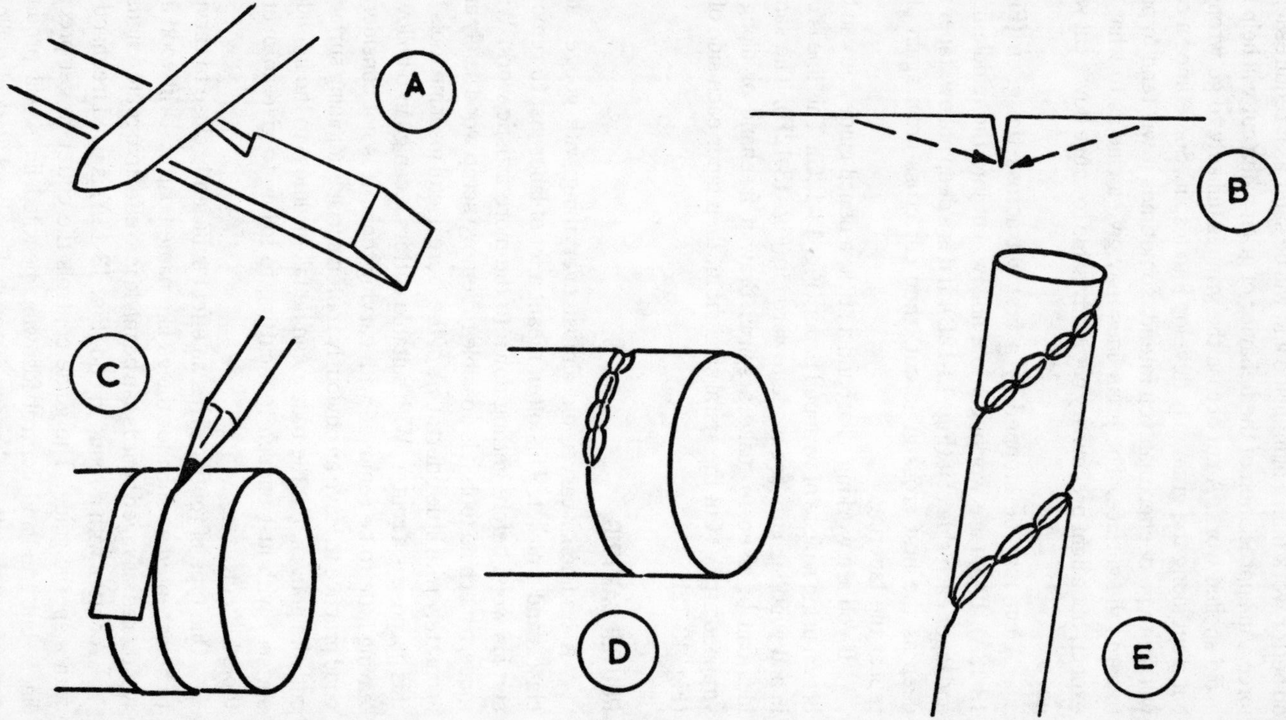

Fig. 13-12. Knife whittling is the simplest type of carving.

letters to be of different sizes and the addition of flourishes (Fig. 13-13B).

With reasonably deep cutting, light and shade may be sufficient to make the name show up, or the cuts can be painted to make them more prominent. This can be done without too much care about paint going over the edges; when the paint has dried, the surplus on the surface can be scraped or sanded off. The whole board should be protected with several coats of exterior varnish, including the back, even if it is to be fixed flat against a wall. This protects the wood from water and consequent warping.

TRADITIONAL CARVING

An oldtime carver had a range of tools that could run to more than one hundred—and he used them all. Modern suppliers have reduced the range considerably, but it is still possible to assemble a carving kit half that size. Fortunately, it is possible to do much interesting carving with just a few tools.

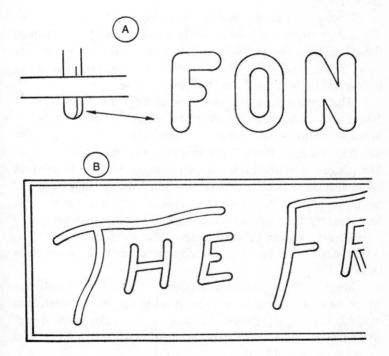

Fig. 13-13. Name boards and signs can be worked with a router.

Most carving tools are gouges. They are sharpened on the outside, although some carvers favor rubbing a slight bevel on the inside. In any case, a carver frequently sharpens his tools; slips in several sizes are needed to rub off the wire edge inside gouges resulting from outside sharpening.

Gouges are made in many widths and with many *sweeps* (the amount of curve, from near flat to quite deep, as in Fig. 13-14A). It is this variety that accounts for the large range of tools. The favored handle is barrel-shaped (Fig. 13-14B). It is possible to use ordinary chisels, but a carver also has some in various widths sharpened on the skew and beveled on both sides (Fig. 13-14C), like lighter versions of turning chisels.

One of your first carving tools should be a V tool (Fig. 13-14D), which is like a double chisel, and is used for making grooves for outlines, veins of leaves, light lettering, and similar operations. There are several angles and widths, but a 1/4-inch in any angle will do at first.

Most tools can be obtained bent (Fig. 13-14E). The curve allows them to get into hollows where a straight tool would catch on the edge. It is also possible to get spoon-shaped versions (Fig. 13-14F) of several tools. Many old patterns are no longer made, so old carving tools in good condition are valuable.

What tools to get depends on what carving is to be done. A "short" kit—including a selection that the maker regards as meeting average carving requirements—is a good start; other tools can be added as you need them. A reasonable selection contains three or four gouges in widths from 1/2 inch down to 1/8 inch in different sweeps. Besides the V tool there may be a 1/4-inch skew chisel and perhaps a 1/4-inch bent gouge. A spooned shallow gouge is useful for backgrounds. A narrow deep gouge may be called a *veiner*, from its use for cutting veins in carved leaves, but it has many other uses. A total of not more than ten tools will allow a variety of carving to be tackled.

Much carving involves pushing the tool by hand, but sometimes—if more force is needed—it is hit with a mallet. Any available mallet can be used, but most carvers like a round one, which may be made from two pieces or turned from a solid piece of heavy wood (Fig. 13-14G).

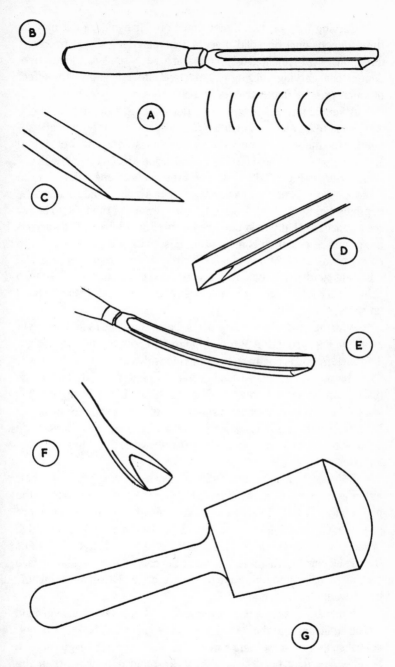

Fig. 13-14. Carving tools are many shapes. A carving mallet is round.

Carving may be two-dimensional on flat panels, or it may be three-dimensional on solid objects that may be viewed from any direction. Tool handling techniques are very similar. Clever two-dimensional carving utilizing perspective effects can give the effect of much greater depth than is actually present.

A simple introductory project is to outline a picture on wood. Any wood to be carved should be firmly secured, for both hands are needed for the work. Clamp the wood in a vise or to the bench top. Draw the picture in bold outline on the wood and go over it with a V tool or veiner (Fig. 13-15A). Control the cut with one hand over the blade, push the handle by hand or hit it with a mallet, and regulate the depth by tilting the tool. Do not let the corners of the tool go below the surface, as that would tear the fibers (Fig. 13-15B). Cuts across the grain are easier to control than those with the grain. Deal with cross-grain cuts first and blend with-the-grain cuts into them. The resulting picture may be left as it is or its grooves may be filled with paint, as a routed sign. Paint or stain of different colors can be used on the spaces between the cuts.

A further step is to outline parts that will remain raised, then cut away the background. A V tool or gouge is taken around the design. The background is cut away by chopping with a gouge (Fig. 13-15C). The characteristic carved background is generally flat, but gouge marks can be seen all over it (Fig. 13-15D). If the background is lowered with a router, enough should be left for the whole surface to be tooled with a shallow-sweep gouge. A deep sweep is more suitable for cutting away waste; a shallow sweep gives better finishing cuts.

For strength in all grain directions, slope the edge of a cut, either as it comes from the V tool (Fig. 13-15E) or rounded from the gouge (Fig. 13-15F). However, the raised design will be more prominent if the edges are not sloped , and even more so if the edge is undercut (Fig. 13-15G). This accentuates perspective and makes the raised part look higher. Undercutting can be used behind surface carving to make something like the curled edge of a leaf seem higher, but it weakens the edge.

For many pieces a flat raised surface and cutaway background will be sufficient, but the raised part can be carved. A badge, symbol, animal shape, or something similar that does not need high relief to be effective may be drawn, the background cut away, then the

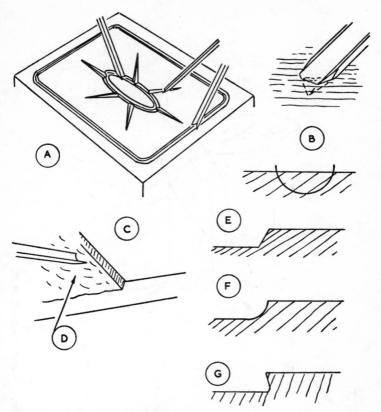

Fig. 13-15. Surface carving is outlined with a V tool and the background cut away with a gouge.

surface shaped with gouges and chisels (Fig. 13-16A). The whole raised surface should be tooled, and none of the original flat surface should show plane marks. Outer curves can be chiseled and hollows worked with gouges, although some carvers prefer a wide shallow gouge to a chisel for outer curves.

The effect of two-dimensional carving comes from parts appearing higher above each other or the background than they actually are. A cross-section should show different levels; some of them can slope to apparently go under other parts. This is often done with leaves, with undulating surfaces and an undercut to a sloping surface as one leaf goes behind another (Fig. 13-16B).

Carving of this type in hard wood is usually left as finished by the tools, without the use of abrasive. Sometimes a part may be sanded

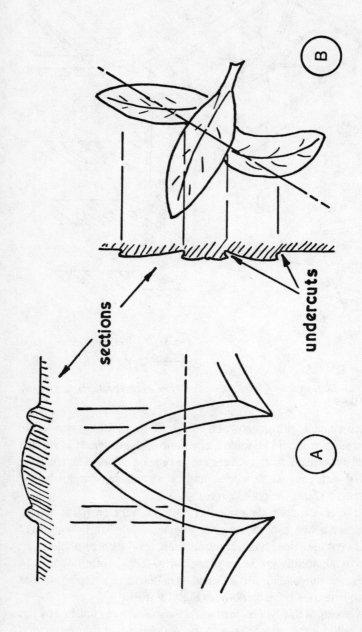

sections

undercuts

Fig. 13-16. Carving techniques give the appearance of greater relief than actually exists.

to contrast adjoining tooled work, as with a coat of arms where the supporting animals are left tooled, but the shield is smoothed so it can be painted.

Carving in the round—three-dimensional carving—depends on visualizing effects of cuts and shapes more than work on flat wood does. Some stylized shapes are not difficult for anyone to do, but to get satisfactory human or animal shapes requires artistic ability that not all of us have. Drawings and designs can provide guidance to a certain extent. A piece of driftwood or a fallen tree branch may suggest a figure, but usually a three-dimensional carving starts as a square piece of wood.

It is helpful to cut an outline one way (Fig. 13-17A) after marking the shape on a surface. If a bandsaw is used the cut will be straight across, but if hand tools are used, mark the design on the opposite surface as well as a guide. With that shape made, draw the design perpendicular to the first cuts. If the waste wood from the first cut came away in one piece, it may be possible to draw the

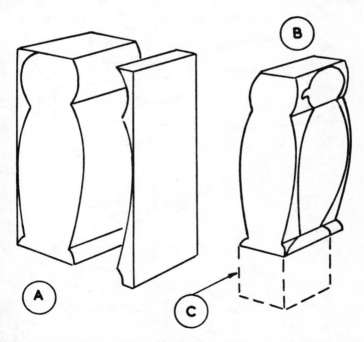

Fig. 13-17. Solid carving is started by getting the shape correct in two dimensions at first.

outline on the flat surface and hold that in position while cutting the other way. Otherwise, marking has to be on the curved surfaces (Fig. 13-17B).

For three-dimensional work it is helpful to leave spare wood that can be clamped in a vise or to a bench (Fig. 13-17C). This is kept on the job as long as possible. It is convenient to be able to move the wood as you work on it: special *carvers' screws* are available that hold a piece of wood to another in a way that allows it to be turned and locked at any position. However, for most carving of salvaged wood, a vise and clamps will be sufficient. Special holding devices are more appropriate for large work.

When the outline has been cut in two directions, the rest of the work is converting the squared sections to curves. Details have to be added, working more by eye than by design. As with flat relief carving, none of the squared shaping should be left on the finished work. Turn the work around and look at it from all directions. As conversion from square section to rounded shape proceeds, there will be high spots to remove; some of these will be obvious only when looked at from several angles, and sometimes from a distance.

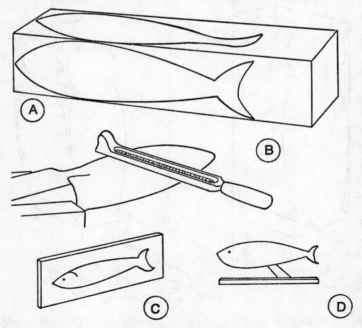

Fig. 13-18. Smooth shapes can be worked with a Surform tool.

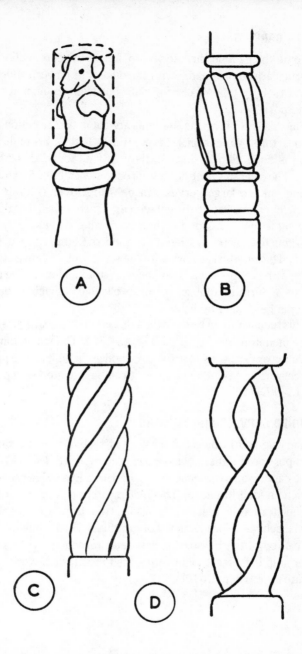

Fig. 13-19. There are some pieces in which carving and turning can be combined.

SMOOTH CARVING

Some things lend themselves to a smooth reproduction. Fish are particularly appropriate. With the advent of power sanders and Surform tools, a type of carving different from traditional carving became possible.

For this sort of carving, outlines are cut in two directions as for traditional three-dimensional carving (Fig. 13-18A). From that point shaping is done with Surform tools with flat, rounded, or tubular blades. They can be used in any direction with little fear of grain breaking out, so large curves can be swept over (Fig. 13-18B). Sharp hollows may have to be cut with a gouge or chisel, but this type of carving is most effective with large flowing curves.

When the shape has been roughed out, the surface can be smoothed by lengthwise work with the same tools, followed by hand sanding with progressively finer paper. A disc sander may be used in place of a Surform tool for some preliminary shaping, but final sanding is best done by hand.

This technique can be used for a three-dimensional figure or half a figure mounted on a flat board (Fig. 13-18C). The whole thing may be polished or varnished to show the wood grain, or it can be painted. If the carving is three-dimensional, it can be mounted on a pedestal (Fig. 13-18D).

COMBINED CARVING AND TURNING

Carving and turning can be very attractive in combination. A turned post or upright may have a carved top (Fig. 13-19A). There may be carving on a turned leg (Fig. 13-19B). Examples can be seen on much antique furniture. The Indian totem pole offers ideas for combined turning and carving. So-called twist turning can be done by special machines in production work, but individual items have to be hand carved after the spindle has been turned (Fig. 13-19C). A further step is to carve right through so the finished work has two separate *bines* (Fig. 13-19D).

266

Chapter 14
Finishing

The term "finishing" includes all ways of smoothing wood and treating its surface. A few woods can be left untreated; their natural oils and resins will provide protection and beauty, but these woods are unlikely to be found in crates and other salvaged items. Some of the resinous softwoods have enough natural resistance to weather to be used without treatment, but although they may be durable, their appearance suffers on exposure. Some form of finish will prevent this.

The finish to use on something made from salvaged wood depends on the type of wood and its condition. If the wood is coarse-grained it would be very difficult, if not impossible, to prepare its surface to take a polished finish. Wood which is comparatively rough after attempts to smooth it needs a finish of the type that builds up a coating to hide the wood. This usually means paint.

The choice of finish is also related to use. If it is a piece of furniture that has to stand by other polished furniture, it would not look right if it were painted; it needs a polished finish or one that looks polished. If the wood is used for outdoor carpentry, protection against the weather is more important then appearance; a polished treatment would be inappropriate, even if the wood were suitable. There are some finishes that will not stand up to water, alcohol and other liquids, so they should not be used for table tops used for food and drink. Some finishes are unsuitable for surfaces used for the preparation of food.

The first step in finishing is preparation of the wood surfaces. This has been mentioned in earlier chapters, but for the finest possible finish, the wood has to be prepared in the following way:

1. The surface is planed as smooth as possible. It is usually advisable to follow machine planing with hand planing. Plane finally in the direction that disturbs the grain least.

2. If the piece is hardwood or very cross-grained softwood, planing may be followed by scraping, paying particular attention to any places that tore up under the plane.

3. Sanding follows, working progressively down through grits to the finest that suits the wood. The harder woods can have finer finishing grits than softer woods. Early stages may be by power or by hand, but final stages are usually best by hand with the paper on a block. If it is a very fibrous wood, it can be wetted and allowed to dry before final sanding. This will lift any fibers that have bent under earlier sanding.

FILLING CRACKS, HOLES, AND OPEN GRAIN

Some wood has such an open grain that the result of direct application of a finish would be unsatisfactory, even after many coats. This applies to both clear finishes that show the wood grain and opaque finishes that hide it. This applies to any open-grained wood, even when there are no flaws or evidence of past use to hide, as there very well may be with salvaged wood.

The compound used to fill holes, cracks, and open grain depends on the finish that is to follow. If it will be transparent, the filler should be as inconspicuous as possible. If an opaque paint is to be used, the color and appearance does not matter, as long as the surface is flat. There is also the question of compatibility. Some synthetic finishes will react adversely when applied over certain fillers. The makers of many modern finishes usually include advice on this, either on the can or in their instructional matter, so decide on the finish before doing any filling.

At one time fillers were made up as needed, but there are better and more convenient fillers which can be bought. Plaster mixed with linseed oil was used (thinned glazier's putty), but it has drying and compatibility problems, so it is better to buy something that matches the intended finish. Grain filler is usually a paste which is applied with a cloth and rubbed in all directions so some of it becomes embedded in gaps in the grain. An excess may be applied and allowed to dry, then the surplus sanded off, but not so violently as to pick up filling from the grain. Fillers can be bought in colors to match certain woods. Other fillers have little color, but will absorb finish and be colored by it. Liquid fillers are intended for woods that are more close-grained, but which tend to absorb finishes unevenly. They bring the more porous parts to about the same condition as the rest.

Fillers for holes and cracks are also pastes, but are thicker than those for grain. Several are like putty, but do not contract as they dry. Plastic wood, wood putty and similar fillers are pressed into hollows with a knife or screwdriver and left to set—usually with a little standing above the surface—then sanded level. Holes and cracks are usually filled before grain. Some hole fillers for use with paint are not applied until after the first coat of paint. Not every wood needs filling, and some finishes provide sufficient filling in and of themselves.

Not strictly filling, but a similar problem, is the treatment of knots in some resinous softwoods. If nothing is done to them under paint, resin will rise and disfigure the paint film. Shellac brushed on provides a quick-drying barrier to the resin. Details of shellac finishes are given later.

There is a limit to the space that can be filled with hole filler. There are flexible fillers that will allow for expansion and contraction of the wood, but this may affect the level that is to be finished. If the hole is clear through, as there might be in salvaged wood where a bolt has been withdrawn, it may be plugged with a piece of dowel rod or a roughly-shaped piece of wood to within a short distance of the surface, then this covered with filler (Fig. 14-1A). It may be better to make a cross-grained wooden plug, so its grain is in the same direction as that surrounding it. It is not good to plug the hole to the surface with a dowel, as its end grain would show through a clear finish and, even with paint, its different absorption would affect the paint surface.

If a plug cutter is available, round cross-grained plugs can be made from the same wood as the work; the result should be inconspicuous. If the plug has to be made by hand, it is better to cut it square or diamond shaped than to try to cut a circle by hand. Make the straight cuts diagonal to the grain (Fig. 14-1B). This plug need not be very deep and may be backed by a dowel. Giving the sides of the plug a slight taper ensures a close fit (Fig. 14-1C). Make a plug before its hole, then draw around its narrower end, so the plug will fit tight and can be planed off. Use glue in any wood plugging.

If you have a piece of wood with good appearance except for a small flaw—such as might occur in dismantling a crate—it is possible to make a diamond-shaped plug to disguise the damage. There is no need to make it very deep (Fig. 14-1D).

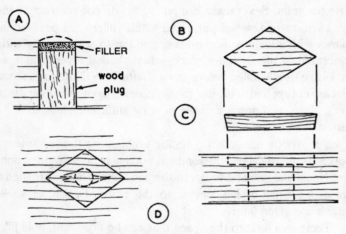

Fig. 14-1. Plugs can be fitted over flaws in wood.

Glue-and-sawdust mixtures are stronger than most fillers, and are useful where strength is an advantage. Using sawdust from the wood being filled, mix enough to make a thick paste with the glue. Fill the hole above the surface and sand level later. Glue without sawdust crazes, so it does not provide strength or a good surface to finish. Glue-and-sawdust mixture does not absorb as much finish as the surrounding wood. This does not matter with a paint finish, but you may need several coats of clear finish to get an even surface.

Painting

Since salvaging yields a variety of woods, there may be several different kinds of wood in some things you make. Usually such an item has to be painted to get an even finish. The alternative is matching wood colors by staining or bleaching.

Paints today are very different from those of not so long ago. Most ingredients are synthetic. These impart qualitites superior to those obtained with natural ingredients, but they also require different techniques of application. It is important to follow the makers' instructions and forget anything applicable to natural paints.

Modern paints do all that is necessary with a smaller variety of paints than used to be needed. In some cases one paint can be used for all coats, but it is more usual to have two or three stages. The first coat on bare or filled wood—the primer—has to enter the grain and grip it. It does not have to penetrate much, but it needs to be sufficiently liquid to soak in. It need not be the same color as the final coat, just grip the wood and provide a base for later coats.

The next coat is an undercoat paint, which is matte and is close in color to the top coat, but usually not exactly the same. Two undercoats may have to be applied. The top coat is usually glossy; only one coat should be used. This means that the one or two undercoats must provide a smooth even surface for it. It is usually better to use more undercoats than to use two gloss coats, as they may not dry evenly over each other.

Paint may be sprayed. This has advantages for large areas and multiple articles, but for single items of moderate size, setting up equipment and cleaning it afterwards is more trouble than it's worth. In any case, the first coat should always be brushed, as this ensures a better grip on the wood.

Brushes should be of as good a quality as you can afford. A cheap brush may not give good results, however carefully it is used. A thick wad of flexible bristles is necessary. Brushes are classed according to their widths in inches. Clean a brush in thinner and by washing with detergent after use. If a hole is drilled through its handle, it can be hung in a jar overnight (Fig. 14-2A). Water can be used to keep air from the bristles for a short period, but it is better to use a thinner. If paint is too thick to brush properly, it can be thinned, but be very sparing with thinners. A small amount stirred in can have considerable effect, and if you over-thin there is nothing you can do except get more paint.

Some modern paints do not need stirring. Check the instructions: some types become less effective if stirred. If paint has a thick sediment under a liquid, it must be stirred thoroughly until its consistency is smooth. A stirrer driven by an electric drill can be used, but stirring with a stick can be effective.

Wood should normally be painted with the grain; this makes brush marks that do not flow out less obvious. Otherwise, brush lengthwise on the work. If there is a choice, on a vertical surface brush up and down; this is less likely to cause excess paint to run into "curtains". Modern paints dry fairly quickly. This reduces the risk of blemishes on the surface, but it means you have to work fairly quickly: overlapping strokes must overlap wet, not dry, paint for a smooth finish.

At one time paint was applied fairly liberally and brushed out in several directions before brushing in the final direction. This ensures a good spread of paint and reduces the risk of curtains, but with many modern paints it is not advised. These paints must be applied with a minimum of brushing, so they are usually brushed only with the grain. Too much brushing may cause the surface to lift and not dry evenly. To avoid marks where new paint adjoins old, brush towards the earlier paint, lifting the brush as it passes over the old edge (Fig. 14-2B).

Where edges or frames have to be painted as well as panels, it is easier to do all the narrow parts first; then any runover onto the panel can be smoothed out with the panel coat (Fig. 14-2C). Edges should be painted before surfaces, but limit spillover onto the surfaces and taper the paint edges by brushing before they harden, as it may be some time before the piece is completely painted.

Old painted wood in good condition may be painted over. If it is dirty, wash it with detergent, rinse, and allow to dry. If any gloss remains, rub it off with sandpaper or a domestic scouring powder. Remove all abrasive dust before painting. It is unlikely that any new paint will react with old hard paint.

If old paint is present but not in good enough condition to paint over, it may be removed with a chemical paint stripper. Follow the maker's instructions, particularly regarding neutralizing afterwards. Beware of any tar-like substances used on crates for marking numbers and other information. This will probably find its way through any paint put over it, so it should be removed with stripper or solvent, or covered with one of the special metallic paints that act as a barrier.

If two or more colors are to be used and they will adjoin, it is usual to put the lighter color on first; then any that goes over the meeting line is more easily covered. Masking tape may help to get a straight line, but with some paints the tape must not be left until the paint is fully set—dry paint that overlaps the tape may break the line as the tape is removed. Apply the lighter color, letting it taper over the final line. Stick masking tape along the line after this coat has hardened. Put on the other coat, letting the brush overlap the edge of the masking tape. When that coat has dried hard enough, peel off the masking tape.

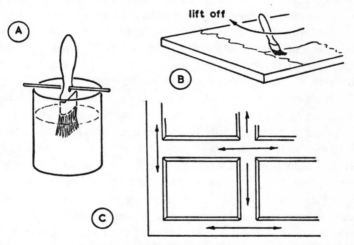

Fig. 14-2. Paint brushes have to be stored so the bristles do not harden or bend. Painting must be done systematically.

Although prepared paints have fairly consistent colors, make sure you have enough for a job before starting painting. A second can may be a slightly different shade. If you are using paint from two cans, mix them before starting. Do not thin paint after you have started using it: this will affect color. If you add thinners, make sure the can is thoroughly mixed, or you may get uneven color rendering.

STAINING

The natural color of many woods is quite attractive and there is no need to alter it. The appearance of others is improved by staining. If something is made of mixed woods, staining may be necessary to get an even final appearance. If a piece of furniture is to be used alongside something of a different shade, it can be stained to match. Staining can make an inferior wood resemble a better one, but the grain will give it away to anyone familiar with woods. However, with mixed woods this will have to be accepted.

Staining makes wood darker. There is no satisfactory stain that will produce results lighter in color than the original wood. It is not usual to alter the basic color of a particular wood—a brown wood may be made a deeper brown, a reddish wood may be made more red. Unless there is a particular need for it, it is undesirable to alter the tone of a piece of wood drastically. Apart from aesthetic reasons, one color over another may not produce the expected result.

It is normally inadvisable to try to lighten the color of wood, but it can be done by bleaching with laundry bleach. This may be needed on crate wood that has become discolored in use, following with stain to match the bleached and surrounding wood.

Stain contains a dye which changes the color of wood without obscuring its grain. Stain is not a final treatment; it must be followed by a clear protective finish. The stains most useful for the type of work this book is about are either water- or oil-based. Spirit stains are based on alcohol. They are quick-drying, but difficult to apply evenly, and are mainly of use in touching up existing finishes.

Water stain is usually bought as a powder. It can be mixed with water in various strengths and can be applied by brush or by wiping on with a cloth. Oil stains are bought as liquids and are brushed on. Their penetration is greater than water stains. Both dry evenly. It is possible to adjust the color to a certain extent by wiping with a cloth before the stain has dried, so as to remove some from the surface. Some furniture is shaded, e.g., the centers of panels are lighter than the border. This is accomplished by wiping before the stain has dried.

Varnish stains are varnishes colored by stain. They allow color to be applied at the same time as a gloss finish, thereby eliminating one coat. The snag is that the stain color is in the finish and not in the grain of the wood: as the finish wears off in use, so does the color. If a quick finish is essential or the article being made is not very important, varnish stain has possibilities, but for the best results it is always advisable to stain as one stage and apply a gloss coat as another.

VARNISH

Varnish is the clear finish of choice for many wooden items. Varnish may be regarded as uncolored paint. There is some with almost no color ("clear" varnish), but most has a slightly yellow or golden tinge that enhances most woods.

At one time varnishes were made with natural lacs and resins and several versions of most brands were available. Modern synthetic ingredients make a more versatile varnish, so fewer versions are needed: varnishes, for example, are suitable for indoor or outdoor use. The toughest varnish is often called boat or spar varnish, but it is suitable for many purposes besides those its name implies.

Most natural varnishes needed special precautions in application. Synthetic varnishes are easier to use, but they still benefit from observing some of the precautions needed with earlier types.

Varnish does not flow well if it is cold. It should be satisfactory in normal room temperatures, but if there is any doubt, stand the can of varnish in a bowl of warm water and make sure the work surface is not cold. Varnish should not be stirred: this introduces air bubbles that cause small marks on the surface.

Varnish does not give a good finish in damp conditions. Do not varnish outdoors when there is a risk of rain and during very humid conditions. Outdoor work should be varnished early in the day; varnish applied later may suffer from night dew. Dampness leaves varnish cloudy and uneven, and may prevent it from ever setting hard.

Older varnishes took up to a day to dry so it was necessary to protect them from dust for a long time. Most modern varnishes are quick-setting. Some are described as "four-hour" varnishes: they are dust-free in about an hour and fully hard in the specified time. Varnish away from drafts and dust. If dust gets on wet varnish, do not try to brush it out of a partly set coat. When the coat is hard, sand it out. If an insect lands on the wet varnish, leave it. There will be surprisingly little marking when it is pulled off the hard finish.

The best paint brushes are often called varnish brushes. This does not mean they are unsuitable for other finishes, but it shows that varnish benefits from the use of the best brushes. Varnish can be used direct from the can. There is no need for a special primer or undercoat, and the same varnish is used for all coats. Some manufacturers advise thinning the first coat to ensure good penetration and grip on the wood.

Also check the instructions about subsequent coats. Some varnishes require that each coat be allowed to harden fully; then they are lightly sanded before the next coat is brushed on. Some makers say the next coat can go directly on the previous one providing it is applied between specified minimum and maximum drying times. Only if the maximum time is exceeded is sanding necessary.

How many coats to apply depends on several factors. Softwoods may absorb two or three coats before an even finish is obtained. The first coat soaks in, and the second coat—even on hardwood—may be uneven. The third coat provides a finish that's acceptable for many purposes, but more coats can be used. Some traditional varnishwork—on coaches and similar things—used as many as twenty coats, with intermediate coats carefully rubbed down with abrasive.

Some varnish makers say their product should be flowed on, meaning it should be put on with minimum brushing. This is not always easy to achieve. Avoid vigorous brushing, which causes air bubbles and disturbance in the varnish so it does not dry evenly. Use only the lower half of the bristles and wipe the brush on the edge of the can or a wire stretched across it. Use only enough strokes to spread the varnish and make final strokes in line with the grain. When working toward an area you've already covered, lift the brush as it goes over the previous work. Thin varnish flows better and is less likely to give trouble than thick varnish. Spread the varnish evenly so as to avoid curtains. If a curtain occurs in semi-dry varnish, don't attempt to fix it at that stage or more damage will be done to the surface. Let it dry, sand it level, then varnish over it.

As far as possible, varnish on horizontal surfaces. If it is a boxlike shape, turn it to bring the work surface to the top if possible. As with painting, deal with narrow border parts before varnishing large areas. Watch for excess varnish over angles and corners—brush it out before it starts to harden. If you must work on vertical surfaces, work up and down if possible, starting at the top.

SHELLAC

At one time shellac had many uses, but modern finishes give better results for most purposes. However, it is a convenient standby still. Shellac is a *lac*—a resinous excretion of the lac insect—that comes in flakes which will dissolve in denatured alcohol. It can be bought already dissolved in various "cuts," or strengths. A strong mixture can be diluted with alcohol. Keep any stock tightly stoppered, as alcohol evaporates rapidly. Have alcohol available for cleaning brushes.

The use of shellac over resinous knots has been mentioned. It dries in a few minutes and keeps resin from coming through to the paint.

Shellac can be used as a primer or undercoat before paint. It is a good first coat on Masonite or other hardboard, to be followed by paint. As a finish in itself it can be regarded as a quick-drying varnish; it is possible to apply several coats during a day. However, it is difficult to get an even finish over a large area. It is better to use shellac for small items, such as whittled figures, souvenir articles and small decorative items. Shellac can also be used over poster paints or other colors that need protection.

Shellac does not have the resistance to liquids and heat that modern finishes have, and this is one reason why it is used infrequently today. Shellac is a good electrical insulator, so it can be used on wood that is in contact with low voltage electricity, as in a battery-driven model railroad.

The traditonal use of shellac was in French-polishing furniture. Much furniture, particularly dating from the turn of this century, has a French-polish finish, which has a very smooth high gloss. It is no more immune to damage from damp and heat than brushed shellac, but much old furniture has retained a good finish for a very long time.

OIL AND WAX

Much very old furniture has a sheen that would be impossible to achieve with any quickly applied liquid polish. In most cases the wood was rubbed with linseed or other oil at long intervals and may have been revived occasionally with wax polish. Neither substance produces much of a gloss, but there is a sort of satin sheen that gives character to certain woods. Hard oak and similar woods with open grain respond best to this treatment.

Linseed oil can be used alone on these woods. It is rubbed into the grain with a cloth and allowed some time to dry. More oil is applied and the whole surface rubbed with coarse cloth, such as burlap. This may be spread over several weeks and followed by more treatment at monthly intervals, so the process is quite lengthy. If you tackle reproduction work or repairing old furniture finished this way, this is the authentic method; otherwise, it is not a finishing method to choose.

There are many waxes, among them beeswax, paraffin wax, and—the hardest—carnauba wax. Wax polishes are blends of waxes and oil. It is unusual to mix these polishes yourself; they are usually bought ready for use. If you're working from bare wood, wax is used similarly to oil, with rubbing and burnishing at long intervals, but today the more common use of wax polish is in reviving the shine on furniture originally polished by another method.

One way of obtaining a quicker wax polish is to varnish or shellac the wood with enough coats to make a basic polish over the wood surface; rub this smooth with fine abrasive paper, then wax and polish over that. Wax is rubbed on with one cloth and polished with another many times to build up the characteristic wax patina. The method avoids the very long intervals that are required if you start with wax on bare wood.

A few woods are considered to have enough character not to require special finishes. The natural oil in others may not accept most finishes. Teak is an example. It is very durable and has a natural resistance to attack by the weather and water. A special teak oil can be bought for reviving its appearance.

LACQUER

Much quantity-produced furniture is finished with lacquer. This is a quick-drying, high-gloss finish based on cellulose or a synthetic material with similar characteristics. Normally application is by spraying. There are brushing lacquers that are similar to varnish, but a good furniture finish can only be obtained with spray. Drying is quite quick and several coats can be applied at short intervals. The finish is hard and immune to many things that would attack other finishes.

As spray equipment is needed, it is unlikely that anyone making individual items would find the technique worthwhile, particularly with the type of products that are usually made from salvaged wood.

PRESERVATIVES

Exterior grades of paint and varnish do much to prevent the entry of water into wood, but if water does get below a paint or varnish film and remains stagnant there, the condition encourages rot. Some woods have a strong natural resistance to rot, but many woods require impregnation with a preservative if they are to survive long in damp conditions.

Tar and creosote are well-known preservatives. In commercial treatment these are forced in under pressure. Applying with a brush may have some effect, but not nearly as much as forced injection. Penetration is much better along the grain than across it, so a post may be stood in a bucket of creosote for some time and allowed to soak it up.

Tar, creosote and bitumastic products cannot be covered with paint or other finish. For much exterior woodwork, a brown preservative finish is acceptable and nothing else is needed, but there are other preservatives that are as effective and can be painted over if required. Some are colorless and a transparent green is common. They may be left uncovered or painted once they have dried. Their preserving qualities are at least as good as creosote.

Section 3
Things To Make

The following chapters offer ideas for things to make. As available materials will vary greatly, many projects may have to be altered to suit what has been salvaged. Consequently, using salvaged wood depends more on individual ingenuity than woodworking projects that are made from wood bought for a purpose and to sizes specified in the drawings.

The drawings that follow and those you come across elsewhere should be valued as much for their ideas and general form as for their dimensions. For many items it does not matter if the wood's section is slightly larger or smaller than specified, or if joints are altered to suit. What does matter is overall size, such as the height of a table. So look at these designs in relation to the wood you have and alter sizes and construction to suit.

Note: All sizes on the drawings are in inches unless otherwise indicated.

Chapter 15

Shop Equipment

If the collector of salvaged wood does not already have a fully equipped shop, some of the early projects may be equipment to use in making other things.

BENCH HOOK

One, or preferably two identical bench hooks will be needed for handwork on the bench top. The base (Fig. 15-1A) should be flat and planed parallel in width and thickness. Hardwood will last longer than softwood, but thick plywood can be used. Use 3/4-inch or thicker stock to keep the wood being worked on well clear of the bench. The length should be enough to accomodate the widest board to be worked on.

The crosspieces should be hardwood. One may be cut back to allow a saw to go through the work without damaging the bench (Fig. 15-1B). If you saw with either hand, cut back one end on the left and the other on the right.

It is important that the crosspieces be at right angles to the sides (Fig. 15-1C). Attach each at one end and pivot it against a try square when fastening the other end.

There should not be any exposed metal on the surface for a saw to hit, so screws should not be used. The best joints are glued with three 1/2-inch dowels at each end (Fig. 15-1D). Alternatively, use glue and screws, but counterbore the screw heads so they can be

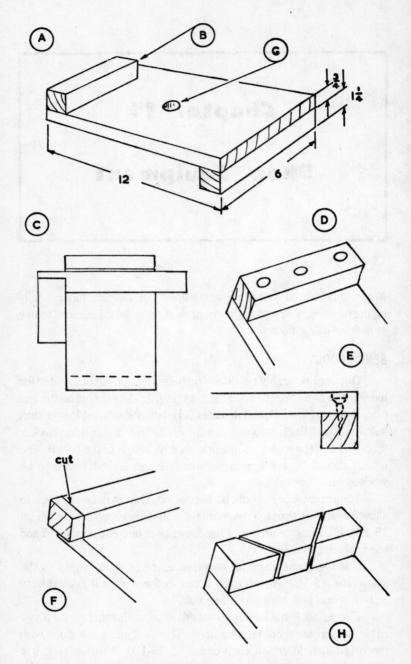

Fig. 15-1. A bench hook is used on the bench top for accurate sawing.

covered with wooden plugs, pieces of dowel rod, or filler (Fig. 15-1E).

True the cut-back end of the crosspieces before attaching. Let the other ends extend past the base, square them after affixing, and saw and plane them true (Fig. 15-1F).

A hole at the center (Fig. 15-1G) allows the bench hook to be hung on a nail on the shop wall or under the end of the bench.

A wide bench hook can have one end piece cut to act as a miter block (Fig. 15-1H). Mark carefully on the finished and glued end with a miter square, including squaring down each side, then carefully saw with the same saw that will be used for making miters.

SHOOTING BOARD

When edges of boards have to be planed true by hand, it helps to have a shooting (shuting) board (Fig. 15-2A). The size shown here suits a jack plane.

The plane base is the important part (Fig. 15-2B). It should be stiff and the top surface flat in all directions. If the board is to be used on the bench against a bench stop, the underside should be true; otherwise there may be a strip (Fig. 15-2C) to grip in the vise.

The top of the wood base (Fig. 15-2D) should come just below the center of the plane to be used on the board. Many boards have the base fixed directly to the plane base, but it is better to raise it so dust and shavings cannot lodge there and interfere with the smooth action of the plane. This can be done with thin plywood or a piece of Masonite (Fig. 15-2E).

Join the parts with glue and screws or dowels from below, so there is no metal on the surface. See that the edge of the base is straight and at right angles to the plane base. If necessary, its top can be planed parallel to the lower base after fixing (Fig. 15-2F).

There is considerable thrust against the stop when planing. It may be sufficient to fix it with glue and dowels in the same way as the bench hook ends, but it will be stronger if it is notched in with a shallow dado joint (Fig. 15-2G). Glue and dowels should still be used. Take care to get the stop at right angles to the planing edge.

An even stronger joint is made by tapering the stop. The edge that takes the thrust remains at right angles to the edge of the wood base, but the other is at a slight taper. The stop is made extra long and driven in before drilling for dowels and cutting to length (Fig. 15-2H).

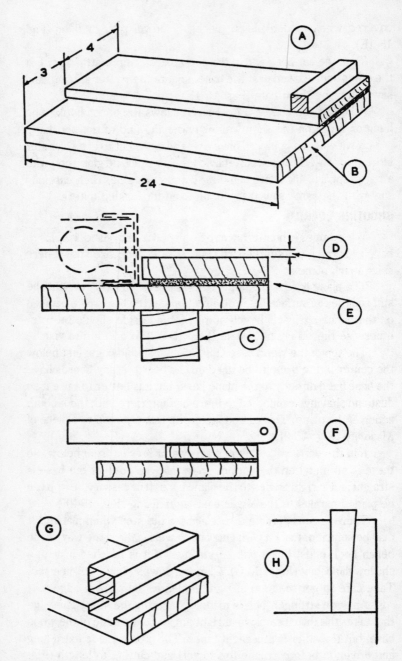

Fig. 15-2. A shooting board is used as a guide for planing straight edges.

TRESTLE

A trestle is needed for hand sawing and many other support purposes. A pair of trestles will support large assemblies at a convenient working height. The top should be stout enough to withstand hammering and sawing without flexing or bouncing. Some trestles have their legs splayed in both directions to put the floor plan outside the area of the top, but this involves difficult joints; it is simpler and nearly as satisfactory to splay one way only.

Make the top true, with squared ends and edges. It doesn't matter if the underside has to be untrue to make use of a particular piece of wood (Fig. 15-3A). Make a drawing of the end view, with a leg in position (Fig. 15-3B) on the floor or on a piece of scrap plywood. This gives the angles to be cut on the legs, each of which notches into the top slightly (Fig. 15-3C). Cut one leg and use it as a pattern for the others, but check angles each time with an adjustable bevel. A power saw will cut square across. If cuts are by hand, mark them on both sides of the wood and saw partly from each side.

Use long screws and glue to attach the legs (Fig. 15-3D). The tops may be slightly overlength, to be leveled after affixing. Use wide crossbars underneath the top (Fig. 15-3E).

It may only be necessary to use one crossbar, on the outside of each pair of legs, or you may use inside pieces as well. Cut them to length after gluing and screwing to the legs. With close-fitting joints and stout wood, there should be no need for further bracing. If necessary you may add lower crossbars (Fig. 15-3F) and a lengthwise brace (Fig. 15-3G).

It is important that a trestle stands level, so test it on a surface known to be true, then adjust as necessary. If a second trestle is made, get its top at the same height, even if the construction materials are of different section.

BENCH

It is important to have a substantial working top that does not vibrate or move in use. The important part is a substantial plank to form the front of the top. Ideally, the entire top should be the same thickness, but if only one suitable board is available, back it with thinner boards, which will act as a tool well (Fig. 15-4A). It is helpful

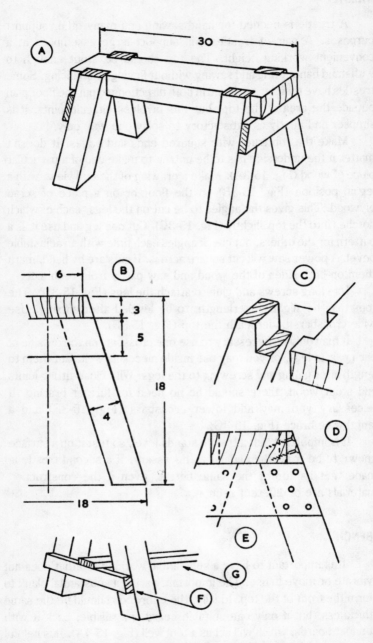

Fig. 15-3. Trestles provide supports for working at knee level.

to brace a bench by attaching it to a wall, but if it has to stand free, blocks on the floor will prevent the legs from sliding.

The important parts of the support are two end frames, which include the legs (Fig. 15-4B). They can be halved, glued and bolted (Fig. 15-4C). Include a diagonal or close the ends with a plywood panel to provide bracing (Fig. 15-4D). The lower rail should be high enough to sweep under. The width of the top is determined by the suitable boards available. An apron at the front stiffens the top (Fig. 15-4E). Join the front to the top, then both to the leg frames with screws, counterbored and plugged. The bench height shown suits hand planing by an average man. If you are exceptionally tall or short, adjust it accordingly.

The most convenient vise for woodworking does not project above the bench top. Its jaws are covered with hardwood, with one piece sunk into the bench front and the other covering the metal of the vise front (Fig. 15-4F). Both are screwed in place so they can be replaced when worn.

The front board should be planed as true as possible. If there is a rail at the back, its top edge should be level with the front board (Fig. 15-4G), so any large work put across the bench is supported level. A crosspiece at the left end of the bench will form a rest for planes so their cutters are kept clear of the bench surface (Fig. 15-4H).

An adjustable bench stop is a valuable piece of bench equipment. This projects through the bench top to plane against. An adjustable metal type can be sunk into a hollow in the bench top, but using a wooden stop removes the risk of hitting metal. The stop shown (Fig. 15-4J) goes through the top and is slotted to go over a coach bolt with a butterfly nut and washer (Fig. 15-4K) in a strip of wood against the leg. Supporting the stop against the leg provides leverage to resist the considerable thrust against the top of the stop. The stop should be a sliding fit through the bench top, so it can be knocked up or down with a mallet when the nut is loosened.

A bench that's open underneath may be advisable if it will have to be moved about, but if it can be kept in one place, it is better boxed in. Besides providing storage space, any framing underneath braces the bench, and the weight of things stored there helps to steady it.

Lengthwise pieces may be notched into the legs, back and front, at the same level as the leg braces (Fig. 15-4L). These will support a platform made up of stout plywood, with intermediate

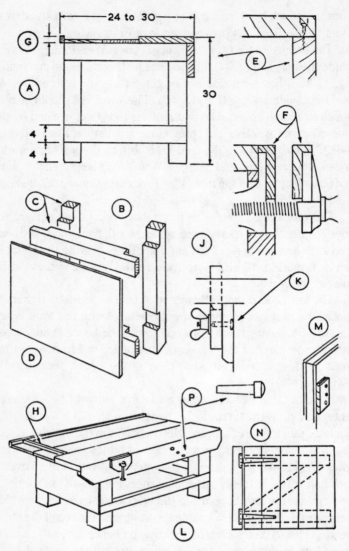

Fig. 15-4. A bench should be substantially made and equipped to allow various processes.

bracing if necessary, or several flat boards. The back is closed with plywood.

Although drawers with fitted compartments for tools may seem attractive, their value should be balanced against the loss of space due to their construction. An open space has much more capacity than one divided into drawers and compartments. It may be better to use boxes that can be lifted out and changed around as storage needs change.

Woodworking activities produce shavings and dust, so if things stored underneath are to be kept clean there should be doors to the storage compartment. How they are made depends on the material available. Framed plywood with panels on both sides is one option (Fig. 15-4M). These are hinged on the legs and overlap the bottom rail, which serves as a stop and a location for catches.

If strip wood is used for the doors, it is possible to make them "ledged and braced," as was often done in the days before plywood (Fig. 15-4N). Place the ledges on the inside face, and put hinge strips down the legs so the hinges can mount on their surface. The brace should slope upward from the lower hinge; it will take the weight of the door in compression and resist any tendency for the door to drop out of shape.

Door or drawer handles should not project forward of the apron so they do not interfere with any wide panel held on edge in the vise. To provide support for long pieces of wood held on edge in the vise, drill holes in the apron at the opposite end for pegs. If a lathe is available, turn pegs with a slight taper and a knob to push into the hole appropriate to the width of board (Fig. 15-4P). Otherwise a piece of wood may be roughly rounded by hand.

If drawers are to be fitted under the bench, they should be made as described later in the furniture projects.

TOOL RACKS

Tools that are frequently used are best racked on the wall above or near the bench. A rack should hold the tool securely, yet allow it to be taken down with a minimum of trouble. There is nothing wrong with a nail for a tool that will hang on a nail, but a more workmanlike rack uses dowels at a slight angle (Fig. 15-5A). If a lathe is available, pegs can be turned (Fig. 15-5B) but otherwise the dowel ends should be rounded. To keep a consistent angle when drilling the back piece for the dowels, rest the wood on an angled piece (Fig. 15-5C) under an electric drill mounted in a stand.

Some tools will hang in U-shaped slots cut in plywood. Angle the plywood up slightly to prevent the tools from falling out, or you may use retaining pieces at the front for some tools (Fig. 15-5D).

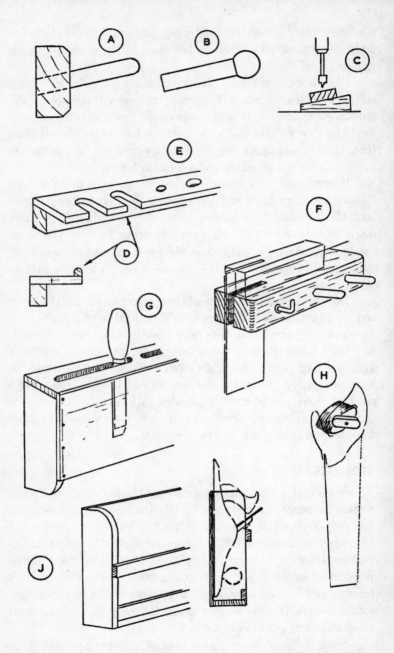

Fig. 15-5. Tools may be stored out of the way, but accessible, on the wall over the bench.

Round tools like screwdrivers may merely drop through holes in a small shelf (Fig. 15-5E).

It will be possible to combine the uses of some racks. A try square can hang with its blade through a slot in a piece drilled for pegs or hooks (Fig. 15-5F).

Edge tools like chisels should have their edges protected. A rack can be divided into slots with a piece of transparant plastic at the front so the edges are covered but visible (Fig. 15-5G).

Saws may hang from pegs, but a shaped block with a turnbutton makes a more positive support (Fig. 15-5H). Planes need their cutting edges protected: the rack in Fig. 15-5J holds several with their edges against a plywood back. Size is governed by the largest plane. Depth back-to-front is enough for the planes' front knobs to pass behind the rail with a little clearance for easy lifting in and out.

Although these racks are shown as units, it is advisable to experiment with the tools to be racked, as many can have combined shelves and supports. The largest rack will probably be for planes; it can have racks for smaller tools on its ends. Other racks can probably be arranged in lines across the wall, using continuous crossbars. Attachments direct to a plywood backboard may not be very secure; crossbars and multiple-use shelves provide better attachment.

TOOL CHEST

At one time a woodworker who moved from job to job carried all the tools of his trade in a large heavy chest. A similar but lighter chest is handy under the bench to hold infrequently used tools and equipment. Construction is of plywood framed with battens, glued and nailed throughout. Size will depend on the intended contents and the material available. The same design can be used for chests for other purposes.

Make the two ends first (Fig. 15-6A), making sure they match. Battens look best if mitered at the corners, but this is not important. As the battens face outwards, plane them to a good finish. The back and front are pieces of plywood which may be slightly oversize at first. Affix battens inside them, tight against the ends (Fig. 15-6B) and plane the plywood to the battens. The bottom is plywood attached to the battens with crossbars added at the ends to lift the bottom clear of the floor (Fig. 15-6C). These strips may incorporate glides or casters if the chest is to be moved much. The handles are

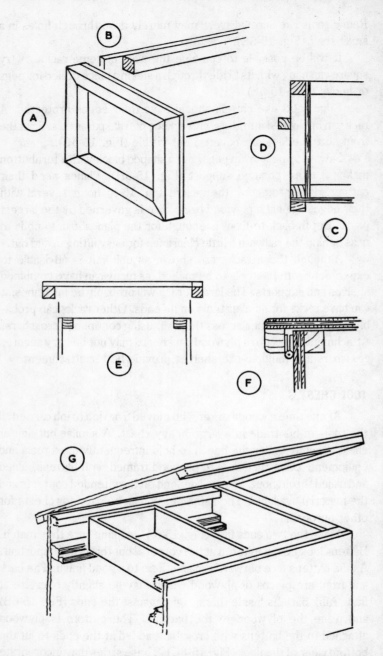

Fig. 15-6. A tool chest can be made with framed plywood and fitted with a sliding tray.

battens across the ends (Fig. 15-6D). Round their centers before attaching to provide clearance for a handhold.

The simplest lid is made from a single piece of stout plywood that does not need framing. If thinner plywood is used, frame around it so the framing pieces fit over the box (Fig. 15-6E). The top may merely lift off; if hinged, the pivot point has to be under the rear batten. Butt hinges can fit between the batten and the side of the box (Fig. 15-6F). If these are not strong enough, strap hinges can be bent around the lid with the knuckle in the same position. Bolts can be used where hinges must be attached to thin plywood.

Too many fittings inside will restrict accomodation, but it is useful to have a sliding tray. Make a tray that fits easily in the width of the chest, with runners back and front locating it just below the top (Fig. 15-6G). If the tray is used for small parts, it can be fitted with divisions.

It may be possible to make racks on the inside of the lid for some tools, but make sure they clear the chest sides and the sliding tray.

PORTABLE TOOLBOX

If work is to be done away from the shop, it is convenient to have a portable toolbox (Fig. 15-7A). It should be large enough to carry a variety of your most-used tools and uncluttered with inside fittings since the tools will vary with the job.

The box's dimensions are governed by the largest tool to be carried (probably a hand saw), space available in the car, and carrying convenience. Construction is strip wood for top, bottom, and sides, with plywood back and front. Thickness—and therefore the width of the strip wood—should be enough to allow a plane to stand in the box and have ample clearance when a saw is fitted inside the closed lid.

The strongest corner joints are dovetails, but a joint nailed or screwed both ways should be adequate (Fig. 15-7B). Make box and lid as one piece, with plywood glued and nailed to the solid wood frame. Mark the cut for the lid (Fig. 15-7C) and arrange the metal fasteners so they clear this line.

Separate the parts with a fine-toothed saw to hold the kerf to a minimum. It may be a back saw used at a flat angle or a fine blade in a jig saw. Clean the edges with a minimum of planing; sanding with a block may be sufficient.

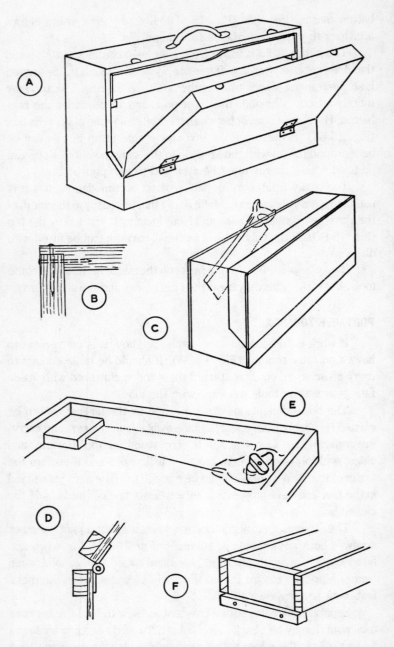

Fig. 15-7. A portable tool box can be made in one piece, then separated. It can be fitted with tool holders and a tray for small items.

Stiffen the hinge edge with strips inside (Fig. 15-7D) wide enough to take screws from the hinges outside. Fit a suitcase handle to the top after painting.

A hand saw may go inside the lid, with its blade in a slotted piece and a turnbutton and block for the handle (Fig. 15-7E). Other tools may go inside the lid on shaped blocks and turnbuttons or in spring clips.

It is useful to have a drawer for small items in the upper part of the box (Fig. 15-7F). There is no space for the usual drawer pull, but a hollow in the front edge will provide a grip. Put runners on the ends of the box. When the box is closed, the saw fitting will prevent the drawer from moving. Two suitcase fasteners hold the lid closed.

Paint is the best protection for the box. A light color inside helps visibility of the contents, but a dark color outside wears better.

MITER BOX

If you do much picture framing or other mitered work, a miter box is a necessity. Sophisticated mitering aids can be bought, but a miter box can be made of well-seasoned hardwood. The wider the box, the better the control of the saw, and the longer, the less the risk of moving the wood being cut. Suggested dimensions are shown in Fig. 15-8A; they can be varied considerably and still be satisfactory.

The three pieces of wood should be straight and flat on their meeting surfaces and the bottom piece should have right-angled straight edges (Fig. 15-8B). The bottom should be deep enough to allow the box to be gripped in a vise and still be high enough for use; if it's not, attach a strip of wood to the bottom to go in the vise (Fig. 15-8C).

Glue the parts and use fairly stout and long screws to reinforce the joints across the grain. The saw slots are the most important parts. Leave them until the glue has set.

A miter square can be used to mark the positions of the slots, but to ensure accuracy, use an adjustable bevel set to a line drawn as a diagonal to a right-angled line on the edge of a piece of wood (Fig. 15-8D). The top edges of the sides should be parallel with the base; use a set square inside as a check (Fig. 15-8E).

A piece of wood may be temporarily nailed across the top edges to act as a saw guide (Fig. 15-8F). Use the same back saw that will be

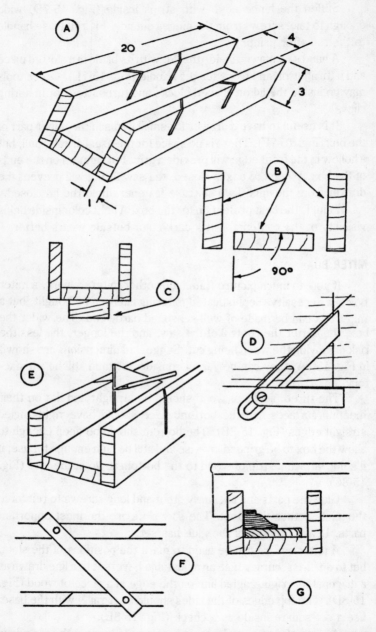

Fig. 15-8. A miter box must be carefully made, but it ensures accurate cutting of moldings.

used for cutting miters. Saw slowly, watching the guidelines at both sides. There is no need to saw all the way to the bottom piece, as it is usual to have a scrap piece of wood under the molding being cut. When mitering, hold the molding tight against the far side of the box and let the saw be guided by the slots, with only sufficient pressure and hand guidance to keep it cutting (Fig. 15-8G).

WOODEN CLAMPS

Many holding and clamping devices can be improvised as needed, but it is helpful to have some already made, particularly if you do not own many regular steel clamps. The main need is for wedges; it facilitates their use if you have a stock all with the same bevel.

The exact angle of a wedge is not important: an angle of about one in six will do. If the wedge is 6 inches long, it will be 1 inch thicker at one end than the other. Not all wedges need go to a thin end, which is weak, but in some clamping situations a wedge that tapers to nothing is needed. A suitable standard to adopt goes down to 1/4 inch (Fig. 15-9A). Wedges are conveniently cut on the end of a long strip, then parted after sawing and planing (Fig. 15-9B).

The basic clamping device has two blocks screwed to a stiff board; the wedges are used with packings if necessary (Fig. 15-9C). The same principle can be used with an adjustment at one or both ends (Fig. 15-9D). If the plywood cheeks extend under the item being clamped, there is less risk of the blocks distorting under pressure than if they were drilled from the top. Although dowel rods may serve as pegs, it is better to use metal rods or bolts.

Wedges can exert considerable pressure. For things like boards edge-to-edge, it is better to use bars on both sides. These can be made up with a fixed block at one end and a series of holes for a peg through a block to suit the work (Fig. 15-9E).

For a four-sided assembly, such as a box or a picture frame, a cord makes a good clamp, particularly used with a set of corner blocks (Fig. 15-9F). Drilling a hole in the corner keeps pressure against the sides instead of directly on the assembly corner. A groove outside prevents the cord from slipping off. Tightening is accomplished by twisting the cord with a rod (Fig. 15-9G). In many cases this can be lodged against the work when tightened, but

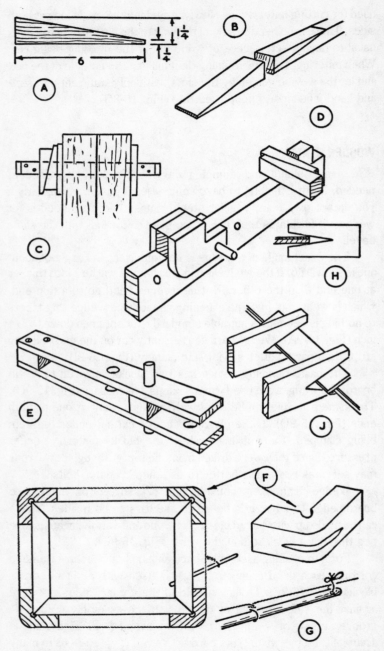

Fig. 15-9. Wooden clamps use a wedge action or the tension of a twisted cord.

otherwise it can have a lace through a hole in the end to tie to the main cord.

For light edge clamping, as when thin pieces are laminated or veneer needs holding, a wedged cut in a block of wood is sufficient. The wider the piece is, the better the spread of pressure (Fig. 15-9H). A wide squeeze can be obtained with two pressure plates fixed in two identical wedged blocks (Fig. 15-9J).

Chapter 16
Small Furniture

There are a great many small items that can be made with offcuts and other pieces of wood not large enough for more ambitious furniture projects. Even when wood is available for making large items, some of it will be cut away, and left over. This chapter is concerned with such items; worthwhile in themselves, they also provide a way to use up the inevitable stock of small pieces.

STOOL

This stool is intended to be of utilitarian rather than ornamental value (Fig. 16-1A). It can be made from a single board, with legs and top of the same width and the sides made by cutting a piece down the middle. Draw a side view of one end (Fig. 16-1B). This will give the angles of the joints. Note that the feet extend as far as the top, so there is no risk of someone standing on the end of the stool tipping it over.

Cut the wood for the top (Fig. 16-1C) and the sides (Fig. 16-1D). Mark out the two legs together (Fig. 16-1E). Drill the holes and saw into them (Fig. 16-1F). Clean the saw cuts carefully with a chisel. The sides of the pieces should be marked with bevels determined from the side view drawing and the distance in for the side cuts marked from the actual pieces of wood (Fig. 16-1G).

Saw the ends to the marked angles. Saw in the angles of the side cuts and down the grain to remove the waste wood. Mark the

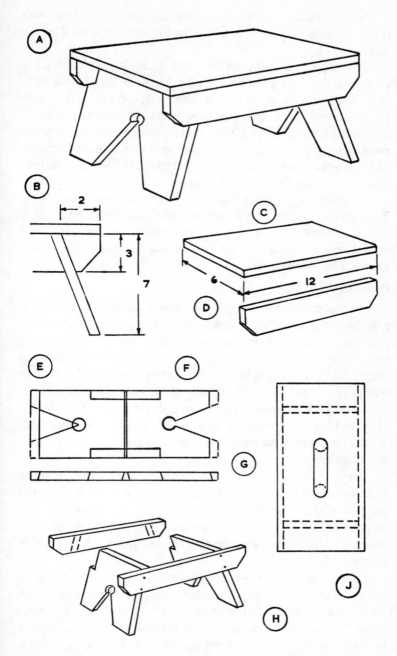

Fig. 16-1. A strong stool is easily made from strips of the same width.

positions of the legs on the side pieces, then glue and fix them with screws or nails (Fig. 16-1H). Plane the top surfaces level if necessary.

The top can be left plain, although it may help in moving the stool around to have a slot for a handhold at its center. This is made by drilling two holes, about 7/8-inch diameter, and sawing the waste away between them. A chisel used bevel downwards can bevel around the holes (Fig. 16-1J) followed by through sanding to give a comfortable grip. Attach the top to the framing with glue and screws. Make sure the stool will stand level, and plane the bottom of the legs if necessary. Sand all exposed angles.

The finish applied depends on the wood and the intended use. For shop use the stool may be left untreated, but even then a coat of varnish allowed to soak in will reduce dirt absorption. Stain and varnish or paint might be used, but avoid a high gloss if the stool is intended for standing on.

BOOKSHELVES

Bookshelves of many types are needed about the home and may be used for other things besides books. The bookshelves described here are a free-standing unit that could be made in sizes other than those shown to suit requirements and available wood (Fig. 16-2A). The depth back-to-front must be enough to take the widest book and to provide stability: 7 inches is the minimum.

If the back is to be plywood overlapping the sides (Fig. 16-2B), sides and shelves are the same width. Rabbetting the sides (Fig. 16-2C) will improve the appearance; the shelves will be narrower by the width of rabbet.

Prepare the wood for the two sides by cutting the rabbets with a table saw or rabbet plane, if rabbet construction is used. Mark out the pair of sides together (Fig. 16-2D). The best shelf joint is a stopped dado (Fig. 16-2E), but ledges can be used in simple construction. More information on making dado joints will be found in Chapter 10 (Fig. 10-7).

If dado joints are to be used, groove the sides before cutting the wood to length. Prepare the ends of the shelves. Assemble the shelves to the sides, with glue and screws from below into dado joints, or down into the ledges. Make the plywood back. Its top can be given a curve or a fretted outline. The important thing is that it holds the shelves true. Check diagonals when the back is fitted.

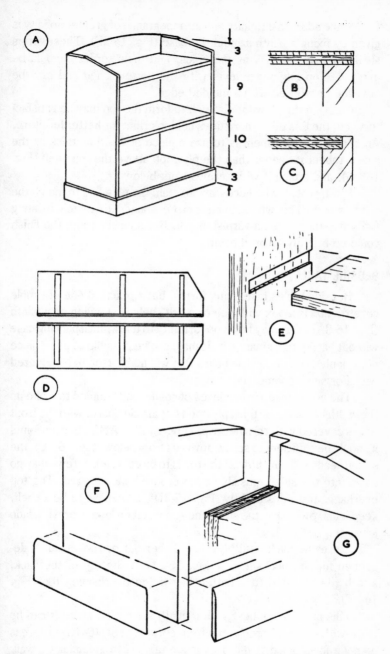

Fig. 16-2. Bookshelves may be built up from boards with a plywood back and a plinth.

Some additional rigidity and an appearance of greater solidity is given by fixing a plinth around the base (Fig. 16-2F). These strips should not be as thick as the sides, and their corners should be mitered. Top edges are level with the bottom shelf and may be bevelled or worked with a molded edge.

Carrying the plywood through to form the top may be satisfactory, but the thin edge there does not look right for better furniture. An alternative treatment is to use a piece of wood as thick as the sides, rabbet it deeper than the plywood above the top shelf (Fig. 16-2G), and attach it with screws from below.

It will probably be necessary to stain the plywood to match the other wood. The whole thing can be stained to match existing furniture, then given a varnish finish. For a child's room the finish could be brightly colored paint.

BEDSIDE TABLE

Bedside tables take many forms, but a practical one of simple construction is a box with one or more shelves standing on a plinth (Fig. 16-3A). This may be an opportunity to use a small packing case without having to dismantle it. It may also be possible to use a piece of thick plywood or particle board that will make a top to be covered with Formica or veneered.

The box is made from pieces of solid wood—joined to make up the width needed—or thick plywood or particle board, with the front edges covered with narrow strips (Fig. 16-3B). At the bottom joints it should be sufficient to screw upwards from below (Fig. 16-3C); the screw heads will not show. If the top is to be covered, screws may go down into the sides, possibly counterbored and plugged. The top overhangs the sides slightly (Fig. 16-3D). If there is to be a shelf, keep it narrower than the sides and support it on ledges or with dado joints (Fig. 16-3E).

Close the back with plywood, either flat or rabbetted as described for the bookshelves (Fig. 16-2). At the top of the back, attach the plywood to a batten below the overlapping top (Fig. 16-3F).

This piece looks best with a plinth set back a little. It can be made with strips mitered at the front corners (Fig. 16-3G). There is no need for a piece at the back if the table is to go against a wall. Attach by using either picket screwing upwards or deeply counterboring from below (Fig. 16-3H). Regardless of the finish used on the main part of the table, a plinth of this type should be black or another dark finish for the best effect.

What is done to the top depends on the material used. If it is attractive wood, the edges can be rounded or molded and a clear finish applied over the plain or stained wood. Otherwise it may be given a veneer pattern, either with wood veneer or plastic substitute, including the edges, or treated similarly with Formica or other mellamine laminate (Fig. 16-3J).

HOT PADS

One possible use for scraps of thinner plywood of good quality is hot pads or table mats. Some may be treated as disposable and not given a very good finish, while others may be made more attractive for dining-table use.

The simplest mat is a plain rectangle (Fig. 16-4A), but the corners should be beveled (Fig. 16-4B) or rounded (Fig. 16-4C). Some mats may be square; larger ones are better rectangular. If they are to be made in sets, it is important that they match. Two edges can be planed at right angles to each other, then these edges used as guides against the fence of a table saw with a fine blade, to ensure a uniform size (Fig. 16-4D). If the pieces are to be cut by hand, a simple saw-guiding jig can be made from scrap wood (Fig. 16-4E).

Corners can also be cut with a jig, into which each pad is pushed (Fig. 16-4F). A jig to take several mats at a time can be used to pass the mats over a table saw. For rounded corners, mark around a can (Fig. 16-4G). Saw away some of the waste and work to the curve by sanding. A disc sander is convenient for this (Fig. 16-4H). Thoroughly sand surfaces and edges and round off any angles.

Circular mats may be drawn with a compass. For elliptical mats, draw an ellipse with string around two nails and a pencil in the slack of the string loop (Fig. 16-4J). The slacker the string loop, the wider the ellipse in relation to its length. Experiment with the spacing of the nails and amount of string. Make one mat, with its outline cut and the edges sanded smooth, then use it as a pattern for marking others.

Some woods may be used as they are. Others are better stained and given a protective coating. The underside can be covered with cloth to prevent sliding on a smooth table top. There are self-adhesive cloth-like plastic materials suitable for this purpose. To fix cloth neatly, cut it oversize, attach it to the wood, then trim it with a sharp knife after the adhesive has set.

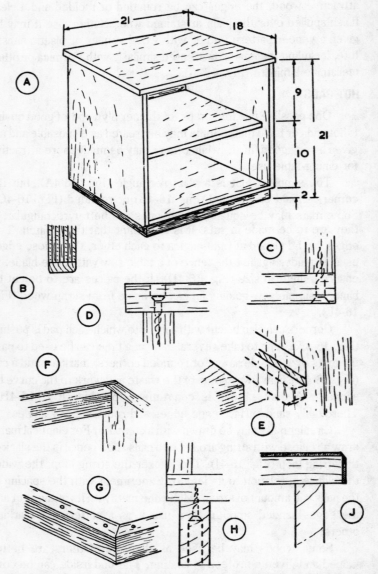

Fig. 16-3. A unit to stand beside a bed can be made from thick plywood **or** manufactured board, veneered or covered with plastic.

It is unwise to give a gloss finish, on which things may slip, but a heat-resisting gloss varnish can be dulled by rubbing with scouring powder or fine abrasive paper.

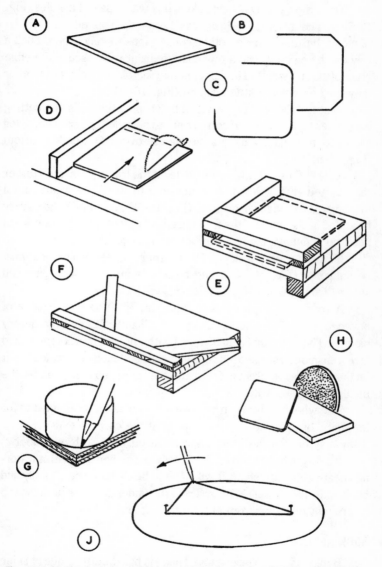

Fig. 16-4. Hot pads use up odd pieces of plywood or hardboard and may be cut uniformly with simple jigs.

TRAYS

Trays are always needed, both nicely finished ones for food in the home or more crude ones for such tasks as holding all the pieces of an item being assembled.

The simplest tray is made like a box with a pair of handles (Fig. 16-5A). The plywood edges are exposed. Top edges may be rounded, but there are no other concessions to decoration. Such a tray can be painted, and a few coats of paint will obscure the edge grain of the plywood. The handles may be plain blocks of wood or they may be given a little shaping (Fig. 16-5B).

Neat handles can be provided by shaping the ends and cutting hand holes (Fig. 16-5C). If corners are to be nailed or screwed, sides can overlap to make a decorative feature over an extended bottom (Fig. 16-5D).

A clear-finished tray looks neater if the frame is mitered rather than butted (Fig. 16-5E). It is possible to work the frame into a molding that provides hand grips (Fig. 16-5F), or metal handles may be added at the ends. If the framing is fairly stout, glued corners will need no additional fixing if the bottom is securely attached.

If extra security is needed in a corner, veneer in a saw cut may be sufficient (Fig. 16-5G). The bottom is attached with glue and screws from below (Fig. 16-5H).

A tray bottom provides an opporutnity to veneer a piece of plywood. It may be a decorative panel (Chapter 12) or a marquetry picture. The plywood could be faced with Formica or a soft plastic to give a cushioned surface for cups and glasses. Such decoration is put on the plywood before it is fitted into the frame, so it goes under the molding (Fig. 16-5J).

The whole bottom can be covered with cloth, as suggested for hot pads, but it is better to use pads at the corners (Fig. 16-5K). They may be pieces of thin plywood faced with cloth or rubber.

If a tray is to be used for food, it should be finished with a water- and heat-proof varnish, as it will have to be cleaned occasionally and hot liquids may be spilled on it. Treat the underside as well as the top to prevent moisture from entering the grain.

BOOK RACK

Book racks are very handy. This one has the advantage of being suitable for taking down for flat packing, or for use when traveling.

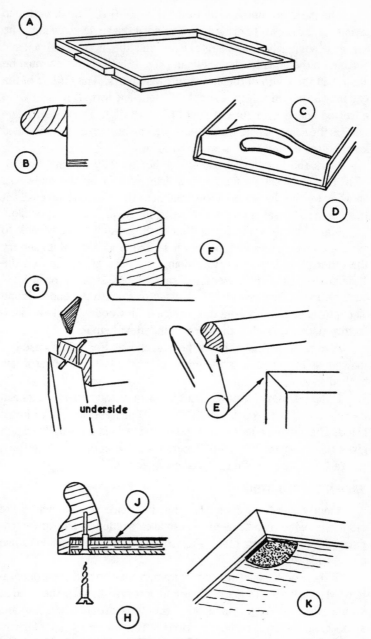

Fig. 16-5. A tray may be made with a plywood base using various methods of forming the surround.

underside

311

The parts are notched together (Fig. 16-6A). The first step in laying out the rack is to draw a book tilted at the angle you want. The corner is obviously a right angle. From this the location of back and bottom on the ends can be drawn in (Fig. 16-6B). Notches must be about half the width of the two lengthwise parts. The outline of the end may be anything from a simple straight-line form (Fig. 16-6C) to a fretted shape with cut-out parts (Fig. 16-6D). The construction work is the same, whatever the outline. The bottom edges will stand level better if they are cut away to form feet.

Mark the lengthwise parts together so they match (Fig. 16-6E). The slots should finally be a firm push fit on the ends but, allowing for the thickness of the finish, cut them to push on easily at this stage. The sawn edges can be trimmed with a chisel or file.

Mark out the two ends together so they match. It is advisable to cut the bottom edges and the feet first, then make the slots and try the other parts in them before doing any decorative work on the ends. Make sure the assembled rack stands steadily on a level surface. If this first assembly is satisfactory, finish the ends. Round all exposed edges and sand the surfaces. Plywood edges look satisfactory under varnish if they are rounded and smooth.

A varnish finish is probably the best choice. For a child's use you may put suitable decals on the ends before the last coat of varnish is applied.

If the takedown feature is not important, the bottom joints can be reinforced with small blocks (Fig. 16-6F) and all of the joints glued. The bottom edges of the ends could be built out with blocks to give broader bases (Fig. 16-6G) and a place for cloth to be glued on if the rack is to be used on a polished table top.

WOVEN-TOPPED STOOL

Good-quality wood of 1 1/4-2-inch square sections will make stool legs, which can be used with smaller-section square or rectangular pieces to make a stool (Fig. 16-7A). It is also possible to use dowel rods for the rails.

If the wood has an attractive grain, it may be sufficient decoration to leave the legs square. Tops and bottoms should be beveled all around (Fig. 16-7B). Make sure the tops are finished flat and smooth, as they will be very obvious in the finished stool. Corners can be given "wagon beveling" (Fig. 16-7C) or hollowed with a chisel bevel downwards (Fig. 16-7D).

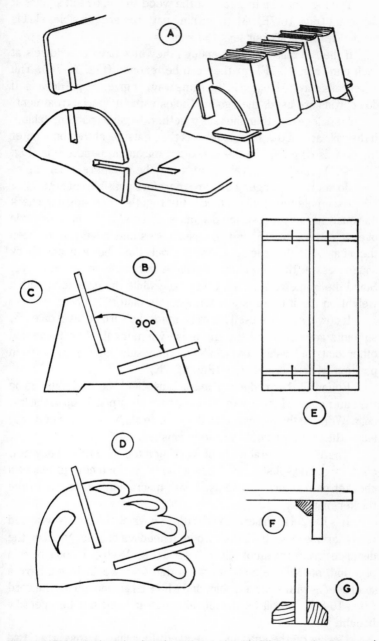

Fig. 16-6. This takedown book rack can be made with different end patterns and in sizes to suit the books.

The legs may be turned, but the wood should be left square at the joints (Fig. 16-7E). Many turning patterns are possible; skill is needed to make all four legs the same.

If the top rails are deep enough they may have two dowels at each end (Fig. 16-7F), or they can be tenoned (Fig. 16-7G). The lower rails may be treated in the same way, or given single dowels. If dowel rods are used, they go into holes without special treatment.

Mark legs together and rails together, to get all parts matching. If the rails are on the same level—as they must be at the top—miter the dowels or tenons in the leg to get maximum penetration (Fig. 16-7H). At the lower level the rails may be at different heights so they do not meet; longer joints are therefore possible (Fig. 16-7J).

Assemble the stool in stages. Put together one side and check its squareness by measuring diagonals. Assemble the opposite side over it so they match. Put the assemblies under weights to keep them flat while the glue sets. Add the rails the other way and check squareness in that direction as well as when viewed from above. Stand the framework on a level surface while the glue sets, with a weight on top if there is any tendency to distort.

If dowel rods are used for rails, mark the surface level on each, so joints are equal and the frame is symmetrical. With these and other joints, a finishing nail can be driven inside the joint to hold it in position while the glue sets (Fig. 16-7K).

Round all sharp edges. The top rails should be well rounded on the outer edges. Finish with stain and varnish or polish, up to the last coat. Working the top may mar the surface slightly, so it is better to leave the last coat until the top is finished.

There are several ways of working a top with rush, seagrass, cord, or plastic substitutes. The method described here produces a checker pattern and can be used with macrame cord or one of the thicker materials.

It is helpful to make a few shuttles on which the cord is wrapped ready for use (Fig. 16-8A). A wooden needle a little longer than the distance across the stool will be needed (Fig. 16-8B). It could be thin plywood, but will be stronger if it's thin solid wood. If you have a steel needle with a curved point and a hole large enough for the cord (Fig. 16-8C), it will be useful, although it need not be specially bought.

Decide on the spacing to be used: four lines across, then two wraps around the rail is reasonable. Tie a knot in the end of the line

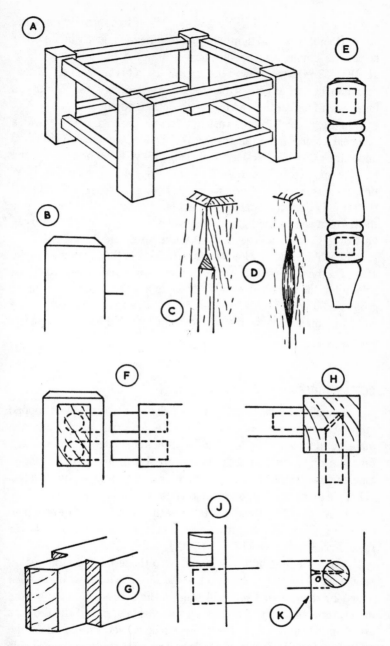

Fig. 16-7. A frame for a stool with a woven top may have square or turned legs and tenoned or doweled rails.

and tack it under a rail (Fig. 16-8D). Wrap four turns across the stool. Do not wrap too tightly or you may have difficulty in the other direction. Laying the needle across may aid even tension (Fig. 16-8E). Wrap twice around the far rail, then twice around the near rail, then four times across the stool, and so on (Fig. 16-8F) until you finish with four strands across at the other edge.

In the other direction work in the same pattern, possibly with a different color. Using the cord in the wooden needle, go over and under the other groups alternately (Fig. 16-8G). Put on wraps at the far side and return underneath to put wraps on the near rail. Next time go across in the alternate manner. Pause occasionally and pull the strands back tight and in straight lines across. Towards the end the pattern will be too tight for the wooden needle, but the cord can be worked across a little at a time; the steel needle will help.

Finish the ends by knotting and tacking in the same way as the start. On the underside the strands may be allowed merely to cross, although it looks neater to work them in a large pattern, say three groups each way. If new lengths of cord have to be joined, knot the ends together underneath where they'll be hidden by the large pattern.

COFFEE TABLE

A small table can be made in a similar way to the woven-topped stool. Dimensions depend on available material, particularly the material suitable for the top. The best-looking tables are about 1 1/2 times as long as wide and the height greater or less than the width. Similar dimensions in two directions is not usually a good design, although there are some pleasing square tables.

It is possible to make a table with top rails deep enough to provide rigidity without lower rails, but this design includes lower rails similar to the stool (Fig. 16-9A).

Make the legs and rails similarly to those for the stool. Mark similar parts together. The tops of the legs are level with the rails, joined by dowels or haunched tenons (Fig. 16-9B). Make up the underframe as for the stool. It improves appearance if the top rails are shaped (Fig. 16-9C). They can also be carved with motifs at the ends (Fig. 16-9D), or with a simple pattern of triangles known as chip carving (Fig. 16-9E).

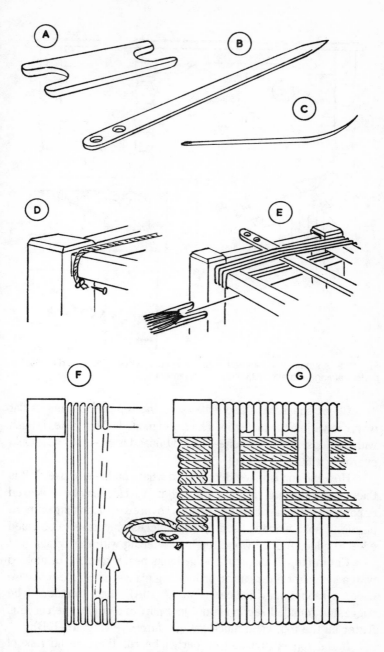

Fig. 16-8. Tools can be made for working a woven stool top. A simple checker pattern in two colors is effective.

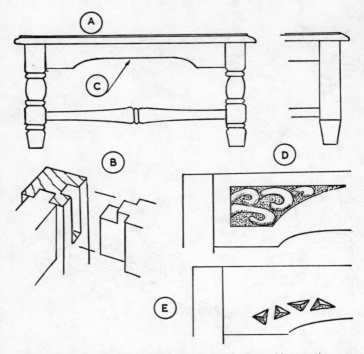

Fig. 16-9. A small table can be treated in several ways, with turned or square parts, carving, and alternative rail arrangements.

Check squareness and make sure the top of the frame is flat where it will join the table top. The top of most modern tables is flush with the legs, but in this one—a traditional design—the top should overhang a little all around.

How the top is made depends on what you have to use. If it is thick plywood or manufactured board, its surface may be veneered or covered with plastic, and the edges covered with molding or more plastic. If solid wood is used, several pieces may have to be glued edge to edge. A solid wood top is in keeping with the design.

Cut the top to shape; the edge looks best if rounded or molded with a suitable router cutter or molding planes. If simple tools are used, a rabbet may be cut (Fig. 16-10A), then rounded. The suggested rounded section is not just part of a circle; the curve is flatter on the top, as in much antique furniture (Fig. 16-10B).

If the top is plywood or particleboard, there is no risk of expansion or contraction, so it can be fixed to the framing with screws driven through pockets cut inside the top rails at about 6-inch intervals (Fig. 16-10C).

If the top is solid wood there is a risk that it will expand and contract in its width. This should be considered in the method of attachment. The top rails can be grooved before assembly and blocks made to fit into them (Fig. 16-10D). The blocks are screwed, and may also be glued, to the underside of the top, but they are free to move in the grooves. Cut the tongues so they pull the top tightly down on the framing and make the intiial assembly so the blocks are a short distance in from the rails to allow for movement.

The finish used will depend on the wood, but this type of table looks best if stained a fairly dark brown and given a moderate gloss finish. If hardwood, you may use one or two coats of varnish rubbed down and finished with wax.

There are variations possible. If the legs are left square, the bottom rails should also be square or rectangular in section. If the legs are turned, it looks best if the lower rails are also turned, although combinations of square legs and turned rails, or vice versa, are sometimes found.

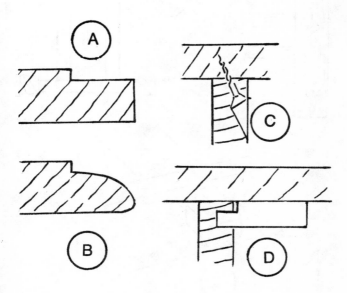

Fig. 16-10. Treatments for table top edges and attaching the top.

There may be double bottom rails (Fig. 16-11A). Besides their decoration, they provide additional stiffness, which may be desirable if the top rails are not as deep as they should be.

Another bottom-rail arrangement—suitable if deep rails provided plenty of rigidity—is normal rails across the ends, but one or two rails joined into them instead of the legs (Fig. 16-11B). The joints should be tenons, which are stronger than dowels.

Another design uses deep lower end rails with a flat rail tenoned through them and held with wedges (Fig. 16-11C). This is a German type of construction and decoration. The wedges in this design are decorative, so the completed joints, including the wedges, may be glued.

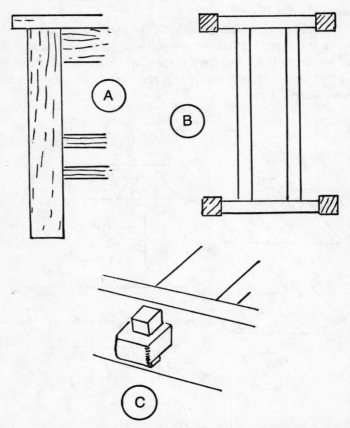

Fig. 16-11. Rail variations can be decorative while providing added strength.

TABLE LAMPS

A lamp to stand on a table does not require much wood. It may have a single stem or it may be more box-like. It needs a broad base to prevent it from tipping, particularly when fitted with a large shade. Pieces of attractive wood that are not big enough for other things may be used for table lamps.

Basically, a lamp provides support for a bulb and its wiring; the design must be planned around these requirements. Fittings should be obtained before work is started so wood can be chosen to suit the fittings.

If the wood has attractive grain, the design can be quite plain so the polished grain becomes the main feature. A square post on a square base with square feet may be sufficient (Fig. 16-12A). If the bottom of the post is broad, it may be held with screws from below; if narrow, it may tenoned (Fig. 16-12B).

The length of your drills limits the height of any one-piece post (Fig. 16-12C). A longer post may be made in halves, grooved lengthwise (Fig. 16-12D) and glued.

A lathe expands your options for making lamps, candlesticks, and similar items. The post is turned to any freehand pattern and a large-diameter dowel turned to fit through the base (Fig. 16-12E). The base should not be turned too much: it must have weight to provide steadiness. A turned-up edge is more stable than a tapered one (Fig. 16-12F). Weight can be added to a base by turning a recess and fitting a piece of sheet lead into it (Fig. 16-12G).

A square stem can be decorated by molding its length with a plane or router (Fig. 16-12H) or by carving. It can be tapered in its length or have a double taper (Fig. 16-12J). There can be edge decoration, either as notches or following lines similar to turned work (Fig. 16-12K).

A table lamp does not have to be high and the post does not have to be slender. A lower assembly with a large shade can be just as effective. A cube-shaped block of wood with its corners cut off to give regular octagonal faces may stand on an octagonal base (Fig. 16-12L). The parts can be joined with screws, drilling is easy, and any type of lamp fitting can be used.

Instead of solid wood, the block can be built up by laminating thinner material—different woods, or the same wood laid in alternate directions. It can also be turned into a variation of a spherical block.

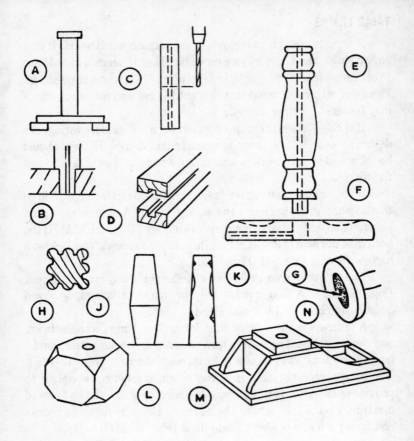

If only thinner wood is available the base can be built up in steps, with feet at the corners. The lamp support can be in the form of a box. It may have its edges flush or they can extend to provide decoration (Fig. 16-12M). Such lamps do not have to be symmetrical: one can be extended to include a small tray (Fig. 16-12N) or act as a base for an ornament.

KITCHEN AIDS

Kitchens are full of plastic and metal, yet many expert cooks favor wood for some things. Wood used in connection with food preparation should be free from resins and oils that might be exuded during use. Light colors look more hygienic than dark ones, but more important than color is closeness of grain. A wood such as sycamore or beech with no obvious pockets in the grain is suitable.

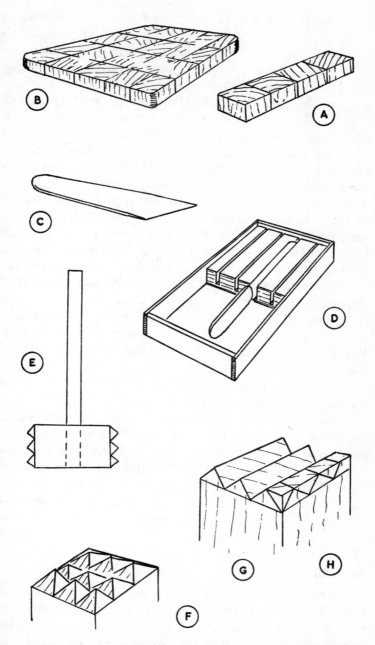

Fig. 16-13. A kitchen chopping block can have an end-grain surface. Knives can be protected in slots. A tenderizing mallet provides some interesting tool work.

One kitchen item that is better wood than plastic is a chopping board; the best type is made like a butcher's block with end grain on the surface. Cut a large number of pieces as long as the board will be thick. Sections need not all be the same, but prepare sets to glue (using waterproof glue) into strips (Fig. 16-13A). After this glue has set, plane the edges true and glue the strips together to make a block (Fig. 16-13B). Plane the outer edges true and round the corners. Use a finely-set steel plane to true the surfaces. Plane in several directions, working in from the edges until saw marks are removed. Check flatness with a straightedge and finish by sanding, wetting the wood to raise the grain before the last sanding.

Wooden spatulas are also favored. They may not last long, but are simple to make and can be made in multiples. They're about the same size as a large spoon (Fig. 16-13C). The handle end is well rounded and about 1/4 inch thick. The other end tapers to almost a knife edge. Smooth the wood well and slightly round all corners.

Kitchen knives need to be sharp, and will not keep their edges if they are mixed with other metal things. Convenient storage and protection of both the edges and the user is provided by a wood block set in a tray or drawer, with saw cuts to take the blades (Fig. 16-13D). All slots can be the same size as a small knife will go into the slot for a large one.

A mallet for tenderizing beef can be made from a block of hardwood, with a turned handle or a piece of stout dowel rod (Fig. 16-13E). The surfaces have small square conical projections (Fig. 16-13F), made by careful hand sawing in two directions. Mark in one direction and saw with a fine backsaw (Fig. 16-13G), but leave one side to use as a guide for cutting the other way. Mark the other direction and saw that (Fig. 16-13H), then remove the remaining slope the other way and clean the cones with abrasive paper wrapped around a sharp-edged block of wood.

BATHROOM CABINET

A bathroom cabinet is a project that will use short pieces of wood. A mirror on the door is almost mandatory; its size will pretty much dictate the cabinet's dimensions. Ordinary hinges are avoided by having the top and bottom of the box overhang so the door pivots on screws (Fig. 16-14A).

The mirror frame must be fairly stout since glass is heavy. In the cabinet shown, the frame gets its rigidity from a stout plywood piece behind the mirror (Fig. 16-14B). Another way of making the front is to use several thicknesses of plywood. This allows the use of a broken piece of mirror: the uneven edge can be hidden in plywood cut to match (Fig. 16-14C). The exposed plywood edge can be hidden by paint or covered with a border strip of wood.

The box part of the cabinet is made of solid wood with a plywood back. It may be satisfactory just to screw the plywood to the frame, but it is better rabbeted. Corner joints are strongest dovetailed. If the back is fitted into a rabbet, cut the dovetails in the upright parts with the rear one cut so as to hide the rabbet (Fig. 16-14D). Number the corners to match and use the dovetails to mark the other parts, then cut them. Glue the frame, then plane the joints smooth.

If simpler joints are needed, the top and bottom may be cut around the sides, which are screwed in place (Fig. 16-14E). For even simpler construction, top and bottom may be screwed to the sides (Fig. 16-14F); since the screws under load are in end grain, they should be stout and long.

If shelves are needed, set them back a little from the front in stopped dado slots in the sides (Fig. 16-14G). Toothbrush slots can be cut in a shelf before it is fitted.

The door should match the width of the front, but there should be some clearance top and bottom. Drill cabinet and door with a drill to suit the tapping size of the screws. Enlarge the cabinet holes to match the necks of the screws. When the parts are assembled, include a washer at the bottom (Fig. 16-14H). Attach a handle to the other side of the door, as well as a catch to keep the door closed. Finish with several coats of paint.

FOLDING STEPS

A small stepladder is all that is needed for the average person to reach to ceiling height in most homes. This need only be two steps high and can be made from strip wood of about 6-inch-by-1-inch section.

Using the dimensions of the wood available, draw a side view of the steps in the open position (Fig. 16-15A). This will give you the angles to mark.

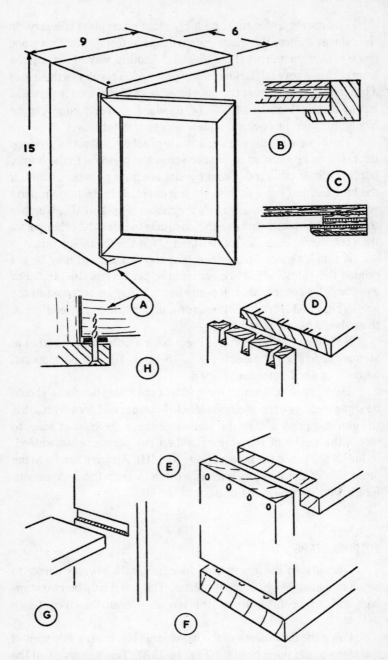

Fig. 16-14. A bathroom cabinet with a mirrored-door can be made several ways, depending on material and ability.

Mark both sides together, using an adjustable bevel (Fig. 16-15B). The top and step are wider than the sides, and pieces may have to be glued to make up their width. The sides are parallel, so joint positions in the top and the step are the same. Mark them together (Fig. 16-15C).

The strongest joint for the top is a tenon taken right through, coupled with a shallow dado joint. The mortise and tenon follow the line of the side and are not at a right angle to the top (Fig. 16-15D). An alternative is to leave out the mortise and tenon and strengthen the joint with a block (Fig. 16-15E).

A similar joint is used with the step, but as this mortise and tenon is perpendicular to the surface of the side, it is easier to make (Fig. 16-15F). When these parts are assembled, join the step into both sides before joining the sides to the top. Check squareness with diagonals. Affix the top strip across the back (Fig. 16-15G).

The leg assembly fits under the back strip. The legs can be made from the same material as the sides, cut down the middle. The crosspieces may be tenoned or doweled (Fig. 16-15H) into the legs. The top piece needs to be flush to allow hingeing, but the bottom rail can be screwed to the surface (Fig. 16-15J). The bottoms of the legs should be cut to the angle they will take when they are fully open. When closed, the legs should be the same length as the sides.

Use T hinges to join the parts, with screws as long as the thickness of the wood will allow. If heavy use is expected you can use metal angle brackets under the bottom step, or wooden brackets can be made and glued and screwed on (Fig. 16-15K).

The legs are kept at the correct angle when open with rope through holes. Drill the sides and the legs, then securely knot the ropes on the outside. Make sure they are the same length to distribute the strain equally.

HANGING RACKS

The simplest hanging rack is a strip of wood carrying hooks on pegs (Fig. 16-16A). If its top is given a shelf, its usefulness is increased (Fig. 16-16B). Such a shelf puts weight at the top, so attachments to the wall should be high on the back. If no pegs are needed—just a shelf—locate the shelf below the back. A shelf for potted plants can be made this way with strips for the shelf (Fig. 16-16C).

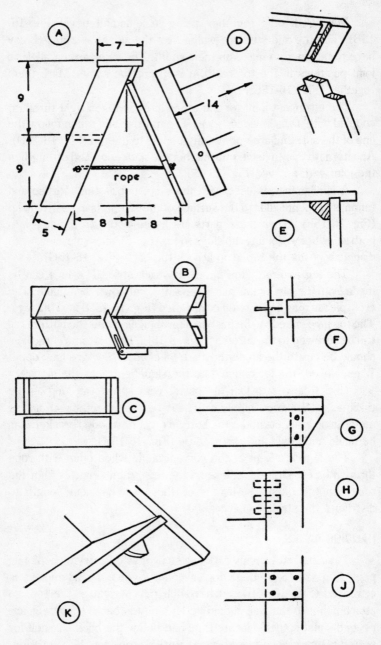

Fig. 16-15. A small stepladder must be carefully and substantially built, but is useful in the home and shop.

A hanging rack for clothes can also incorporate a mirror framed by wood (Fig. 16-16D). The parts can be halved or tenoned together. A rabbet for the glass can be cut with a plane, saw or other power tool in sides and bottom. The short rabbet under the top edge can be cut with a router or chisel.

Towel rails can be made single or double (Fig. 16-16E), with square, octagonal, or round rods, and the ends tenoned to the back or merely screwed from behind. A different rail arrangement provides a shoe rack (Fig. 16-16F).

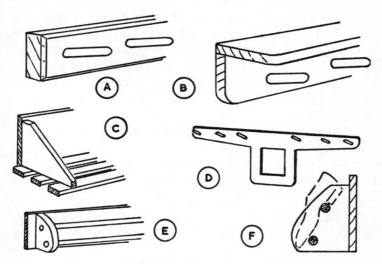

Fig. 16-16. Strip wood and dowels will make many types of wall racks.

MAGAZINE RACK

There are several ways that a rack can be made for magazines and periodicals, but the one shown is constructed without elaborate joints and can be adapted to suit available wood and magazine sizes (Fig. 16-17A).

The central member (Fig. 16-17B) is plywood about 1/2 inch thick. Shape its top and cut the hand hole, then thoroughly round the exposed edges of the hole and the part that will project.

The other plywood parts are made the same width as the center piece, but their heights are arranged to suit the width of your magazines, leaving enough room to grip and lift it out. The edges can finish flush (Fig. 16-17C), which would suit a painted finish, or they may project and be rounded (Fig. 16-17D) under stained and varnished finish. When calculating the sizes of these panels, allow for the thickness of the spacers that fit between them.

The spacers may be strips of rectangular-section wood, although it makes a better rack to have them slightly tapered (Fig. 16-17E). They should all be the same thickness and the top ends should be rounded.

Construction is in steps so nail or screw heads will be hidden. Attach the sides of the smaller rack to the main front panel first, then nail or screw on its sides (Fig. 16-17F). Add the center piece (Fig. 16-17G). This leaves the rear end pieces, which will have to be fastened the opposite way. This is best done by counterboring deeply for screws (Fig. 16-17H). There is no need to plug over the screw heads. The two outer panels are attached with glue and decorative screws, or finishing nails punched below the surface and covered with filler.

To avoid the rack tipping over easily, the feet should project farther than the width of the top (Fig. 16-17J). If the panels project with rounded ends, the feet should be rounded. If the panels are flush, the feet ends might be simple bevels. In any case, cut back the center. This allows the rack to stand solidly and also allows the feet to be screwed under the sides (Fig. 16-17K). The feet can be fitted with glides or non-skid rubber.

CHILD'S DESK

The length of time a child can use a piece of scaled-down furniture is very limited, so there is little justification in spending much on it. An inexpensive child's desk (Fig. 16-18A) can be made from salvaged strips, mostly of the same section, and a few pieces of plywood.

Seat height controls the dimensions. Determine the appropriate seat height, then make the underside of the desk high enough to clear his knees and the top a few inches above that. The back edge of the top should be only an inch or so forward of the front edge of the seat. The sizes shown give an indication of proportions, but can be modified considerably to suit the age and size of the child and the available materials.

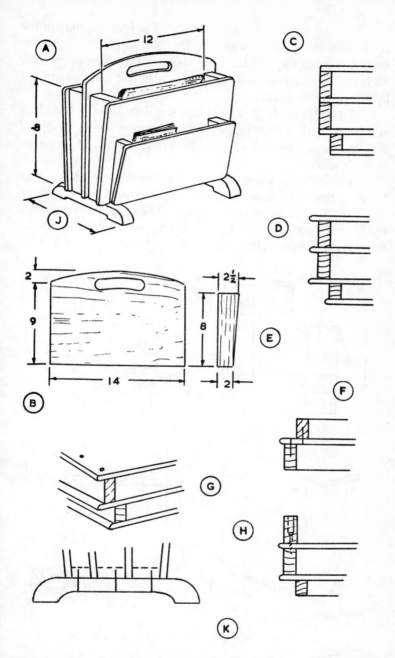

Fig. 16-17. A magazine rack can be built with plywood panels and strip wood, with nailed or screwed joints.

The seat is made like a small form. The legs and top are the same width and are nailed together. The sides can be from the same wood cut down the middle, then nailed to the other parts (Fig. 16-18B). Check squareness during assembly with a try square and by measuring diagonals.

The bottom rails fit outside the seat legs and the desk legs attach outside the rails, so allow for this when marking the lengths of desk top parts. The desk legs may fit outside the top, which can be made as a unit.

Build the top as a box with a sloping edge (Fig. 16-18C). It may be made from boards of the same width as used in the seat, or slightly narrower. Nailed corner joints can be reinforced with inside blocks or, better, joints can be dovetailed or notched. There can be some inside division, but it is probably better to leave most of the

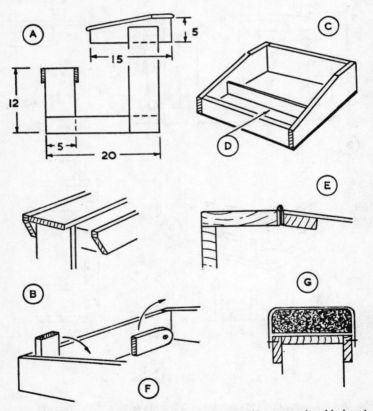

Fig. 16-18. A child's desk may be built as a unit with a lifting top and padded seat.

space open and just have a front compartment for pencils and other small items (Fig. 16-18D).

The flat top has to match the sloping top to allow for hinges. Both may be solid wood, thick plywood, or manufactured board, but it may be necessary to build up the sloping part with thinner plywood and framing strips. Let these be wide enough to bear on the desk sides. In any case, the top parts should overlap the box parts slightly so the edges can be rounded and gripped for lifting. The flat top has a right-angled edge, and the sloping part is beveled to match it. Use butt hinges between these parts (Fig. 16-18E).

There may be occasions when a level surface will be more useful than a sloping one. This can be arranged by having two turnbuttons inside (Fig. 16-18F). Round their bottoms, but cut the tops square; keep them close to the corners to give wide support to the top.

The desk can be finished to match other furniture or painted in bright colors, then suitable decals added to the sides.

The seat could be upholstered with a pad of plastic or latex foam, cut to size, and held in place with a piece of plastic-coated cloth tacked around the sides (Fig. 16-18G). The working surface of the desk top could also have a piece of plastic glued on, if this is preferred to bare wood.

The dividing line between large and small furniture is arbitrary, but for purposes of this book, large furniture is regarded as those items that require large pieces of wood.

Small things can always be made from large pieces of wood, but the reverse is rarely true. It is possible to splice and laminate so as to make larger items, but it is wiser to keep large pieces of wood for large projects. Of course, if you plan no large constructions, it makes sense to cut down large pieces of wood, but the keen collector of salvaged wood will hesitate before doing this. Clean, quality wood should certainly be kept for furntiure. A piece of wood with damage on one surface can often be worked into a piece of furniture so only its good side is visible.

Straightness and flatness are important. If a large piece of wood has twists and undulations, it may be used for garden carpentry, but not for furniture. If its faults are modest twists or general bending, it is often possible to work the wood into a structure that pulls it flat and straight. A piece of salvaged wood that is flat and true is the material for a project where the wood has to keep its shape without outside help—as in a long shelf or bench.

Large furniture is not necessarily more difficult to make than small furniture. There is just more wood, so the labor may be greater although the degree of skill required is no higher. Some large pieces of furniture present opportunities for refined construction and decorative skills, but modern furniture tends to be comparatively plain in outline. This suits most salvaged wood, which may be quite good in its plain state, but would not be very amenable to carving or intricate work.

Some people want their furniture to look as though it was made from crates, and enjoy seeing crate markings through the finish. However, much salvaged wood is as good as what you buy; there is no reason why it cannot be given a good furniture finish. Such wood should be planed and sanded before use.

SHELVING

It is possible to build-in furniture in most homes: shelving in a recess gives you a bookcase; with doors on it, it becomes a cabinet. Shelving can be mounted flat on a wall for similar purposes. In both cases the structure of the house serves as part of the furniture. The result is additional utility without using up as much floor space as free-standing furniture would.

The simplest construction is a single shelf in a recess (Fig. 17-1A), a straight board resting on two battens. Bevel the fronts of the battens and bevel or round their lower edges. Attach with screws into studs, or use the special fasteners intended for hollow walls. For stone or brick walls it will be necessary to use a masonry bit and plug the wall. Make sure the shelf is level in both directions. It may be adequate to measure parallel with the floor, or check with a carpenter's level.

The shelf can be stiffened by a batten across the back, which can also be attached to the wall, and another under the front. It may be set back and the front of the shelf rounded (Fig. 17-1B) or covered with molding.

If you have no suitable large boards, it is possible to use plywood stiffened on its edges. The simplest way is to nail the plywood to the battens and cover the front with a strip of wood (Fig. 17-1C). Better construction is to fit the plywood into a rabbet (Fig. 17-1D).

A bookcase or block of shelves can be built the same way, but appearance is improved if the mounting battens and shelf ends are covered by vertical pieces. The shelves may be notched around them or may stand out, especially if doors are to be fitted.

The simplest doors overlap the shelves, although the top or bottom (or both) shelves can extend over the doors. The simplest

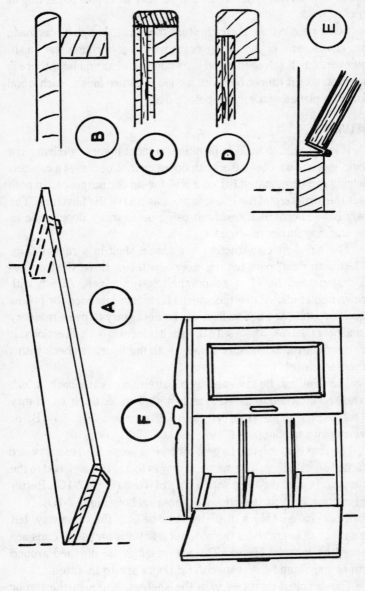

Fig. 17-1. Shelves can be built into a recess or on the surface of a wall and elaborated by the addition of ends and doors.

light doors that will resist twisting are made of two plywood panels with solid wood framing. They swing on strips attached to the front edges of the shelves (Fig. 17-1E). Catches can be arranged centrally on a shelf.

The plainness of such a fitting can be relieved by a shaped piece over the top or a pattern of molding on the doors (Fig. 17-1F).

A wider shelf at table height will make a working surface, a desk, or a stand for a sewing machine. With other shelves above it and storage space below, the whole recess becomes a useful unit. One easy way of providing storage space below is to use a deep frontal stiffener with a curtain rail behind it (Fig. 17-2A).

Shelves mounted on a flat wall require brackets. If one end is in a corner, it can be supported the same way as in a recess. A single shelf may be bracketed directly to the wall, but it is better to fasten battens to the wall and attach the brackets to that. It is also a good idea to have a horizontal batten under the back of the shelf, with the other pieces halved to it (Fig. 17-2B).

Ready-made brackets can be used, but it is possible to use shaped pieces of solid wood attached to battens (Fig. 17-2C). For a

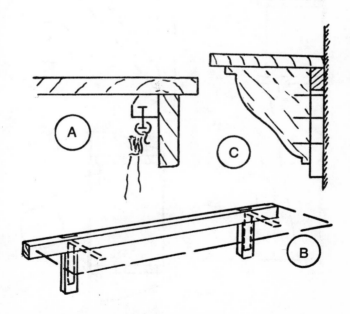

Fig. 17-2. Details of shelf brackets and stiffeners.

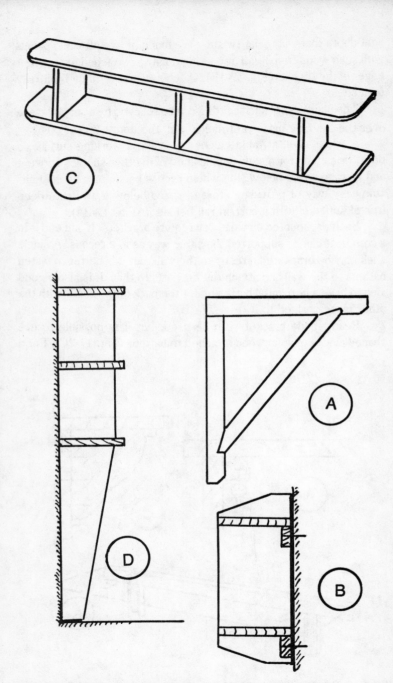

Fig. 17-3. Variations of shelf support, attachment, and backing.

338

heavy load or a wide shelf, wooden brackets can be built. The diagonal fits into notches (Fig. 17-3A). With any bracket it is advisable to make the angle a few degrees more than a right-angle. Even if it does not actually sag, a right angle tends to make the shelf look like it.

It is possible to support a bank of shelves with brackets mounted on vertical battens, but for such constructions as bookcases it is better to join ends and shelves with dado joints and probably add a plywood back (Fig. 17-3B). There is no need for brackets unless the shelves are very long; then brackets or spacers will be needed intermediately (Fig. 17-3C). Such an arrangement can extend across an entire wall if you have boards of sufficient length.

With any sort of wall assembly, the supports that take the greatest load are at the top. If attached to a hollow wall, some of the top fasteners should be long screws into studs. Lower fastenings take some of the load, but they do not get much strain, except when a load away from the wall is put on the bottom of the assembly.

Much of the advantage of shelving is in providing storage without reducing floor space, but in some situations it may be advantageous to extend one or more legs to the floor. This can be decorative and relieves wall fasteners of some of the load. You may use a single central leg—perhaps tapered—or legs at the corners (Fig. 17-3D).

WINDOW SEAT

Plywood and stout strip wood will make a seat with built-in storage space against a straight wall, or in a recess or window bay. In a bay or recess, mark the height around the sides, taking care to keep the lines horizontal and allowing for the thickness of the top. A comfortable seat level is not more than 16 inches from the floor. Even if the sides of a recess are uneven, the front of the seat must be parallel with the back (Fig. 17-4A).

Battens are fastened around the top of the box and the front is arranged to attach to more battens at the sides and on the floor (Fig. 17-4B). The front is a panel of plywood. For a very wide seat or to use smaller pieces of plywood you may join the front sections over vertical battens (Fig. 17-4C). Ideally the batten framework should be halved or tenoned, but it is satisfactory to use nailed joints.

A lifting top requires parallel sides and must swing clear of any framing around a window or other projections above it. If cushions are to be used behind it, the hinge line should be located forward enough that the lid can swing up without removing the cushions. Frame around the top of the box to allow for this, with a top surface level with that of the lid. It usually looks best for the lid to overlap the front, so the framing at the sides should project to support it (Fig. 17-4D).

The top framing can be fastened directly to the battens attached to the wall. The greatest load comes on the hinge rail, which should extend across the recess to be supported at the walls. The pieces that form the sides of the opening may be halved to it.

Using reasonably stout plywood in a small recess, it may be enough just to frame around the edges of the top, but there are occasions when such a seat may be stepped or jumped on, so it is advisable to have plenty of intermediate framing (Fig. 17-4E). Such framing is rather ugly and may be visible when the lid is lifted: if thin plywood is available, panel the underside of the lid.

In a small recess the lid may be satisfactorily supported by the hinges and the front edge, but if the seat is very big it is advisable to include ledges under the sides and back of the opening so the lowered lid rests on them (Fig. 17-4F).

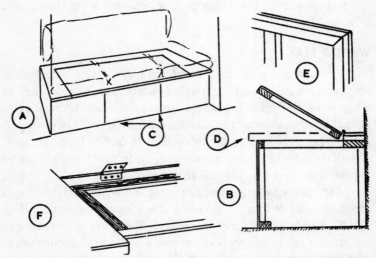

Fig. 17-4. Framed plywood makes a window-recess seat with storage underneath.

This completes the basic construction woodwork. With cushions on the top, the only visible part will be the front, which can be painted or stained and varnished to match the rest of the room. Plainness there can be broken up by a pattern of molding on the plywood surface.

Vertical cushions at the back are not as comfortable as sloping ones. If there is enough back-to-front depth, sloping plywood can be arranged from near the hinge line back to the wall. With the cushions fitted, there should be at least 15 inches of seat depth to provide comfortable sitting.

It is possible to arrange this sort of fixed seating in a corner. One end is then the same as in a recess, but the other end is cut square and closed in like the front. If the seat is away from a corner, both ends can be enclosed this way. At an open end, framing can extend up the wall and above the box level to prevent cushions from sliding off.

This type of seat/chest is useful in a bedroom for storing spare bedding, in which case the chest can be lined with plywood or hardboard, then possibly covered with plastic padding or cloth over a thin layer of cotton batting. The underside of the lid should be treated the same way, but any padding should be kept within the boundary of the chest framing.

BED

Pieces of plywood with attractive grain may suggest bed ends. As little more than the panels will show, other parts can be made of available strips and the whole bed framework stained and varnished to match. Dimensions will depend on available plywood panels, but 30 inches is a minimum width for a single bed and 48 inches for a double one. Length is usually 6 feet, 6 inches. Besides the wood available, standard mattress sizes should be considered before any wood is cut.

In the construction shown, the panels are made independently of the legs. The plywood panel is carefully squared and the framing parts made and fastened to it (Fig. 17-5A). The side pieces should be wide enough to accept fasteners from the legs. Since the edges are covered there is no need to miter the frame corners. Fasten the plywood to the framing with glue and finishing nails, which can be punched and covered with filler. Plane the finished edges if necessary and see that they are at right-angles to the plywood surfaces.

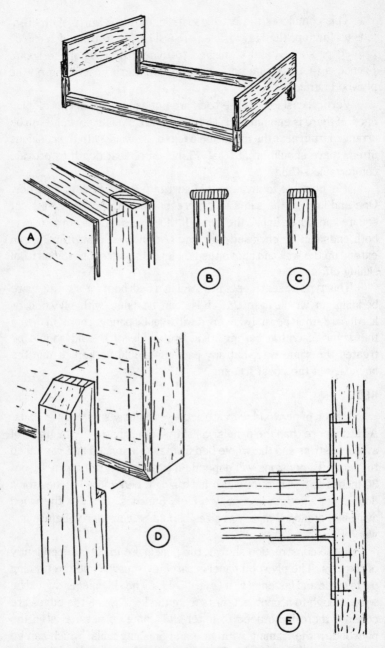

Fig. 17-5. Framed plywood makes bed ends; stout lumber is needed for legs and rails.

The strips around the edges may be any wood not more than 1/2 inch thick, and will produce an interesting effect if they're of a color different from the plywood. The strips may overlap in the finished bed end (Fig. 17-5B) or they can be put on with a little to spare and planed flush (Fig. 17-5C). In both cases, round all edges and the top corners.

The legs should be 2 inches square (or slightly more) and notched over the ends slightly (Fig. 17-5D). At the foot end their height should allow for the panel lower edge being only a little higher than the bottom of the mattress. At the head end it should be near the top of the mattress. Attach the legs with glue and the longest screws that can be used without risk of breaking through.

How the lengthwise parts are arranged depends on the support the mattress needs. If it is framed it will only need two rails, which may be 2 × 4s held to the legs with steel angle brackets (Fig. 17-5E). Tenons or other more permanent joints will make dismantling difficult if the bed has to be moved.

When deciding on the bed height, it is advisable to allow for casters fitted to the legs. Allow enough clearance for the mattress to fit easily.

LOUNGE CHAIR

A comfortable chair can be made almost entirely from strips about 3 inches by 1 inch, such as may be recovered from pallets. Padding is provided by cushions which lift out; the available sizes will determine the chair's dimensions. Springing can be by rubber webbing or by steel coil springs. Coil springs may be bought with hook ends and perforated steel strip to hold them. Material for springing should be obtained before making the frame.

The chair sides consist of plywood panels with framing extended to form legs (Fig. 17-6A). Although the seat slopes, the bottom rail looks better if it's parallel with the floor. Make the sides as a pair so they match. The seat bottom slopes (Fig. 17-6B). Leave its top flat for rubber webbing, but slope (Fig. 17-6C) or rabbet it to take the metal strip for springs. If square material is unavailable, a piece of wider board cut down the middle and joined will do.

The back is of material similar to the side framing, arranged at right angles to the seat sides (Fig. 17-6D) and screwed through the plywood into the framing. A strip inside each back piece takes the webbing or springs, but it need not be as thick as the seat pieces.

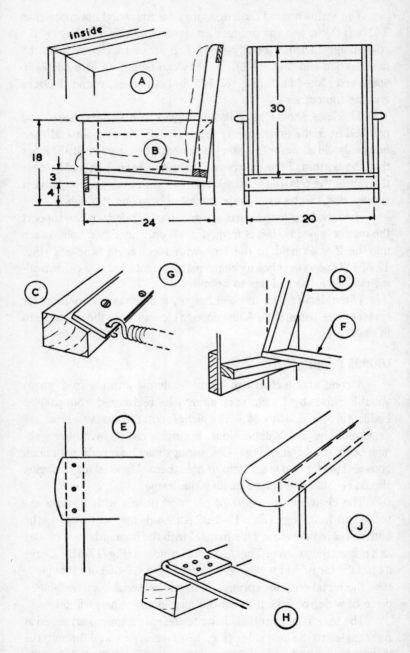

Fig. 17-6. A lounge chair can have plywood sides and lift-out cushions supported on springs or webbing.

The tops of the back sides can be rounded. There are a minimum of three cross members, which can be notched into the sides. Although they could be flush, top and front pieces may project and be rounded (Fig. 17-6E). At the back of the seat there is a crosspiece on the spring strip (Fig. 17-6F). Besides stiffening the chair, this prevents the back cushion from dropping through. Further stiffening is provided by another strip on edge. With the usual low seat height of this type of chair, the short legs should be stiff enough, but if the wood is of light section, it may be thickened inside behind the cross piece.

If coil springs are used, the metal plates are screwed in place and the springs stretched to fit (Fig. 17-4G). With webbing, turn back an end and tack it into the rail at one side (Fig. 17-6H). Stretch it slightly and do the same at the other side. If the space between webbing strands is about the same as their width, that should give enough support. It may be advisable to use a double thickness of webbing across the front.

Arms (Fig. 17-6J) should be well-rounded. Finish the chair to match other furniture and drop in the cushions to make the chair ready for use.

WALL MIRROR

A mirror on the wall is useful in any room. It might be fitted to the back of a door. Its usefulness is increased with a shelf below; this assembly might serve as a dressing table in a small bedroom. Dimensions depend on the mirror available.

The frame should have a rabbet deep enough to take the mirror and a piece of plywood backing (Fig. 17-7A). These sizes will determine the thickness of wood to be used. The border should be about 3 inches wide. The bottom, which should be wider, could be two pieces with their joint hidden by the shelf.

Prepare strips for the frame by cutting rabbets in strips of wood, a little long to allow for the corner joints. Several corner joints are possible. The expert's joint is a mortise and tenon (Fig. 17-7B). This can be arranged so the tenon comes in the rabbet and one shoulder is stepped over the front of the mortised piece. Taking a tenon in about 1 inch should be enough.

Another way is to use dowels, also kept inside the rabbet for simplicity in drilling (Fig. 17-7C). One piece has to have its end

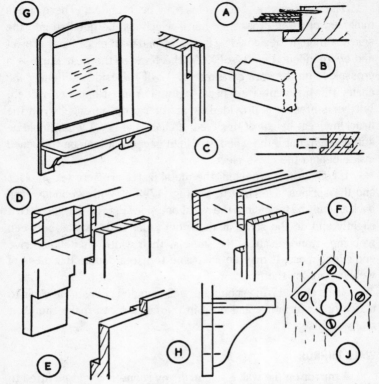

Fig. 17-7. A wall mirror is simple to make and may be fitted with a shelf.

stepped over the other, but for convenience in drilling for dowels the step cut should not be made until the holes have been drilled.

The corners could also be halved, going right through at the top corners (Fig. 17-7D) and only part way at the wider bottom (Fig. 17-7E). These joints should be screwed from the back, as well as glued. If facilities for cutting a rabbet are not available, it is possible to make the frame of two thicknesses of wood all around. This forms the rabbet; the strips can be arranged at the corners like halving joints (Fig. 17-7F).

The outline need not be severely plain. The top edge may be curved or otherwise shaped. The sides can project below the bottom, which could also be shaped (Fig. 17-7G).

If there is to be a shelf, its depth depends on the situation. In a narrow passageway it should not be more than about 4 inches, but in a bedroom it could be deeper.

Wooden brackets look better than metal ones. Let the angle be very slightly more than a right angle so the shelf does not look as if it is sagging. Also, things on it will not tend to roll off. Fasten the brackets and the shelf with screws from the back (Fig. 17-7H). Most shelves will hold to the brackets with glue only, but a wide shelf may need screws, which can be counterbored and plugged.

Glass is a heavy material, so allow for secure hanging. There can be a screw in each side about one-quarter of the depth down from the top. Another way to provide invisible hanging is to use keyhole plates over holes at the back (Fig. 17-7J) to hook over projecting screws in the wall.

A mirror reflects the inside of a rabbet. If the assembly is to be given a dark stain and varnish finish, carry this into the rabbet. A lighter finish can also be treated this way, or it may be better to use black stain or paint inside the rabbet.

TABLE

If the crate side is a size that suggests a table top with little or no modification, that may be the best thing to use it for. In making a table, it is the large area of flat top that is usually most difficult to obtain. The other parts are more easily found.

In a fairly large table with no lower rails, the usual construction has rails tenoned or doweled into the legs. The height is about 30 inches, which is convenient for working at when standing, or for sitting. So knees can go under the table, the rails should not be more than 5 inches deep, but depth is obviously valuable in stiffening the legs (Fig. 17-8A). The top may be solid wood or particle board with wood edging. It may be plywood stiffened by framing and with wood edging. If the top is to be plywood from a crate, its framing may have to be made up to suit the legs and rails. There should be enough width of solid wood under the top to extend over the rails (Fig. 17-8B). How much stiffening to put across the plywood depends on the thickness and stiffness of the plywood, but crosspieces at about 15-inch intervals are advisable, even if the plywood seems stiff, so sagging will not develop in use.

As the top determines other dimensions, it should be made up first. Legs should be fairly stout: 2 1/2 inches square is the minimum, but many tables have legs as much as 4 inches square at the top, relieved by tapering to the bottom. For a kitchen or dining

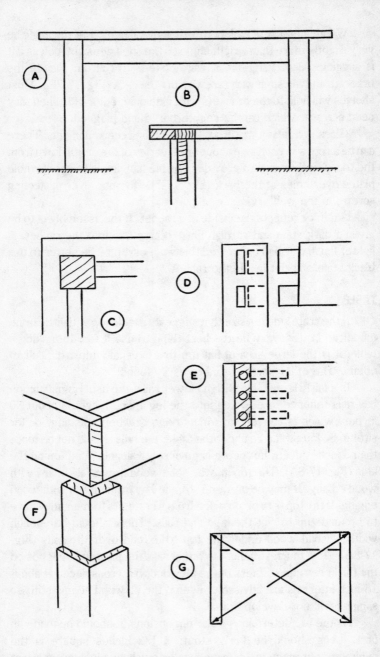

Fig. 17-8. A table can have tenoned or doweled rails, or the legs can be fitted inside a framed top.

table the rails may be about a 5-inch-by-1-inch section. In conventional construction the legs are set in about 2 inches and the rails are a little farther in (Fig. 17-8C).

The rails may be tenoned (Fig. 17-8D) or doweled (Fig. 17-8E). All the rigidity of the table depends on these corner joints, so they should be cut carefully and glued adequately. A simpler construction, which should be strong if carefully made, has the rails arranged under the table top like the sides of a box. The legs are notched to fit inside, so they reach to about half the thickness of the rails (Fig. 17-8F). If the rails are fairly close to the outside edges of the top, the legs can be put in without notching, but notches are neater and stronger. The joints should be securely clamped while gluing and reinforced with screws.

It is very important—for appearance—that the assembly is square and upright. Make one side and check its diagonals (Fig. 17-8G), then assemble the opposite side on it. When the glue has set, attach the sides to the other rails and check the new diagonals. Let the glue dry with the table on a level surface.

If the top is plywood, it will not expand or contract, so it can be attached with slot screws; if solid wood, use blocks to allow movement.

Bottoms of legs should be flat and given a slight bevel all around to reduce the risk of splitting or catching in mats or carpets.

WALL UNITS

A fitting close to or attached to a wall can serve as a piece of built-in furniture. Basically it may be a bank of shelves, but parts may be enclosed with doors, there can be flaps to let down to serve as desk tops, and a record player may be built in with its speakers at the sides. It is possible to make up the assembly as modular units which can be rearranged, or the units can be fixed in position.

How the work is planned will depend on available wood. There are two basic ways of approaching the design. The through lines may be mostly vertical (Fig. 17-9A). This suits modular construction, as several units can be stood alongside each other. For a more permanent construction the through lines can be horizontal, so the assembly is based on a series of long shelves (Fig. 17-9B).

The back-to-front depth should be decided. This will depend on the widest thing to be accomodated, but even if there is nothing very

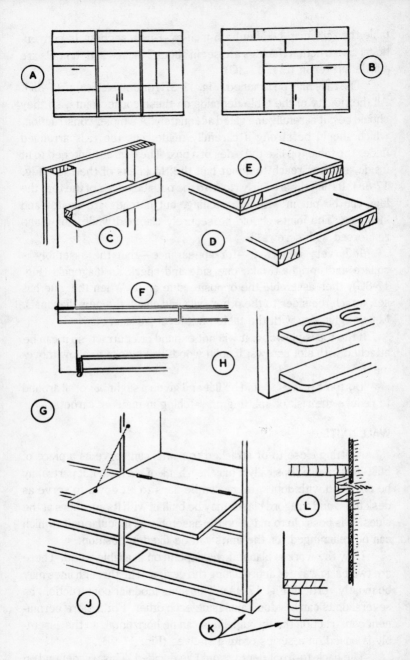

Fig. 17-9. Wall units can be based on horizontal or vertical lines. Construction may use framed plywood.

wide a depth of about 15 inches is advisable, although this may be modified to suit available wood.

Solid wood may make the major parts, although framed plywood uprights are convenient for attaching shelf supports where needed (Fig. 17-9C). Shelves can also be framed plywood. Those below eye level only need panels on top (Fig. 17-9D), but higher shelves need panels below for the sake of appearance (Fig. 17-9E).

Watch squareness in all construction. It may be possible to have the units with their backs open to show the wall, but plywood or hardboard backs serve to hold the other parts square, as well as cover the wall.

Doors may be surface-mounted to give greatest access to the space behind and avoid the need for very careful fitting. A small door may be thick plywood, but others should be made of plywood on both sides of strip framing (Fig. 17-9F). Doors may fit inside their openings (Fig. 17-9G). There should be stops on the shelves. Ensure that door lines are parallel with the vertical and horizontal lines of the unit. There can be racks inside doors for glasses or bottles. (Fig. 17-9H).

A flap to function as a working surface may be made like a door and hinged horizontally (Fig. 17-9J). It is possible to arrange supports to swing out below a flap, but a folding strut or piece of chain is simpler.

The bottom of a unit is best with set-back plinth (Fig. 17-7K). A crossbar below one or more shelves will provide a strong place for screwing to the wall (Fig. 17-9L).

STORAGE TABLES AND STOOLS

A unit that acts as a stool or table, yet incorporates storage space, is useful in many ways. It can be a sewing box. It may contain shoe-cleaning material with its top a suitable height to put a foot on. A large chest may store bedding and have a top suitable for a seat. Equipment for games may stow inside, while the top serves as a seat for spectators.

Several methods of construction are possible. A plywood box end may have legs fixed outside, with a matching crossbar at the top and a narrower rail at the bottom (Fig. 17-10A). If the legs do not project they should be nearer square. Sides are plywood panels reinforced inside with strips (Fig. 17-10B). The bottom fits within

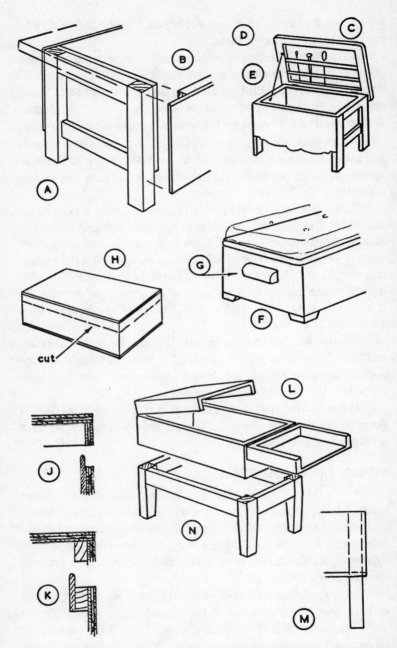

Fig. 17-10. A table with storage space may be framed around table legs or made as a box on legs.

the sides, which may have shaped bottom edges. The top may be a single piece of thick plywood or particleboard, or thinner framed plywood (Fig. 17-10C). It may be possible to utilize the framing for fittings to hold needles or other tools (Fig. 17-10D). If the lid overlaps, it is advisable to have a cord or chain inside to prevent it from being forced back, straining the hinge screws (Fig. 17-10E).

If maximum storage space is needed, a box can be made without built-in legs, all framing inside, and blocks under the corners to act as feet (Fig. 17-10F). The lid may be an overlapping top. If the chest is to be moved about, there should be blocks on the ends to serve as handles (Fig. 17-10G).

An alternative to a flat top is to make a lid part of the box construction. The plywood structure on framing is made as one unit with no fasteners near where cuts will be made. The lid is sawn away from the box (Fig. 17-10H). If the plywood alone is stiff enough, there may be a lip put around the inside of the box for the lid to drop over (Fig. 17-10J). If stiffening is needed, the lip comes inside that (Fig. 17-10K).

A variation on this is a sewing box with a two-part lid which hinges outwards on the end of the box (Fig. 17-10L). Some stiffening along the hinge lines may be needed, but stout plywood may serve for other parts of the lids without stiffening.

This type of box may be made into a table by using legs in the framing extending through the bottom (Fig. 17-10M). Another way is to make the box as a unit, then make up table framing to fit underneath (Fig. 17-10N) and attach it to the box with pocket screws inside the rails.

CHAIR FRAME

Much fully upholstered furniture is based on a wooden frame that is hidden in the finished article, except for short legs or feet. In most cases the frame is built up from strip wood, such as might be obtained from crates or pallets. It will be impossible to get at the frame once it is covered, so it should be made of sound wood with secure joints, but since appearance is not important, this is a project where wood that is unsuitable for furniture surfaces can be used. It is not usually necessary to plane chair-frame wood, but a very rough sawn surface should be smoothed enough to prevent snagging covering material or interfering with the fit of joints.

There is very little shaping to a modern chair frame: nearly all parts are straight and flat. In a typical armchair or club chair there are two matching sides (Fig. 17-11A). Most joints are doweled and glued. The arm is the only part that is not rectangular, with its front wider than the back. The bottom rail provides stiffness (Fig. 17-11B), so its joints should be good. The narrow rail above it is a "gut rail" (Fig. 17-11C), needed when the side is covered. The bottoms of the legs will project to form feet, so they should be planed and sanded.

Front and back rails match the side bottom rails (Fig. 17-11D), forming a box in which the pattern of springs will be arranged on webbing. Other cross members provide stiffness, with one forming the top edge of the back. There may be a lower horizontal member and a gut rail to serve the same purposes as those on the sides (Fig. 17-11E).

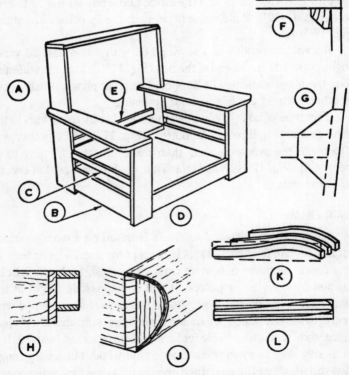

Fig. 17-11. A frame for upholstery can be built of salvaged wood. Shaped parts may be laminated.

A weakness of such a design is that in all directions it is four-sided—a pattern with little resistance to distortion. Blocks put in corners where they will not interfere with the covering resist distorting loads (Fig. 17-11F). In some places diagonal bracing may be provided by a piece of plywood (Fig. 17-11G).

In some chairs the front of the seat projects beyond the arms. If this is to be a square edge, it is arranged by building out the front of the frame. The front rail may be brought forward or, using smaller springs at the front than in the body of the chair, extended with ledges (Fig. 17-11H).

Other fronts are founded. This can be done with shaped blocks on the front rail and thin plywood bent over (Fig. 17-11J). Arms may have curves in both directions. This can be arranged by vertically laminating several thicknesses of wood cut to shape individually (Fig. 17-11K). When these are glued together, the shaping in the other direction can be done (Fig. 17-11L). So that the opposite arm can be an exact match, use a hardboard or cardboard template that can be turned over to mark the shape.

DRAWER UNITS

The making of drawers by traditional methods calls for accurately cut wood of good quality and uniform size. Salvaged wood may not always come up to these standards, but it is possible to make blocks of drawers with wood of lesser quality if overlapping fronts are used to disguise any variation in wood sizes.

When planning a block of drawers it is always advisable to taper drawer depths. If they are all the same depth, an optical illusion makes the lower ones seem shallower.

The chest should be made like a box on edge mounted on a plinth (Fig. 17-12A). It could be solid wood or framed plywood. If plywood framing is used, the drawer runners will have to be built with guides (Fig. 17-12B). The runners should be the same depth as the front rails. These may allow the drawer fronts almost to meet (Fig. 17-12C), or, with a deeper rail, there can be a gap. Although the runners need not be as deep as the rails to support the drawers, shallower ones would require "kickers" to prevent drawers from tilting when partly withdrawn (Fig. 17-12D).

The drawers are boxes made to fit easily in their space. If the drawers are not the full depth of the box, there should be stops on the runners (Fig. 17-12E).

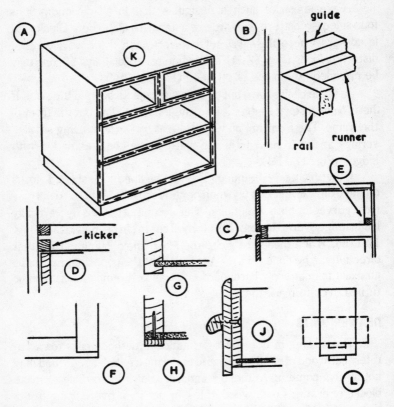

Fig. 17-12. Drawers can be made as boxes with overlapping fronts, fitted between strips in framed plywood chests.

In the best construction, the corners would be dovetailed, but it is simpler to let the sides into the notched inner front (Fig. 17-12F). A plywood or hardboard bottom can be let into a groove (Fig. 17-12G) if tools are available for making it. If the bottom has to be nailed on, allow for a thin strip of wood glued on to travel on the runner (Fig. 17-12H).

See that the drawer runs correctly and the front is flush when shut before fitting the outer front. This is a piece that overlaps all around. Its edges may be rounded and screws may be driven from the back to help glue hold it. If a wooden handle is made, it also can be screwed from the back (Fig. 17-12J).

Drawers should be the same width but they vary in depth. In a large chest of drawers there may be two half-length drawers above the others, with handles in line (Fig. 17-12K). Large drawers are easier to make than small ones where there is less margin for error, so large furniture is simpler than making a dainty drawer in a small cabinet. A drawer that is deeper back-to-front than in its width will slide more easily than one which is wide and shallow (Fig. 17-12L). If a drawer needs lubricating, rub the wood with candle wax.

Besides their use as free-standing units, blocks of drawers can be built into other things. Two stacks of drawers with a top across them will make a desk or a sewing work table. With only one stack of drawers, the top can extend to one side and be supported by legs. Drawers and their contents are useful for making a piece of furntiure stable. There may be drawers up to table height, then lighter shelves for display items, as in a Welsh dresser.

Chapter 18
Outdoor Woodwork

There are many uses for salvaged wood in making items for the yard, garden or other places outside your home. Sometimes this is an opportunity to use wood that is not good enough for indoor use, but many outdoor things benefit from the use of good material just as indoor things do. Outdoor woodwork has to stand up to much more severe conditions than that in the shelter of a house, so it is false economy to use wood that might be better burned. However, often good wood that cannot be brought to a furniture finish has uses outdoors.

USING THIN STRIPS

Fruit crates are often made of wood that is no more than 1/4 inch thick. If it can be cut into strips of uniform width on a table saw, there are several small things that can be made from it. Markers or pegs are needed at the ends of rows of planted seeds. Instead of any odd twig, it is convenient to have a stock of pegs (Fig. 18-1A), preferably with one surface given a coat of flat white paint so markings are easily seen.

Three thicknesses can be put together to make a trowel that will be appreciated by the window-box gardener (Fig. 18-1B). One end is pointed and the other thinned and flat. Glued joints should be enough. Edges should be rounded.

Pieces can be put together to make a low sectional picket fence (Fig. 18-1C). Various patterns are possible, but a number of these can be used to border a flower garden. Use glue and clenched nails for the joints (Fig. 18-1D). Clench diagonal to the grain to prevent splitting.

A trellis can be made in the same way. If it is to be of fixed shape, strips can be nailed directly to posts, but it is usual to arrange a trellis to fold, so it can be taken down and used in another place. Sizes will depend on the length of the strips you have, but cut and mark all pieces the same (Fig. 18-1E). Lay the pieces across each other at about right angles, and nail through the marked points (Fig. 18-1F). The trellis may then be folded anywhere between closed and open to make square or diamond shapes.

WINDOW AND PLANT BOXES

A box to contain soil in which something will grow must be strong and able to withstand damp conditions. Some woods have a natural resistance to dampness, but others will need treating with a preservative. This must be applied and allowed to dry thoroughly before soil is used; some wet preservatives may affect seeds.

The simplest box is a rectangular one, but it is stronger and looks better if the bottom is contained within the sides, instead of being nailed on (Fig. 18-2A). There should be holes in the bottom and the box should be raised slightly to permit drainage (Fig. 18-2B). Battens across the tops of the ends (Fig. 18-2C) provide something to grip if the box has to be lifted and reinforcement for the sides, to prevent them from bulging away from the ends. Most windowsills have a slight slope; a box can be made deeper at the front than the back to allow for this (Fig. 18-2D).

Boards are often thrown away because one edge—the "waney edge"—follows the outside of the tree. This uneven edge can become a feature in a box. The box can be raised at the ends with uneven edges along the bottom of the sides (Fig. 18-2E). A box to stand on a wall may have the uneven edge overhanging the wall (Fig. 18-2F).

Square potted-plant holders can be made with small offcuts of wood, but let the grain go across, for strength, even if the box is higher than it is wide. A moderate taper presents no problems, but a very wide tapered box needs special angles at the corners. If two

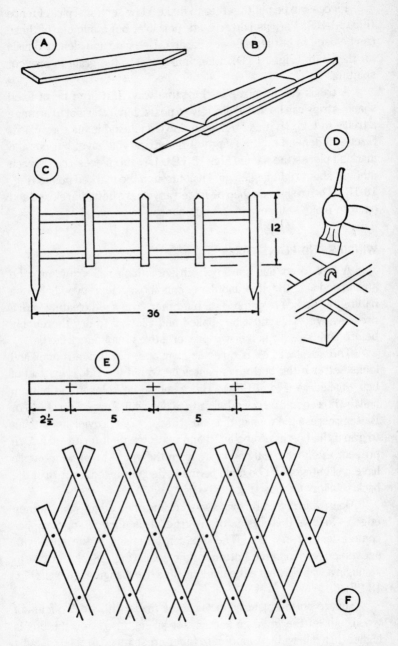

Fig. 18-1. Strip wood can be used to make small garden tools, fencing, and trellis.

sides overlap the others, they can be shaped for decoration (Fig. 18-2G) and will be stronger than sides cut close. All boxes should have drain holes in the bottoms, even if the plant they hold is in its own pot.

If plants in a number of identical pots have to be accomodated, there can be a board with holes to take them, either arranged as a rack—if the pots are decorative or the foliage is expected to hide the support (Fig. 18-2H)—or built into the top of a decorative box (Fig. 18-2J).

Boxes can be painted to match existing decor, but boards with a natural edge look better if given a clear finish. They need not be planed, although this improves them, but a few coats of varnish brings out the natural features of the wood.

SEED BOXES AND PROTECTORS

Trays in which to start seeds may have only a temporary use, but if well-made they should last for many seasons. The wood need not be very thick; it may be possible to use up thin wood on the sides, with thicker ends for stiffness (Fig. 18-3A).

If plywood is used, it should be exterior or marine grade, bonded with waterproof glue. Strips used on the bottoms may have narrow gaps, sufficient for drainage but not wide enough to let soil through (Fig. 18-3B).

Corner blocks will stiffen construction and their projecting tops will allow boxes to be stacked, at least until their contents have grown a few inches (Fig. 18-3C). If sides project a little below the ends, this will help to keep stacked boxes in position.

When seeds are planted in the open there is the problem of protecting them from birds. This is often done with strands of cotton or thread. Better than using odd sticks at the ends is the use of prepared supports, which can be made from salvaged wood.

The simplest arrangement is a crossbar supported on two or more pieces that push into the ground (Fig. 18-3D). This can be made long enough to go over more than one line of seeds. The thread attaches to a series of partly driven nails. Their spacing may depend on experience, but 2 inches should be enough (Fig. 18-3E).

More complete protection of a single row comes from using semicircular shapes. They could be barrel ends or parts of round offcuts obtained from a furniture manufacturer. They could be cut

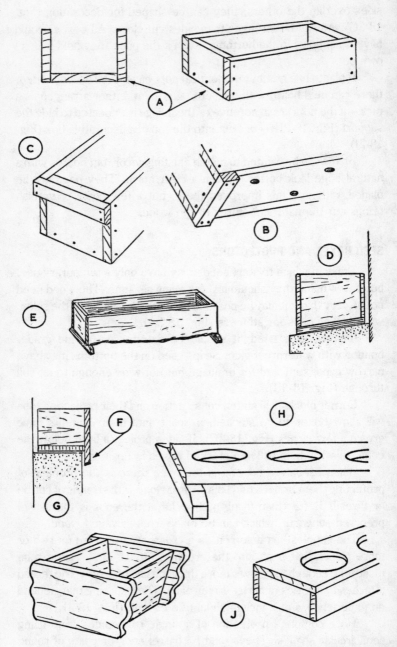

Fig. 18-2. Window boxes and plant-pot holders are simple nailed constructions.

from thick plywood that is known to be bonded with waterproof glue, or several strips of wood can be used, held together by the strips that push into the ground (Fig. 18-3F). Protection may be just as good if the outlines are not true curves, but your idea of craftsmanship may suffer every time you look at an irregular shape. A variation could be half an ellipse instead of part of a circle.

The bottoms of the pieces that go into the ground should not be too sharp (Fig. 18-3G). A fine point is too easily broken or split when it contacts a stone.

GARDEN TOOLS

Many garden tools need to be metal, but many of them have wooden handles. Suitable salvaged wood can be kept for replacement handles. A handle need not have a truly round section; a square piece of wood can be brought to a close approximation by planing. The corners are planed off until a reasonably regular octagonal section is obtained. This may be done by eye, or diagonals may drawn on the end and half a diagonal measured on each face from each corner (Fig. 18-4A), marking the border of a regular octagon. The next step is to plane off the eight corners. This will leave a shape that is probably acceptable for a tool handle, but if a smoother shape is wanted, the strip of wood can be held by sitting on it while it projects over the edge of a trestle and a strip of abrasive worked around it (Fig. 18-4B). The end of a handle should be rounded, and the other end may have to be tapered to fit the socket on a tool. Anyone unused to manual work will appreciate having at least the part that is handled smoothed and varnished.

Several things can be made incorporating rounded strips. A planting stick or dibber is one (Fig. 18-4C). These are often made from broken-off tool handles, but a long one can be used without stooping. A piece of steel rod across it will allow a foot to be used to help push into hard ground (Fig. 18-4D). The handle is best fixed with a tenon (Fig. 18-4E), but if the shaft is hollowed to take the handle, both parts can be drilled to take a dowel (Fig. 18-4F).

Another use for rounded strip stuff is a garden line winder. One piece is pointed and the top is rounded for ease in pushing into the ground. It can have a hole drilled through it to take the line (Fig. 18-4G). It need not be thicker than 3/4 inch, but if thicker it might also double as a dibber.

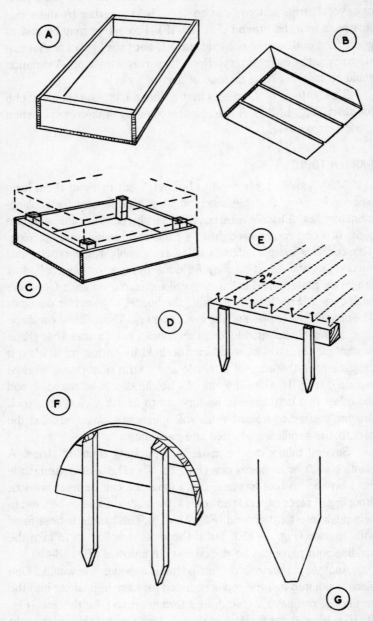

Fig. 18-3. Seed trays can be designed to stack. End frames can be made to protect young plants.

The other part is similar in size, but near the top a flat is cut to take a piece of exterior plywood (Fig. 18-4H) which is shaped so the line can be wound on it. Rounding the edges makes a neat job. Drill a hole in the plywood for the end of the line. A well-made winder deserves a paint finish—green if it is to blend into the garden, red if you want to find it among the foliage.

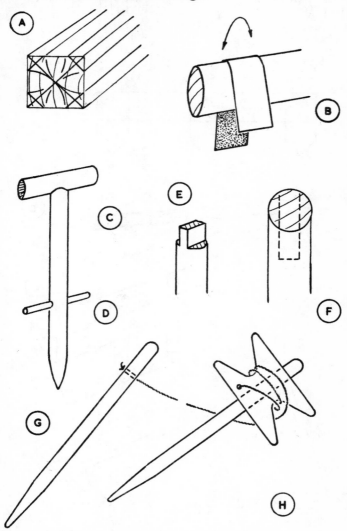

Fig. 18-4. Square wood can be made round to form planting sticks and line winders.

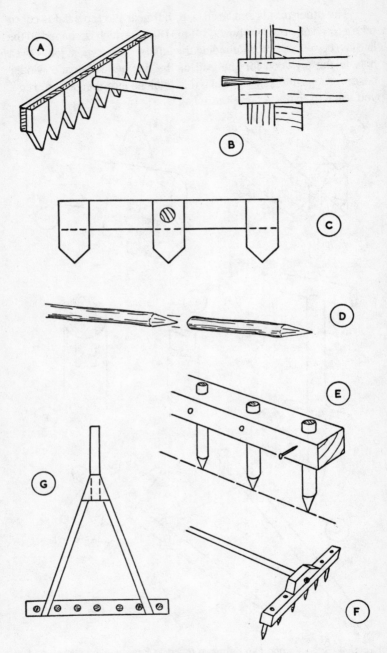

Fig. 18-5. Wooden rakes for several purposes can be made in many sizes.

RAKES

Some garden rakes have to be made of steel, but those used for gathering cut grass or leaves are better made of wood. A large wooden rake is much lighter than the equivalent metal one, and therefore is more effective as it is easier to handle.

A simple type for leaves has a number of strips of wood identically pointed, fastened to another piece with its grain going across them (Fig. 18-5A). The handle is a rounded rod taken through a hole and wedged (Fig. 18-5B). The end and the wedge should not be cut off: if the handle loosens, its other end can be hit on the floor to drive it further in, then the wedge tightened.

A similar tool can be made to make drills for planting seeds in rows a set distance apart. The points are cut at wider angles than for a rake and arranged according to the intended spacing (Fig. 18-5C).

A better type of rake for grass or straw has a large number of tines made of rounded pegs. These should be stout hardwood, such as hickory or ash, but any heavy crate wood should be strong enough.

Wood for the tines can be cut square on a table saw in lengths enough for several, then the edges planed off and the wood roughly rounded. A point can be cut with a chisel or knife (Fig. 18-5D), then that tine cut off and another point made.

The tines all fit into a stout crossbar. The best way to get an even projection is to let the tines go through until all points are level, then drive nails to fix them (Fig. 18-5E).

The center of the rake is thickened enough to allow a hole to be drilled for a handle (Fig. 18-5F). If a very wide rake is made, to gather the maximum amount of straw with each pull, the handle can be made into an A frame, with the part that is gripped projecting from where the sides meet (Fig. 18-5G).

SCOOPS

Much garden work is picking up things: grass cuttings, gathered weeds, fallen leaves, etc. Once the debris has been brought together, it is helpful to have something to pick it up with.

Two large pieces of plywood can be used to pick up leaves and such. They can have hand holes, but keep these far enough from the edge to allow your palms to lever on the surface of the wood (Fig. 18-6A). Round the parts that are gripped. A coat of paint will show

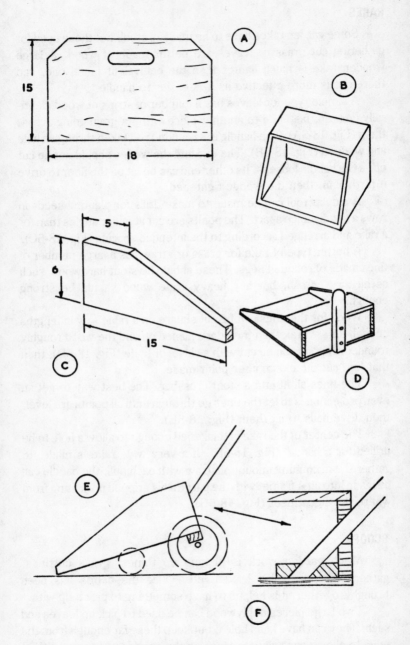

Fig. 18-6. Scoops are needed to pick up leaves and garden waste. They may be for hand use or fitted with wheels.

others that these are not just scrap wood to be used for other purposes.

It is useful to also have a scoop which could be a salvaged box cut across (Fig. 18-6B). If a scoop is made up, the sides have to provide strength, so make them first and let them be fairly stout (Fig. 18-6C). The bottom is best made of one piece of stout exterior plywood, with the underside of the front edge thinned slightly for ease in picking up. Too much thinning will weaken it. The back can be thickened where the handle fits; a simple and effective handle is a post standing up (Fig. 18-6D).

A further step is to make it larger and provide it with its own wheels, so it can be taken away and emptied. Suitable wheels may come from discarded toys and other things. They should not be too small or narrow, nor so big that they tilt the scoop too much.

The available wheels and axle may determine the size of the scoop. Locate the wheels towards the back if they are large, nearer the center of the sides if they are smaller (Fig. 18-6E). Thicken the bottom of the scoop for bolting through the axle or taking brackets to hold it.

The handle can be a simple pole. To give it strength and leverage, it can be taken through the back to a strengthened bottom (Fig. 18-6F).

FENCES AND GATES

Much salvaged wood is suitable for making fences, but avoid using non-durable woods without protection. Many hardwoods and some softwoods that are resinous have a good resistance to rot without treatment. Other woods need soaking in preservative. Painting it on is not enough, particularly near ground level. If a brown color is acceptable, soaking in creosote is a satisfactory treatment. Other preservative chemicals are either colorless or a light shade that produces a transparent effect. Even if a fence is to be painted, it is advisable to treat many woods with preservative first, but check that the particular preservative is suitable for use under paint.

Fence posts are usually square. If they are not, let the greater dimension be across the fence. Usually the post goes into a dug hole and is driven further. Do not cut too fine a point, which may break, but leave some flat on the end (Fig. 18-7A). How far the post goes into the ground depends on many factors, but allow for about one

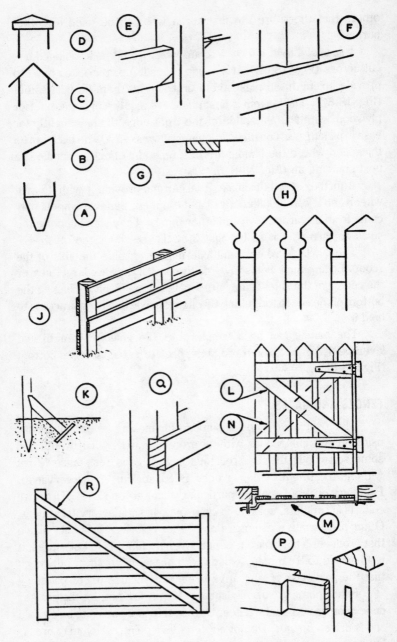

Fig. 18-7. Fence posts and rails can be made from salvaged wood. Gates are built up to match.

quarter of the above-ground length. It is advisable to leave a post extra long for driving, then cut to length after a row of posts have been driven. Bevel around the top to minimize the risk of splitting when driving in.

Mark the tops of a row of posts from a cord stretched along the row. The finished ends may slope or be cut to a point to shed rain which might otherwise enter the grain and cause rot (Fig. 18-7B). Alternatively, cap the post with sheet metal (Fig. 18-7C) or a shaped wood block (Fig. 18-7D).

Wood available will determine the lengths of rails, but for a field fence about 8 feet is the limit. For a garden fence the posts should be closer. Rails may be nailed to the posts directly, but a better fence has the rails in slots, with joints made with overlapping angles (Fig. 18-7E). The rails can also be notched slightly into the surface and nailed (Fig. 18-7F). If the fence is to have pales fixed to the rails, they should be let flush into the posts (Fig. 18-7G). If cutting away the post for the full thickness of the rail might weaken it too much, cut some from the rail. Joints are made between rails by cutting them to meet diagonally on the post.

A fence can be made with upright pales, either close or at intervals, with the tops decorated in some way (Fig. 18-7H). Use a cord to level the tops and a piece of wood as a gauge between pales. Close-boarding a fence gives privacy, but if it is in an exposed windy position, air pressure on it may be considerable. An alternative that gives almost as much privacy, but lets the wind through, has boards fixed horizontally on opposite sides of the uprights (Fig. 18-7J). A low fence of this type can be made from pallets, with the thicker parts as posts and the surface boards as rails.

Where fence posts come at corners, there should be struts to steady them. These can be notched into the posts or blocks nailed above them. At the lower end a piece is driven across to take thrust (Fig. 18-7K). This should also be done at an end post, particularly if it is to support a gate.

A small garden gate may be made to match the fence, but it is important to triangulate it to prevent it from dropping out of shape. This is usually done with a strut going across from near the lower hinge position (Fig. 18-7L). The ledgers can continue the line of the fence rails and the size of gate be arranged so the pales match those of the fence.

Hang this type of gate with T or strap hinges on the surface, usually on the rail side of the fence, then allow plenty of clearance at the other side, so the gate swings against a stop and there can be a secure catch (Fig. 18-7M). Gates always tend to settle, so allow a new gate to be slightly higher on the side opposite the hinge at first.

If a gate is more than about 30 inches wide, brace it with another diagonal the opposite way. The first is in compression between ledgers, but the second will be in tension and will take the load better if it overlaps and is securely nailed or screwed at the ends (Fig. 18-7N).

For a gate that is wider than it is high, a different method of construction is needed and the hinge post has to be substantial and firmly fixed. Such a gate can be made of 3-inch-by-2-inch stock, preferably joined with mortise and tenons, which are then doweled (Fig. 18-7P). In a simpler construction the joints could be lapped, but to avoid weakening either part, let the rails stand out from the uprights (Fig. 18-7Q).

A diagonal can go from the top of the hinge side to the bottom rail at the far end. If it can start even higher, the effect is attractive and the bracing better (Fig. 18-7R). Fasten securely everywhere the brace crosses another part. In a large field gate this should be by bolts. Another diagonal may go across the gate in the opposite direction.

There is no need for a high finish on many fences unless they are to be painted, but a gate is touched more, so should be given a smooth finish and all sharp edges removed. The gate rails may be closer toward the bottom to keep smaller animals in. Upright pales can be fixed to match adjoining fencing, but they should be additional to the normal construction and not in place of any of it.

SHED

A complete building may be made from crate material, from a small place to store garden tools to a roomy shed to use as a workshop. Large crates may provide subassemblies without full dismantling. The construction may be planned around these basic shapes.

Any shed should give standing headroom in at least part of the area it covers, and the roof should slope to shed water. This can be arranged with a ridge roof having an inside height of at least 6 feet, 6 inches (Fig. 18-8A) or a sloping roof with that height at the front (Fig. 18-8B). It would be better to have greater height so there is more room to move about and the doorway can have a clearance of over 6 feet. For a shed to be worked in, there should be standing headroom everywhere.

A shed can be made as units, or ends prefabricated and the sides and roof added in position. For unit construction the corner posts overlap and are bolted through (Fig. 18-8C). Parts should be framed as much as possible to give rigidity. Cladding will usually be exterior plywood, which provides stiffness, but this should be related to inner framing. At doors and windows, framing members should be carried through (Fig. 18-8D). Uprights should usually be stouter than horizontal members and may be notched in to give a smooth surface against the plywood (Fig. 18-8E). Corners could be bridle joints nailed through (Fig. 18-8F). Check squareness of each assembly and try opposite sides against each other.

Doors and windows should be framed with strips that cover the plywood edges; there should be a sill below each window with a groove under it to prevent water creeping back underneath (Fig. 18-8G). It is usually best to let the bottom rail cross below a door, to help retain the shape of the assembly. The door may shut against this.

When sides and ends are assembled, check diagonals and put temporary diagonal braces on to hold the shape if necessary. Purlins can be notched into the ends to support the roof (Fig. 18-8H). Alternatively there can be a central member for a ridge roof and the roof sections made up with plywood on framing that fits inside the upright parts (Fig. 18-8J). In any case, allow a good overhang. This looks better and provides protection from the sun, as well as keeping some rain clear of the walls. The two sections that meet at the apex can have strips to cover the joint (Fig. 18-8K). Attach these after roofing material is put over the plywood.

A shed may be erected on a concrete base, although a platform can be made from crates. In any case it should be fastened down, particularly in areas with high winds.

A plain shed may serve its purpose, but its appearance can be improved by adding bargeboards to the ends, possibly with a decorative finial at the ridge (Fig. 18-8L). If the main part of the shed is painted a dark color, the door and window framing and barge boards may be a contrasting lighter color.

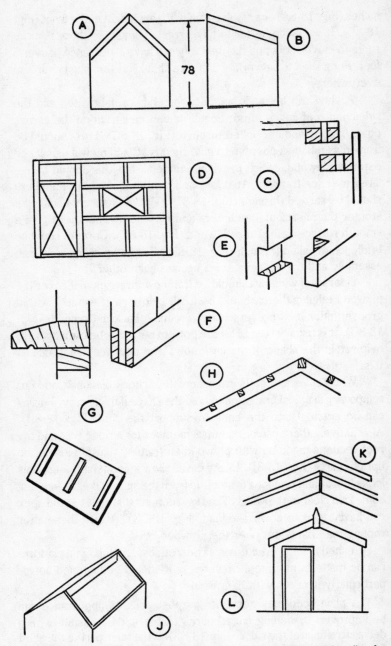

Fig. 18-8. A shed has to be planned to suit needs and may be framed to allow for sectional construction.

A storage shed may have no lining, but for all-weather use it is advisable to line with plywood, preferably with insulating material between the two skins.

DOG KENNEL

A dog kennel may be constructed like a small shed, but there are a few special considerations if it is to be satisfactory. Size depends on the dog, but allow plenty of room back to front so the animal may get away from the entrance in bad weather. It should be able to get through the opening easily, but it should not be unnecessarily large. Sometimes the roof is made to lift off for cleaning, but this design allows for the kennel to lift from its floor.

The floor is framed plywood raised for dryness and warmth (Fig. 18-9A). Make this first as it determines other sizes. Make the back with plywood to overlap the floor. Frame it inside (Fig. 18-9B), allowing notches for lengthwise parts.

Make the door end, using the back as a template for shape. As the roof is to overlap and act as a porch, the notches for lengthwise roof members should be cut right through. Round the edges of the door opening thoroughly. Fix a piece to the front edge of the floor to match the door gap (Fig. 18-9C).

Fix the lengthwise side members. The one at the eaves should be beveled to match the slope of the roof. Let them extend enough to make the porch. Add the plywood sides. The whole assembly should fit over the floor firmly, but it should be possible to push the floor out. Outside strips around the sides and the back will stiffen and allow fastening down.

Nail on the plywood roof. At the front you may add strips under the porch over the doorway (Fig. 18-9D). Allow the plywood to overlap at the sides and stiffen below with a strip of wood (Fig. 19-8E). Decorative barge boards can be attached to the front of the porch. Weatherproof the top with a strip of plastic or roofing material. See that all joints are tight to prevent drafts, and finish the kennel with paint.

A wooden platform to put in front of the kennel will help to keep the kennel clean and provide a dry area for the dog during the day. It should have a plywood deck at the same level as the kennel floor and be framed enough to provide stiffness (Fig. 18-9F). If the dog tends to push his eating and drinking vessels around, there can be a ledge

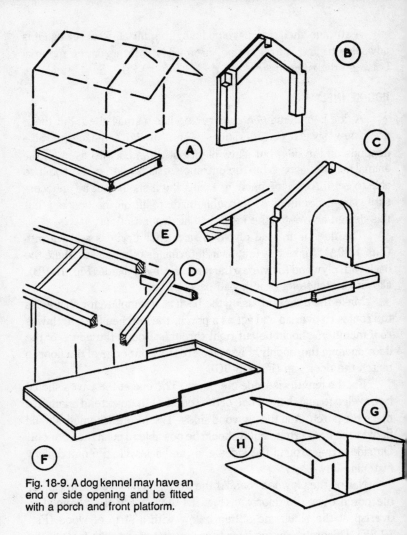

Fig. 18-9. A dog kennel may have an end or side opening and be fitted with a porch and front platform.

around one end of the platform or frames or blocks into which the vessels can be placed.

A kennel with an opening in the end is the most common type, but one with a door in the side gives better protection against the weather, as the dog can better get away from the door. This may be made like the other kennel, but an opening cut at the end of one side, or the kennel may be made with a single slope to the roof (Fig. 18-9G).

The roof may overhang a few inches to provide some protection for the door, but it is better to attach a separate roof over the full length of the porch (Fig. 18-9H).

COLD FRAME

The next best thing to a greenhouse for starting seedlings and protecting them from frost is a cold frame with a sloping glass top,

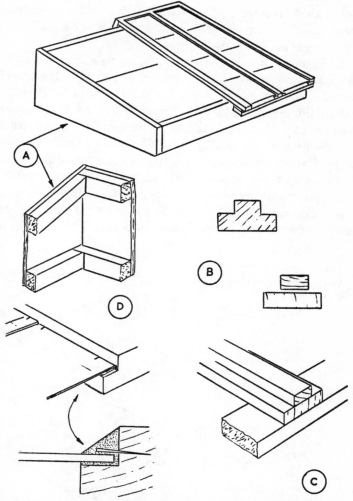

Fig. 18-10. A garden cold frame can be planned to suit surplus glass and made with solid wood or framed plywood.

preferably arranged so it faces south. Size may depend on the availability of salvaged glass. The panes do not have to be large, but a number of them should be the same width so they can overlap.

Size will depend on the wood and space avaialble. The sides may be solid wood or they can be framed plywood (Fig. 18-10A). Make them first. If the frame is light and there is a risk of it moving, the corner posts can extend downwards into the ground.

Back and front can be solid wood, with several pieces making up the width if necessary, or plywood may be used with stiffening across top and bottom. Bevel the top edges, at least partially, so the top will bear evenly on the frame.

The top could be hinged at the back, but for a large frame it can be made in two or more parts that can be lifted off. The glass is puttied in, so rabbets are needed. These can be cut in thick wood, or built up with strips (Fig. 18-10B). Top and bottom edges are made of stout pieces, with flat strips notched into them. Other pieces put on top provide the rabbets (Fig. 18-10C). These should be strong pieces of wood—although they need not be of very good quality—as glass is heavy and wood which flexes may cause the glass to crack.

Space the pieces to suit the glass available. Panels about 10 inches wide are suitable. One section may consist of three such panels, but if the whole frame is much wider than this, it would be

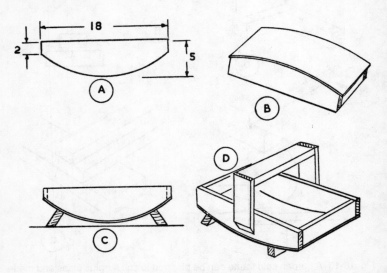

Fig. 18-11. A garden trug is made from small pieces of surplus wood.

better to have more sections. Apart from the problem of size and handling, you may wish to open part of the frame in suitable weather.

Glazing should be done so water runs off. There may be wood across the high end, but the glass should overhang at the bottom. Arrange pieces of glass to overlap. Put a thin layer of putty in the rabbet, then secure the glass with small nails (Fig. 18-10D) before puttying over.

Wood and putty should be protected with paint. As the bottom edge of the frame rests on he ground, it may be advisable to use a preservative, but select one that the makers say will not harm growing crops, either by seeping into the soil or giving off a vapor.

TRUG

When working in the garden it is convenient to have a handled box, sometimes called a trug. Some used to be woven with thin cleft pieces of wood, but an equally useful one can be made from plywood and oddments of solid wood.

The sides are matching pieces of solid wood cut with curves (Fig. 18-11A). Solid ends are arranged between them. Thin plywood is sprung around and nailed on. Make this slightly oversize and plane the edges level after fastening (Fig. 18-11B).

Make two feet of sufficient height to lift the center of the bottom clear of the ground and nail them on from inside (Fig. 18-11C).

The handle is a crossbar between two uprights. It could be a round rod, but better control of a heavy load is given by a flat piece with rounded edges. This is nailed between two uprights, which are nailed to the box sides (Fig. 18-11D).

There is no need for a high finish on the trug, but sharp edges should be removed and paint or varnish will stop the wood from absorbing dirt and make it easier to clean.

Chapter 19
Recreational Woodwork

Many things can be made for children to play with: for use in games, for activities such as camping, and for use with the car or recreational vehicle. Sturdiness is often more important than finish, so wood that is not good enough for furniture may be used. Children will get satisfaction out of quite simple toys that may not seem sufficiently sophisticated to adult eyes.

TRUCK TOOL BOX

A box to fit over the open body of a truck against the back of the cab may be bought in metal, but it can be quite satisfactory in wood, and it provides a means of using up comparatively narrow strips of plywood. Sizes depend on the truck, but the back-to-front dimension can be whatever is needed for the tools, fishing equipment or other things to be carried. Making it yourself allows tailoring the box to its intended contents.

The main supports are two stout strips (Fig. 19-1A) which could be planed 3-inch-by-2-inch softwood, although lighter-section hardwood should be stiff enough. The width of the truck sides governs the width of the box. The box depth is limited by the depth of the bed of the truck (Fig. 19-1B).

Make up one side with the supporting crossbar and necessary framing (Fig. 19-1C), and use this as a pattern to assemble the other side. Join these parts with cross bars, preferably notched into the framing (Fig. 19-1D). If the contents are not heavy, the bottom can be plywood nailed on, but strips may be provided for screws (Fig. 19-1E). For a heavy load it is better to arrange the bottom inside the framing (Fig. 19-1F).

Frame the ends (Fig. 19-1G), with extra bearing surfaces where the box will rest on the truck sides.

There are several ways that lids can be arranged. If long things are to be carried the lid should open across the truck, although it can be in two parts (Fig. 19-1H).

To give the lid clearance to lift behind the truck cab, the hinge line is a few inches from the edge, with a stiffener built in plywood over it. To provide some protection against rain running through the joint, there can be a piece below the hinge rail. The lid top is framed plywood with a lip that hangs a short distance over the box (Fig. 19-1J). If the lid is in two parts, there should be a strip across the center of the box for the parts to rest on.

It is convenient to get at smaller contents if two lids are hinged near the center (Fig. 19-1K) with a fixed center section to carry the hinges. The two lids can be made as the long lid, but it is also possible to arrange them to close flush with the sides (Fig. 19-1L). If this is done, the lid framing should match the box framing with pieces around the inside of the box for the lid to fit over, making a weatherproof joint. For easy closing, these pieces can be tapered slightly or the lid can be made slightly oversize.

For ease of access from the sides these covers can be tapered so they are deeper at the sides, but there must be enough depth left there for strength. One way of making tapered lids is described for the portable tool box (Chapter 15). The sides and lid are marked out on one piece of plywood, then the lids are sawn out, the edges cleaned up, and stiffening provided inside (Fig. 19-1M). Pieces inside the box for the lid to fit over will provide weatherproofing.

Hinges should be the butt type for security, as the screws are covered, but T or strap types can be used on the surface (Fig. 19-1N), with bolts taken through and their ends riveted. On a long joint, allow hinges at not more than about 18 inch intervals; otherwise there is a risk of the hinge line warping.

If the box will not always be used for the same things, it may be advisable to leave the inside without fittings, but for many purposes it is convenient to arrange a sliding tray on runners (Fig. 19-1P) to

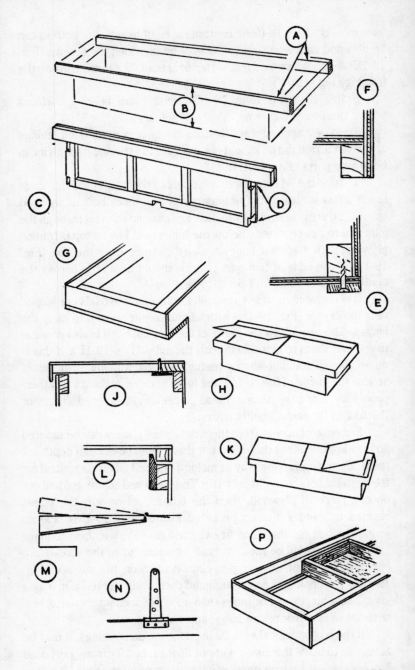

Fig. 19-1. A tool box for a truck made of framed plywood, with optional lids.

hold small things. If the runners extend across, the tray can be used at either side or pushed out of the way when something long is to be loaded.

Finish the box with plenty of paint inside and out. Even with exterior or marine-grade plywood there is a risk of moisture entering any exposed edges and causing trouble. These edges can be given a coating of glue as extra protection before painting.

SURFBOARD

A short surfboard (belly board) on which a swimmer lies to ride to a beach needs an upturned front to grip with the hands, clear of the surface so knuckles are not rubbed. This cannot be arranged with one piece of plywood, but two thin pieces can be laminated to keep the shape (Fig. 19-2A). The sizes shown should suit most adults and children.

Cut two pieces of 1/4-inch plywood to size, but do not shape the ends. A form is needed; this can be used for making any number of surfboards. Cut a piece of stout wood (about 1 inch thick) to the curve required and make two others to match it (Fig. 19-2B). Join these pieces with crossbars let into the edges, making the assembly slightly wider than the surfboard is to be (Fig. 19-2C). Let the crossbars project a little.

Bend a piece of plywood around this shape. It will bend more easily if the grain of the outer plies is across the curve. Leave a few inches of the flat projecting at the bottom. Nail the whole assembly securely together. This completes the form (Fig. 19-2D).

Try a strip of plywood around the form. Use a strip of scrap wood and clamps across the upper edge to pull the wood to the form (Fig. 19-2E). Although cross-grain plywood may bend more easily, the board will be stronger if the outer plies are lengthwise. The board could be made with one piece with lengthwise grain and one crosswise. When you are satisfied that both pieces will bend to the form, coat them with glue and bend them together. Besides clamps around the form, have other clamps or weights on the flat part (Fig. 19-2F). Do not disturb the board until the glue has set.

Round the forward edge a little, then round the four corners. Thoroughly round all edges in section. Besides making the board more comfortable to use, this will reduce the risk of splintering when it rubs on sand. The forward corners may be drilled to take a short

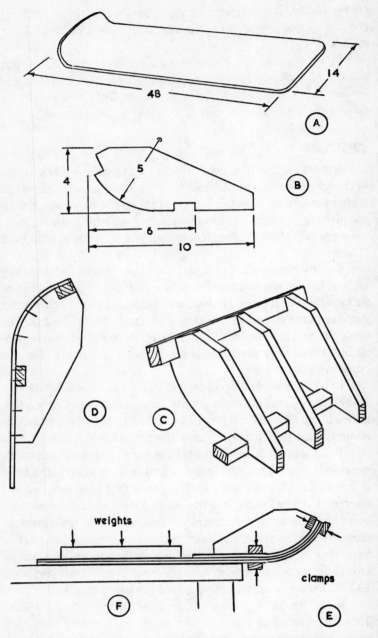

Fig. 19-2. The curve in a small surfboard is made by laminating two pieces of plywood around a jig.

rope bridle for holding. Do not use a long piece of rope, as it may tangle with a swimmer's legs. This is a belly board, for supporting the flat body, and is not intended for standing on.

Finish the board with several coats of paint. Bright red or orange will help in locating the board if it goes adrift. A personalized decorative pattern on the top will help to identify your board.

THROWING GAMES

Several games using rings or quoits—or even horseshoes—use wooden targets that can be made from salvaged wood. Round rods are needed as pegs, but they could just as well be square material which has been planed octagonal. This sort of stock is most easily made in a long length, then pieces cut off as needed.

A board for outdoor use with large rings can be made with six similar strips crossing (Fig. 19-3A). Pieces should be at least 2 inches by 1 inch. A little weight prevents the assembly from moving in use. The top could be covered with a sheet of plywood, either round or square, or individual pieces can be placed at every crossing with holes drilled for pegs, which are glued in (Fig. 19-3B). Paint the assembly in bright colors and add score numbers at each of the pegs.

Although rubber or rope rings can be used, plywood rings can be cut (Fig. 19-3C). If only thin plywood is available, several pieces can be laminated to make up thickness.

For a board to hang on the wall there may be a similar arrangement of pegs (Fig. 19-3D), but it will be necessary to slope the pegs upwards. They should be thinner and longer than pegs used on a board that lies on the floor. There is a tendency for rings to bounce back from a hanging board: it makes the game easier if you shape the pegs with a fret or jig saw (Fig. 19-3E).

For horseshoes there should be a single taller peg. Its base can be a disc of plywood over two crossing pieces with holes through which spikes hold the target to the ground (Fig. 19-3F). If iron horseshoes are used, the post should be about 1 1/4 inches thick. If plastic or wooden horseshoes are used, it can be a little thinner. Horseshoes may be cut from 3/4-inch plywood, or laminated from thinner pieces.

Another throwing game gives practice in throwing a lifeline or a rope ashore from a boat. The target consists of a strip of wood. Its size depends on the length of the throw: for outdoor use it should be about 72 inches long. It can be scaled down for indoor use. Pegs are mounted in drilled holes (Fig. 19-3G), and crossbars under its ends prevent it from tipping. The lifeline is a cord or rope weighted with a large knot or a bag of sand. The highest score is for a central throw.

Bags of sand, beans, or other filling can be thrown at a target with holes. This is a piece of stout plywood with a pattern of holes, raised above the ground (Fig. 19-3H). The holes may be all the same

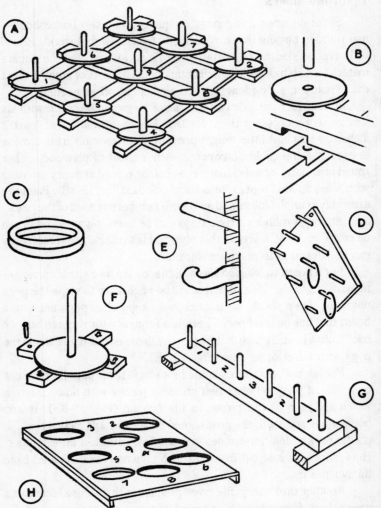

Fig. 19-3. Ring and throwing games can be made with strip wood and pegs or dowels.

size, or there can be larger holes for lower scores. To guard against disputes, a box can be fixed under each hole to retain any bag that goes through. As with all the games, finishing in bright colors makes it more attractive to children.

BLOCK TOYS

Many small wooden toys need wheels. Some may be salvaged from discarded items, but they can be made from wood. The simplest are pieces of broom handle or other rod sawn across (Fig. 19-4A). Surfaces can be rubbed smooth on a piece of abrasive paper and the center found by trial and error. If a wheel does not run true, that probably improves the toy in the eyes of its youthful owner! If a lathe is available, wheels can be turned individually or in sets of four (Fig. 19-4B), with each one drilled and sawn off in turn. Wheels can turn on screws between washers (Fig. 19-4C).

The simplest pulling toy is a flat board with two crosspieces to take the wheels (Fig. 19-4D). This can be made into a box with a load of cubes to go in it (Fig. 19-4E). If a pattern of different sizes and shapes is built, the toy becomes educational, teaching how to fit things together. A block at the front and youthful imagination makes it a car or truck (Fig. 19-4F).

Wheels and metal fasteners can be avoided if a tug and barges are made with interlocking shapes like loose rounded dovetails (Fig. 19-4G), so the assembly can be pulled along the ground. The same idea can be used for an interlocking snake that wiggles as it is pulled along.

Exact cubes are difficult to cut accurately; it is better to make rectangular building blocks. To get uniform size, it helps to make a simple sawing jig. This is like a bench hook, with a stop for the wood to be pushed against and a guide for the saw (Fig. 19-4H).

Wood-block toys are better made of close-grained hardwood than softwood, which may splinter if thrown about. In any case, sand surfaces smooth and round all edges and corners more than with an adult construction. Screws used for wheel axles should have round heads so there are no sharp edges above washers. Nails used in toys should be punched below the surface and covered with filler. Construction should be strong enough to stand up to abuse without joints opening, exposing nail points.

Ideally, all parts of a wood-block toy should be too large to be put in a child's mouth. Any paint used should be a non-poisonous type. Salvaged wood that contains grease or other liquid absorbed from its previous use should not be used for toys.

CAR CREEPER

It is useful to be able to lie on your back on a platform that can be moved about when working under the car. Retrieving some substantial casters from a piece of salvaged furniture or industrial equipment

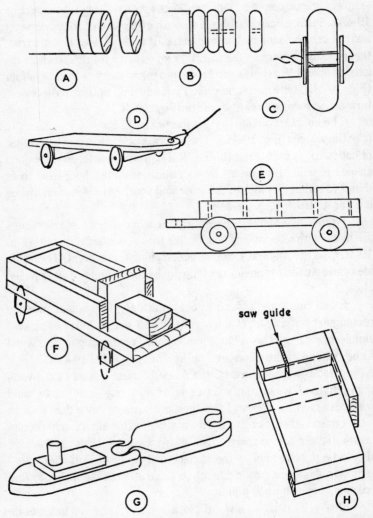

Fig. 19-4. A pulling toy can have wooden wheels and be made to carry blocks.

may suggest making such a creeper. Although it should be big enough to support your body, it should be no bigger than necessary to give the maximum adaptability in a confined space.

The base is a piece of plywood stiffened at intervals across its underside, and with strips lengthwise on top (Fig. 19-5A). At one end there should be a pad for your head. This can be a piece of wood faced with sponge rubber or plastic encased in a piece of plastic fabric (Fig. 19-5B).

How the casters are attached depends on their type. Corner blocks provide a solid place to which their plates can be screwed (Fig. 19-5C) or for holes drilled to take their stems.

Finish the wood with varnish or paint to reduce absorption of dirt and grease, and lubricate the casters so they swivel easily. A tray can be made to fit on one side of the creeper to carry tools, but keep it narrow so it does not interfere with movement under the car.

STILTS

Stilts for a child to walk on should be carefully made. The main shafts should be straight-grained and without flaws. For a heavy user they should be a tough hardwood, but for a young child a lighter, straight-grained softwood is better. The handle size needs to be comfortable to grip, but even for a small child, 1 1/4 inches square is

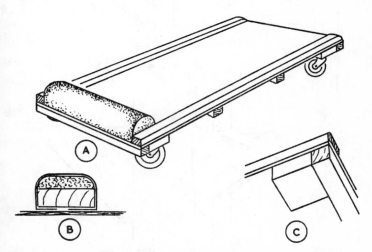

Fig. 19-5. A crawler for use under a car may have a padded headrest and run on casters.

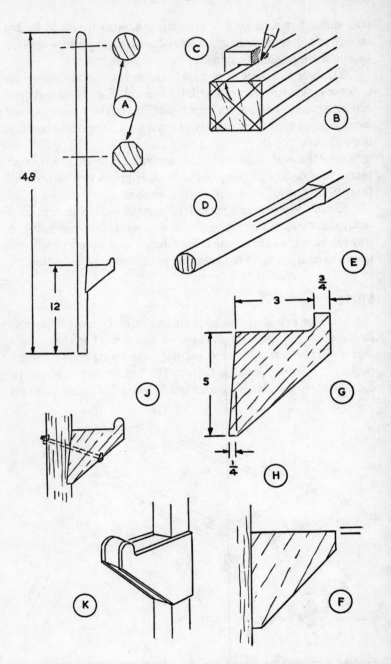

Fig. 19-6. Stilts should be substantially made and of a size to suit the user.

the minimum section. Length should be enough to go behind the armpits. The amount of projection above the shoulders is unimportant, so long pieces allow for growing.

The shafts should be square for much of their length, but they can taper to octagonal, then round towards the top for comfortable grip (Fig. 19-6A). Draw a regular octagon, using the diagonals of a square to give the outline (Fig. 19-6B). Notch a piece of wood and use this with a pencil as a gauge (Fig. 19-6C). Use a chisel, bevel downwards, to cut in the ends of the octagonal part, then remove the rest of the wood with a plane (Fig. 19-6D). Towards the top, take off the corners of the octagon and make the handle round. A strip of abrasive paper worked around the wood will round it sufficiently, then finish by rubbing the paper lengthwise. Round the top. At the bottom, take off the angles to reduce the risk of splitting, but do not bevel much as this would reduce the bearing surface.

The foot blocks or steps may have flat tops or be cut with ends to prevent the foot from sliding off (Fig. 19-6E). If flat, cutting at a slight angle helps to retain the foot (Fig. 19-6F). The block should be fairly thick and made of hardwood with the grain upright or approximately parallel with the angled edge (Fig. 19-6G).

The block may be notched into the shaft, but keep the notch shallow so as not to weaken the wood (Fig. 19-6H). Glue the joint and use either long, stout wood screws, or a bolt at an angle (Fig. 19-6J).

An alternative uses plywood cheeks (Fig. 19-6K). Use plywood about 1/2 inch thick with the outside grain across. Assemble with glue and screws. Let the plywood cover the full width of the shaft and extend downwards for extra stiffness.

Take off all sharp edges by sanding. Finish with paint, preferably in bright colors. To reduce the risk of slipping, the bottoms can be given rubber feet, either the type used on shoe heels or pieces of sheet rubber nailed on. Finally, check that the stilts match each other.

DOLL'S CRIB

A crib or cot for a doll can be anything from a simple box upwards. If it can be made to rock, that will be an additional attraction to the young owner. The design shown (Fig. 19-7A) provides scope for the owner of a jig saw, but it could be made with straight lines or

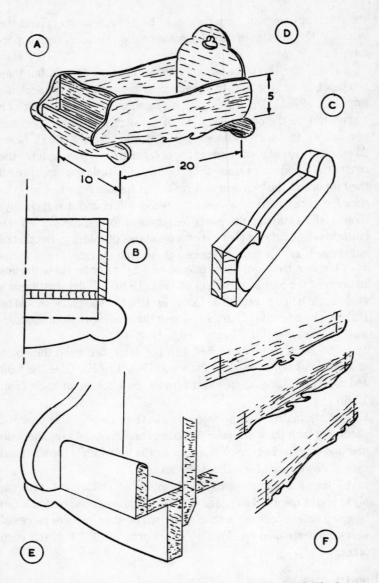

Fig. 19-7. A doll's crib that rocks can be simple or elaborately finished.

just a few large curves. Size will depend on available wood and on the dolls.

It will help to draw a full-size end view, either full width (to better visualize the final appearance) or just one side of the center line (Fig. 19-7B). Make the two rockers. The curves on which they rock should be smooth parts of a circle. Shape the two together and mark them so they are assembled facing as shaped, in case the curves are not exactly symmetrical (Fig. 19-7C).

Make the two ends and fasten them to the rockers with glue and screws from inside. The foot end can be straight across, but the head can be raised and decorated by shaping (Fig. 19-7D). German cribs of this sort have the head and sides elaborately carved. Some carving could be included if this is intended to be a reproduction crib.

The bottom fits inside the sides and ends; attach it with screws from outside. Plane its sides level with the ends.

The sides are parallel. They may be cut flush with the head end or can be carried over a little and shaped. At the foot they should extend enough to be given a decorative outline. They could go far enough to take a small rock or shelf for small doll items (Fig. 19-7E). These parts fit between the sides and are glued and screwed.

The upper edges of the sides may be straight or given a slight hollow for easy access, but all of these edges and projecting parts of the ends should be well rounded. In a basic crib the lower edges of the sides could be straight, but there can be some shaping with the jig saw (Fig. 19-7F). Clean the outline with a chisel and Surform tool, then remove any sharpness by sanding.

The sides may be attached with glue and screws, but the screw heads may look rather obvious in the finished crib. It's better to counterbore and plug or fill the holes with filler. A traditional crib was left in the natural color and finished with polish or varnish, but it may be better to use bright paint and maybe add some fairy-tale decals to the sides and head.

OARS AND PADDLES

A nicely-shaped wooden oar is attractive to look at and use, but those made in the traditional way have given way to more functional, less attractive oars made by quicker methods. Canoe paddles have not all gone the same way, but some of these are not as attractive as older versions. Cutting oars and paddles from solid wood was wasteful, but with modern waterproof glues it is possible to build them up more economically to get the same effect.

The wood has to be straight-grained. For inland and occasional sea use, oars may be softwood. For sustained salt-water use a hardwood, such as ash, is better. If suitable wood is obtained from salvage sources, making a pair of oars or one or more paddles can be an interesting project.

An oar is made from a square-section piece with pieces glued on each side to make the blade (Fig. 19-8A). Use a cardboard template to mark the shape of the two sides of the blade. Cut the outline and mark a center line around the edges, with other lines about 1/8 inch each side of it (Fig. 19-8B). Plane the shaft and blade edges to these lines. Delay further shaping there until some of the surplus wood has been removed from the rest of the shaft.

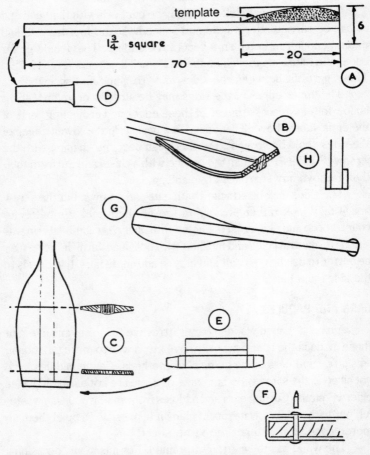

Fig. 19-8. Oars and paddles are built up by gluing pieces together, then shaping them.

Do this in stages. Work to an octagon first, using a notched piece of wood as a gauge (Fig. 19-8B and C), then take off the eight corners by planing. It is helpful to hold the oar with one hand in a position where the light comes diagonally across it. This will show up ridges which can be removed with a light plane in the other hand. Follow this by using coarse abrasive paper or cloth pulled around the wood until all plane marks are gone, then sand along the grain until the abrasive marks are removed.

Blend the shaft into the blade, curving, thinning and rounding with a spokeshave, curved Surform tool, or a disc sander. The main part of the blade will come to a ridge at the center in its upper part, but this will reduce to parallel near the end (Fig. 19-8C).

A parallel shaft is satisfactory, but the greatest strength is needed where the thrust comes against the oarlock, so some oars were made thicker there and tapered slightly towards the blade and to the grip. It is difficult to taper towards the blade without weakening the shaft, but the other end can be given a taper, or the oar can have the end reduced to form a grip (Fig. 19-8D).

Wrap a strip of paper around the end, pencil along its edge, then reduce it to size with a chisel.

The tip of the blade needs some protection. This could be one or two layers of fiberglass tape laid in resin or—the traditional method—a piece of copper or aluminum wrapped around and riveted. Make a paper template (Fig. 19-8E) and cut thin metal to match. Wrap this over the blade and drill for thin nails (the same metal if possible). Support a nail head on an iron block, so the point can be cut off and the other end riveted (Fig. 19-8F).

A canoe paddle (Fig. 19-8G) is made in a very similar way, except that pieces glued at the top are shaped to form the grip (Fig. 19-8H).

Much time should be spent with abrasive getting oars and paddles to smooth outlines, with all parts rounded and blending into each other. Finish sanding along the grain so any remaining scratches are disguised. Give the oars or paddles several coats of marine varnish. The grip at the end of the oar may be left plain or its varnish can be rubbed matte, to give a firm hand hold.

SLED

In parts of the country where snow is only experienced for a brief period in an average year, there may be no justification for an expensive sled, but one that can be made from crate or pallet wood at no cost has obvious attractions. Dimensions will depend on available wood, but those shown will serve as a guide (Fig. 19-9A).

The sides should be thick enough to retain stiffness without risk of cracking. Curve the front edges as part of an ellipse rather than part of a circle, so the curve is shallow at the bottom. This can be drawn freehand, but shape both sides together (Fig. 19-9B).

The crossbar at the front serves as a footrest when the sled is sat on or as a handgrip when lain on. This is let into the sides; there are other pieces notched in or merely nailed in place (Fig. 19-9C).

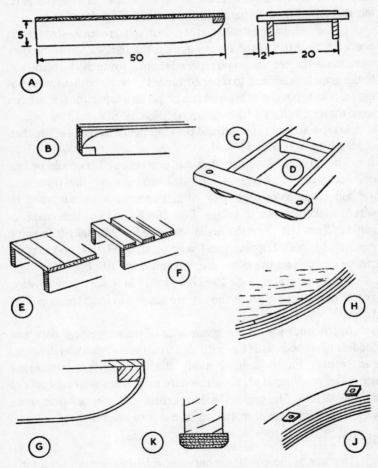

Fig. 19-9. A sled should have laminated runners for best performance.

The top assembly provides some stiffness, but crossmembers hold the sides firm. If they are deep enough to touch the snow, hollow their lower edges (Fig. 19-9D).

The top is made from cross strips. They can fit close or have gaps between them. If the pieces are of different widths, close fitting is preferable (Fig. 19-9E), but if pieces of equal size are available, they can be rounded and finished with varnish (Fig. 19-9F) for a superior appearance.

Drill holes in the front crossbar to take a rope bridle. Another large hole in the center of the rear crosspiece will serve for hanging the sled when out of use.

The edges of the runners take the wear. For occasional use, the wood of the sides may be allowed to wear, and trued when worn too badly. Obviously, there is a limit to how often this can be done. Most wear comes when the sled is used on thin snow and the runners touch stones underneath.

It is better to cover the edges with strips (Fig. 19-9G). A single strip may be bent around, but if the curve is too severe for this, the strip can be laminated. This can be done with strips from fruit crates or other thin strips unsuitable for other things. Inner pieces need not be full-length (Fig. 19-9H). The finished laminated thickness should be at least 1/4 inch, preferably 1/2 inch.

So there are no nails or screws on the surface, glue the laminations, but inner ones may be nailed permanently. The outer laminations can be held with temporary nails driven through scraps of plywood (Fig. 19-9J). When the glue has set, they are levered out.

The laminated runners need not be planed to the thickness of the sides if they are stout enough to be left a little wider. The bearing surface should be mainly flat, but the edges should be rounded (Fig. 19-9K) or they will soon splinter.

The whole sled should not be very heavy, but if lightness for carrying is important, part of the top can be left open or the crossbars spaced quite widely. Deep sides can have openings cut in them for lightness, but be careful not to weaken the structure.

FISHING BOX

Most anglers have a large collection of small items to carry and also need a place to sit. A box that is a suitable height for sitting on and can be carried by a sling over the shoulder can be made of plywood, with a few strips of solid wood. The box shown is wider at the base, for steadiness (Fig. 19-10A).

Mark out and cut the two sides first (Fig. 19-10B). Frame them with strips, which need not be very thick—1/2-inch square on 1/4-inch plywood should be enough. Join the two sides with the plywood back (Fig. 19-10C). If there is to be a lift-out tray, arrange a support for this across the back, with a piece behind it to match the thickness of the top framing piece (Fig. 19-10D).

The front could have a support for the tray arranged the same way, but because of the taper it would be thicker and interfere with access to the lower part of the box. It is better to arrange supports inside the ends (Fig. 19-10E) and not have one on the front.

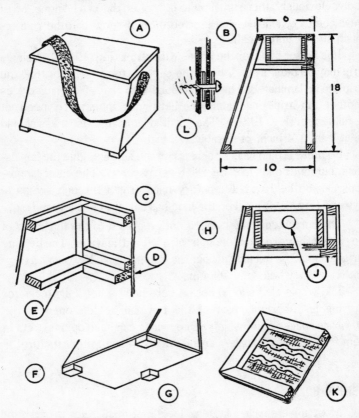

Fig. 19-10. The fishing box has a broad base for stability, and storage arranged to suit small items.

Nail on a plywood bottom (Fig. 19-10F). There should be some feet to lift the bottom of the box off the ground. On uneven ground three feet will stand firm when four might wobble, so arrange blocks under the front corners and at the center of the back to give a triangular arrangement (Fig. 19-10G).

The tray is a box that rests on the supports and comes within about 1/8 inch of the top. It should be an easy fit within the framing (Fig. 19-10H). How the box is made depends on the quality of finish intended. It may be sufficient to merely nail the corners, but for the best finish the corners would be dovetailed. Some divisions in the tray will probably be wanted. Drill two 3/4-inch holes before assembly to provide finger holes for lifting the tray out (Fig. 19-10J).

The simplest lid is a piece of stout plywood. The rear edge should be flush with the box, to take hinges. The other edges should overhang a little and be rounded. The lid could be thinner plywood framed inside with strips wide enough to rest on the box. The recess can be lined with cloth and fitted with tape loops (Fig. 19-10K). Pins or hooks can go into the cloth and other small items held by the loops.

Fit the hinges into the edge of the box so the lid will shut flat. If a fastener is needed, it can be arranged under the front of the lid to reach down the front of the box.

The sling is a piece of leather or webbing strap. Attachment is by screws into the sides at the tray-support level. Arrange these towards the back of the box and have large washers under and over the straps (Fig. 19-10L). The inside of the box should be painted a light color so the contents can be seen easily, but the outside may be a more durable, darker color.

Index

Index